ISLAMIC FUNDAMENTALISM
IN EGYPTIAN POLITICS

Also by Barry Rubin

REVOLUTION UNTIL VICTORY? The History and Politics of the PLO
ISTANBUL INTRIGUES
MODERN DICTATORS: Third World Coupmakers, Strongmen, and Populist Tyrants
SECRETS OF STATE: The State Department and the Struggle over U.S. Foreign Policy
THE ARAB STATES AND THE PALESTINE CONFLICT
PAVED WITH GOOD INTENTIONS: The American Experience and Iran
THE GREAT POWERS IN THE MIDDLE EAST 1941–1947: The Road to Cold War
HOW OTHERS REPORT US: America in the Foreign Press
INTERNATIONAL NEWS AND THE AMERICAN MEDIA
THE POLITICS OF TERRORISM: Counterterrorist Policies (*editor*)
THE POLITICS OF TERRORISM: Terror as a State and Revolutionary Strategy (*editor*)
BOOKS ON ISRAEL, ESSAYS ON POLITICS, CULTURE AND SOCIETY (*co-editor*)
CENTRAL AMERICA CRISIS READER (*co-editor*)
THE ISRAELI–ARAB READER (*co-editor*)
THE HUMAN RIGHTS READER (*co-editor*)

Islamic Fundamentalism in Egyptian Politics

updated edition

by Barry Rubin

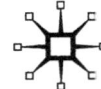 ISLAMIC FUNDAMENTALISM IN EGYPTIAN POLITICS
Copyright © Barry Rubin, 1990.
All rights reserved. No part of this book may be used or reproduced in
any manner whatsoever without written permission except in the case of
brief quotations embodied in critical articles or reviews.

First published in 2002 by PALGRAVE MACMILLAN™
175 Fifth Avenue, New York, N.Y. 10010 and
Houndmills, Basingstoke, Hampshire, England RG21 6XS.
Companies and representatives throughout the world.

PALGRAVE MACMILLAN IS THE GLOBAL ACADEMIC IMPRINT OF THE
PALGRAVE MACMILLAN
division of St. Martin's Press, LLC and of Palgrave Macmillan Ltd.
Macmillan® is a registered trademark in the United States, United
Kingdom and other countries. Palgrave is a registered trademark in the
European Union and other countries.

ISBN: 1-403-96074-7   ISBN-13: 978-1-403-96074-0

Library of Congress Cataloging-in-Publication Data available from the
Library of Congress.

First Palgrave Macmillan edition: September 2002
10 9 8 7 6 5 4 3 2 1

Contents

Preface to the Updated Edition	vii
Preface to the Original Edition	ix
Overview	1

1 Introduction — 3
- Factors Promoting Fundamentalism — 4
- Factors Opposing Fundamentalism — 5
- Prospects for Fundamentalism — 6
- Organization of this Study — 6

2 Contemporary History of Fundamentalism in Egypt — 10
- The Fall of the Muslim Brotherhood — 10
- The Second Round — 14
- Sadat Revives the Brotherhood — 16
- Confrontation and Assassination — 19
- Mubarak Tames the Opposition — 23
- Conclusions — 26

3 The Muslim Brotherhood: Ideology and Program — 28
- Al-Tilimsani's Policy — 29
- General Strategy and Electoral Politics — 31
- Attitude toward Radicals, Violence and Demonstrations — 35
- Internal Factions — 38
- Conclusions — 39

4 The Jama'at — 41
- General Ideology — 43
- Al-Jihad's Ideology — 44
- Sayyid Qutb — 49
- The Critique of Jahiliyyah — 50
- Motives — 53
- The Islamic Liberation Organization and Al-Takfir Wal-Hijrah — 56
- Al-Jihad — 57
- Survivors from [Hell] Fire — 59
- Rivalry among the Jam'at — 60
- Conclusions — 61

5	**The Radical Jam'iyat**	**63**
	Jam'iyat on University Campuses	63
	The Jam'iyat's Appeal	65
	Islamic Action in Asyut	67
	Student Elections	69
	Reasons for Jam'iyat's Growth	70
	Community-Based Jam'iyat	72
	Charismatic Preachers	75
6	**Popular Islam and Official Ulama**	**79**
	Al-Azhar and State Control over Religion	80
	The Debate with the Radicals	83
	How Should Al-Azhar Counter Extremism?	86
	The Mainstream Clergy and the Shari'ah	88
	The Popular Moderate Islamic Revival	88
7	**Attitudes toward Foreign Policy Issues**	**93**
	Stages of Egyptian Foreign Policy	96
	The Fundamentalists and the United States	98
	The USSR	106
	Israel	107
	Iran and the Arabs	115
	The Arabs and Arab Nationalism	121
8	**Strategy and Doctrine**	**125**
	Muslim Brotherhood: Political Party or Electoral Alliance?	126
	Critics of Brotherhood Strategy	130
	The Shari'ah as Rationale	131
	How to Implement the Shari'ah	132
	Reform or Revolution?	137
9	**Assessments and Conclusions**	**150**
10	**The Islamist Revolt**	**156**
	Problems within the Revolutionary Movement	157
	The Anti-Tourist Campaign	161
	The Muslim Brotherhood	162
	Government-Appointed Leaders	169

Appendix	174
Notes and References	186
Bibliography	206

Preface to the Updated Edition

Islamic radical fundamentalist political movements have a long history in Egypt, where they have posed as the most important alternative vision and ideology to the dominant, state-sponsored Arab nationalism. These groups have challenged the Egyptian state but have failed to take over either the regime or the society. Their defeats have arisen from the success of governmental policies, including repression and cooptation; internal ideological and organizational divisions among the fundamentalists themselves; and the Egyptian people's rejection of their radical message and interpretation of Islam.

One of the most important ideological debates has been whether the primary target of fundamentalist action should be the Egyptian regime or an anti-Western campaign. This book examines Egyptian fundamentalist groups, with particular emphasis on how ideological differences have led to distinctive attitudes towards violence and terrorism. Chapter 10, new to this edition, analyzes how internal debates, coupled with the defeat of the anti-government insurgency, led many Egyptian radical fundamentalists to join Usama bin Ladin and focus on attacking America. A new appendix includes excerpts and an analysis of the writings of Ayman al-Zawahiri, a veteran leader of the Egyptian movement who became Usama bin Ladin's right-hand man and helped plan the September 11, 2001 attacks on the United States.

Events in the 1990s and afterward confirmed the correctness of this book's original analysis. The revolutionary Islamists in Egypt were defeated; they were unable to overcome their own organizational, doctrinal, and strategic divisions; and they certainly failed to win mass support among Egypt's people. The Egyptian government clearly won the war launched by the Islamists though, of course, it could neither destroy these forces entirely nor dismantle the factors which inspired them in the first place.

At the same time, as this book explains, the government's triumph was based in part on its own extensive Islamic assets and its ability to show that the regime was pious. This was achieved through various social, cultural, and intellectual concessions to Islam and Islamic activists (though not to radical Islamists). It could be said that these actions constituted a sort of surrender to the opposition or an extension of its influence.

In fact, though, the government's strategy was also highly successful in preserving a safety valve to diminish dissent and reduce the level of violent conflict. Of course, government-sponsored religiosity and Islamic measures also maintained a milieu capable of giving rise to future insurgencies and maintained the status of Islamism as the main opposition ideology in Egypt. Government policy also constrained the regime regarding closer relationships with the United States or contributing to furthering the Arab-Israeli peace process. The broader result of government actions in domestic terms was to preserve stability while blocking democratic and other modernizing developments.

BARRY RUBIN, 2002

Preface to the Original Edition

Following the Victory of Iran's Islamic revolution in 1979 and the murder of Egypt's President Anwar al-Sadat in 1981, many studies were undertaken and published on radical Islamic fundamentalist movements in the Middle East. Given these events, that research stressed the importance of such groups, focusing on reasons for their rise and possible future success.

During the following decade, however, Islamic fundamentalist movements did not come to power in any country. Furthermore, they failed to show the kind of growth in power, size or influence which many observers had expected. Consequently, it is necessary to analyze why the fundamentalists have not done better.

This study deals with Egypt, the most important country in the Arab world. Certainly, Egypt had many problems in the 1980s which might conceivably have strengthened radical Islamic groups, whose apparent assets seemed to include a long-established Muslim Brotherhood and a revolutionary underground capable of murdering the country's ruler. This book considers why other, contrary, factors remained uppermost in Egyptian politics.

The book began as a research project for the Orkand Corporation. Raymond Stock did a massive amount of translation with admirable speed and accuracy. Dr Ami Ayalon and Professor Jerrold Green read the manuscript and made extremely helpful suggestions. Enthusiastic support from Simon Winder is also acknowledged with pleasure.

BARRY RUBIN

Overview

Revolutionary Islamic fundamentalism in Egypt is capable of episodes of terrorism and urban disorder, but lacks the capability to overthrow the government. A careful examination of the ideologies of Egyptian Islamic groups reveals deep divisions among them and their espousal of doctrines which do not appeal to most Egyptian Muslims. These constraints, which create conflicting approaches to how national political power should be gained and used, are unlikely to be overcome under the current leadership of the fundamentalist movement.

Four main forces, each demanding a more Islamic society, are currently active in Egypt. The first of these, the Muslim Brotherhood, has made a strong commitment to a reformist strategy because of severe repression in the past. The Brotherhood presents itself today as a responsible and moderate force in an effort to broaden its base and to gain a fully legal status from the government.

The second grouping, the jama'at, are small, underground groups that seek a violent revolution. They are badly divided among themselves, however, and have suffered greatly from the government's countermeasures. The jam'iyat, the third grouping, are campus or neighborhood associations – some led by charismatic preachers – which have varying ideological views. Their interest in continuing to function openly, however, cautions them against confronting the authorities.

These radicals tend to accept the doctrine of *jahiliyyah*, which declares that Egypt's rulers and much of its society is pagan and anti-Islamic. It is difficult for average Egyptians to see themselves as having deviated from their own religion, a fact making it harder for the revolutionaries to win many converts. Moreover, their ideology deviates in other ways from Islam as most Egyptians understand it.

The fourth group, the mainstream clergy, tends to be pro-government. This attitude is based on a combination of factors – the clergy's distaste for the radicals' innovative ideas, its professional rejection of the revolutionaries' anti-clericalism, and the fact that the government controls its jobs and salaries. Thus, while there has undoubtedly been a popular revival of Islam in Egypt, much of this movement has been of an apolitical and traditionalist nature which does not necessarily coincide with the views of extremists.

The fundamentalists are extremely suspicious of the United States, the USSR, and Israel. Non-Muslims are often seen as anti-Muslim forces. The view that Western culture is subverting Egypt's traditional way of life and religious piety encourages these attitudes as much as does any political question. The fundamentalists preach nonalignment.

Despite the fundamentalists' passionate feelings about foreign policy issues, they are more focused on internal affairs. Their main complaint about the United States is what it does inside Egypt – especially its alleged control over the government and the high profile of Americans throughout the country – rather than what it does in the region as a whole. There is an underlying isolationism which conditions their views of external matters and the lower priority these hold in their agenda. Very few of them have any sympathy toward Iran; Khumayni's ideology is seen as a handciap for the Egyptian fundamentalist cause.

The most important domestic issue for the fundamentalists is the implementation of the Shari'ah. The mainstream clergy hopes that the government will enact the Islamic code as the basis for all Egypt's laws. The Brotherhood hopes to persuade others through parliamentary means, while the revolutionaries believe that the authorities have no intention of enacting the Shari'ah.

Both the mainstream clergy and the Brotherhood criticize the use of violence. The jam'iyats use low-level violence on local matters but are restrained by the concern about repression. The revolutionaries say that only armed struggle can bring about a change in Egypt.

Within the fundamentalist community, the more moderate forces – the bulk of the clergy, the Brotherhood, and some jam'iyats – campaign for an institutionalized Islamic society. The jama'at and some jam'iyat demand an Islamic state. The Mubarak government has clearly played on these divisions by promoting the moderate clergy and allowing the opposition to function as long as it does not exceed certain limits. At the same time, it threatens revolutionaries or those using violence with extreme punishments. Although Egypt's growing economic difficulty and its effect on living standards are causes for concern, a serious fundamentalist upheaval does not seem likely in the short- to medium-term future.

1 Introduction

The purpose of this book is to identify and analyze the political positions of Egyptian Islamic fundamentalist movements and their chances for seizing power. In addition, it assesses fundamentalist attitudes toward international issues such as Egypt's relations with the United States and the Soviet Union, Israel, and the Iranian revolution. This study also addresses fundamentalist prescriptions for seizing power in Egypt, attitudes toward reforming the existing political system, and visions of an Islamic revolution or state.

The nature of the fundamentalists' world view has a great effect on how Egyptian authorities might cope with the threat and on how the activities of these groups might affect U.S. interests. Moreover, the ideology of Egyptian fundamentalists provides important clues on their likely popular appeal as well as their choice of strategy and tactics. These ideas also suggest how they would act if they attained power.

Egyptian fundamentalist movements have become the main opposition forces within the country and are the most likely source of domestic political instability. The assassination of Egyptian President Anwar al-Sadat by an Islamic revolutionary group in October 1981 demonstrated the potential for even small fundamentalist forces to have a disproportionate effect on the most important country in the Arab world.

Among the key questions this study addresses are the following:

- Are Egyptian fundamentalists capable of united action or are they badly divided over issues of doctrine and strategy?
- Can anti-regime fundamentalists seize hegemony as the legitimate representatives of Islam or are they stymied by progovernment clerics?
- Is it possible for large elements of the fundamentalists to become reformists rather than revolutionaries in exchange for some government concessions?
- Does the ideology of the fundamentalists make them more or less palatable to Egypt's masses?
- Are fundamentalists innately opposed to the United States or might they adopt positions friendlier to America?

- How do these groups stand on the U.S.–Soviet competition?
- Might they favor some peaceful resolution of the Arab–Israeli conflict?
- Do significant numbers of Egyptian Muslims support Iran and its revolution?
- Are fundamentalists likely to increase their power in Egypt and are they likely to gain power there?

FACTORS PROMOTING FUNDAMENTALISM

There are a number of structural factors which both strengthen and constrain the appeal of fundamentalism in Egypt. Egyptians are predominantly, roughly 90 per cent, Muslim. Those who oppose a strong role for Islam in public life – Christians, Marxists, liberal secularists – are well-advised not to express their own views too loudly. Islam is respected as the foundation of Egyptian life. Open criticism of its role and teachings is constrained and not politically profitable. Yet even Egyptians who consider themselves good Muslims are often satisfied with the current role of religion in their own lives or in the society. Most of them do not want a revolutionary Islamic state which will impose a set of values and a code of behavior which a small group of would-be leaders define as properly Islamic.

Fundamentalists can, however, draw on the underlying strength of Islam as an ideology and a belief system. Some particularly powerful assumptions in Egypt are that Islam is *right*; Egyptian law *should* be based on the Islamic holy law (the Shari'ah); Islamic values – or more properly traditional values – are *better* than Western, imported ones. On the role of women, the structure of the family, and its concept of social justice, Islam is the basis of the customs by which most Egyptians live.

The crises through which Egypt passed after its defeat in the 1967 Arab–Israeli war created an ideological vacuum which pushed many people toward Islamic fundamentalism. As the Nasirist system declined, Egyptians began to comprehend the regime's failures and the problems it had left them. Saad Eddin Ibrahim noted six such issues which led to an upsurge in fundamentalism: "The social question" refers to the debate over whether Egypt's current system provides social justice and opportunity fairly among the citizens. "The political question" defines the amount of popular participation and democracy in Egypt. "The economic question" assesses the

Introduction   5

rulers' competence in wisely using resources and promoting development. "The patriotic question" analyzes whether the system preserves independence and avoids subservience to a foreign power. It should be noted that while Islamic fundamentalists are generally opposed to nationalism, they are interested in Egypt's sovereignty since only a country free of foreign, non-Islamic control can be Muslim. "The nationalist quesstion" is the search for Egypt's role in the "greater Arab nation" and the way to deal with Israel. Finally, "the civilization question" addresses the relative balance between Westernization or preservation of Egypt's own historic traditions.[1]

In the 1970s and 1980s a variety of groups had to decide their stand on the role of Islam in their own lives and in Egyptian society. These sectors include veterans of the Muslim Brotherhood returning home from Nasir's prisons, students in Egypt's rapidly growing universities, lower middle class artisans and merchants whose livelihoods were threatened by modernization, poor immigrants in the burgeoning cities, and clerics who were disturbed by both growing secularism and the threat of radical fundamentalism. In a country facing so many problems, Islam seemed a familiar creed which provided both a powerful link with the past and a promise of a utopian future.

FACTORS OPPOSING FUNDAMENTALISM

There are also several factors which limit fundamentalism's appeal. While the society as a whole accepts Islam as an integral and leading element, the state and the mass of Egyptians also have their own *interpretation* of Islam. This view and daily practice do not correspond with the radicals' theories and the resulting conflict poses a great problem for fundamentalists who wish to translate their theories into political power.

The first factor is the nature of the fundamentalists, particularly the revolutionaries. In fact, fundamentalists are not traditionalists but innovators whose ideas are often at odds with mainstream and historically prevailing Egyptian views. Moreover, the practice of Egyptian culture is frequently in contradiction with its supposed fundamentalist values. Egyptians may praise Islamic piety but do not want it imposed on their own personal lives. Islamic fundamentalist groups themselves are divided in terms of their leaders, institutions, and ideologies. Dr Mustafa Kamil Murad, chairman of the Liberal Party, shrewdly points out that fundamentalists come together only occasionally. "Afterwards, however, followers of the religious tendency go their separate ways . . . because each one of them has his own agenda." The Muslim Brothers reject with abhorrence the radical ideas of Sayyid Qutb, ideological father of the contemporary radical fundamentalists. "If that continues to be their position, there can be no agreement between them and the [radical] groups" which follow Qutb's view that contemporary Egyptian society is pagan rather than Muslim.

While changes in Egyptian society have created sentiments favoring fundamentalism, they have also made it more difficult for that ideology to gain broad support and to triumph over its competitors. Western values, ideas, and culture have been coming into Egypt for well over a century and have a strong foothold there. There are also interest groups which oppose an increase in fundamentalist practices either because they find them personally threatening – Coptic Christians, many urban women, and intellectuals – or politically dangerous – the nation's leaders, high officials, and military officers.

From the point of view of Egypt's rulers and elite, the survival of the state and geopolitical considerations require compromises which run contrary to the fundamentalists' ideology. For many years, for example, Egypt tried fighting Israel and rejecting the United States, but it eventually discovered there are concrete advantages derived from peace with Israel and alignment with the United States. The state is quite willing to suppress groups which use violence or which threaten revolution. Arab and Egyptian nationalism are counter-ideologies to Islamic fundamentalism which attract many people.

PROSPECTS FOR FUNDAMENTALISM

Thus, while fundamentalism has become an important factor in Egypt, it is a distinctly minority force. Still, one should not underestimate its potential appeal. Some Egyptian politicians and intellectuals have panicked, saying that "at present a Muslim mood prevails in Egypt" or that "Egypt has now become an Islamist's dream."[2] While not exaggerating, observers must understand this doctrine's appeal for Egyptians. As Professor Fouad Ajami notes, Islam offers a message of certainty and hope in a world marked by military defeats, confusion over identity, and economic hardship. "Its tracts offer some easy solutions, faith instead of detail, but they also tell the truth about treaties, diplomacy, the corruption of officials." It calls on believers to take their lives in their own hands, "a contrast to an official political culture that reduces citizens to spectators and asks them to leave things to the rulers. At a time when people are confused and lost and the future is uncertain, it connects them to a tradition that reduces their bewilderment."[3]

When fundamentalists criticize the existing order, they make sense to many people who may also be moved by their confidence that Islam provides all the answers to Egypt's problems or needs. The influential Muslim Brotherhood leader Shaykh Salah Abu Isma'il strikes a chord when he points out that "Egypt has been living on promises since the July 1952 revolution, and gaining nothing but disappointment." And he blames all "our economic hardships, military weakness and social unrest to the absence of the Shari'ah."[4]

All Muslims, of course, are bound to respect Islam and its commandments, which include a full range of guidelines and prescriptions for everday life and social organization. Yet there is much disagreement over how these should be interpreted. This explains the gap between the theoretical appeal of the Muslim Brotherhood or radical groups and the much smaller constituencies they actually possess. For example, there is a Qur'anic injunction that reads, "Who so desires another religion than Islam, that will not be accepted of him, and in the hereafter he will be among the losers." The radicals have claimed that this condemns nominal Moslems who do not act properly – i.e., the rulers and their supporters – and thus one can wage jihad (holy war) against them. The fundamentalists claim the right to institute what amounts to a dictatorship of the pious to right society's wrongs. Most Egyptians have found this idea unacceptable and can base this interpretation on passages that imply more tolerance: "There is no compulsion regarding religion, uprightness has been made distinct from tyranny."

Furthermore, while some Egyptian intellectuals think the fundamentalists are sweeping forward victoriously, Islamic radicals themselves feel besieged by modernity and believe that Egypt is being inundated with Western culture: education, movies, foreigners, and the changing roles of women. While Iran proves to them that fundamentalists can win, few Egyptians have any fondness for that Persian, Shi'ite state. They also know that there is a powerful Islamic establishment in Egypt which serves the government as a bulwark against them. As one Egyptian fundamentalist writer states, "What is lacking are ulama [clergy] free of the chains of office, function, and dependence, ulama who cannot be hired and fired at will, and are economically independent, hence impervious to pressures."[5]

Thus, Islam is popular and fundamentalism has a strong potential appeal in Egypt. Yet the possibility of a fundamentalist revolution seems most unlikely. An attempt to resolve this apparent paradox must rest on a careful examination of the evidence. We have thus attempted to look at all available sources for understanding the ideology and practice of Islamic fundamentalism in Egypt.

ORGANIZATION OF THIS STUDY

This study presents the history, structure, and ideology of the different kinds of Islamic forces active in Egypt today on three levels: history, groups, and specific issues. Chapter 2 discusses the history of Islamic fundamentalist movements, pointing out the previous wave of activist challenge to government – the Muslim Brotherhood, suppressed by Nasir in the early 1950s and the emergence of revolutionary underground and campus-based groups, Sadat's efforts to suppress these movements, his assassination in 1981 and the reemergence of fundamentalist groups within certain restrictions in the 1980s.

Chapters 3, 4, 5, and 6 take up four different categories of fundamentalist groups. Chapter 3 assesses the Muslim Brotherhood, by far the largest and oldest of Islamic groups, which has adopted a reformist strategy and participated with some success in the electoral process. Chapter 4 analyzes the jama'at, the radical and mostly underground small groups which have carried out Islamic terrorism and see themselves as revolutionary. The most important of approximately three dozen sects are al-Jihad and al-Takfir wal-Hijrah.

The jam'iyat, campus and community-based militant groups which number in the hundreds and function legally, are examined in Chapter 5. They see themselves as radical and may be recruiting grounds and reserve troops for the jama'at, whose ideology they often echo in somewhat diluted form. Some of these groups are built around fundamentalist preachers whose followers congregate around their mosques and buy their taped sermons. Two of the most influential are Shaykhs Kishk and Hafez Salamah. The pro-government clergy is assessed in Chapter 6. The two most prominent members are those holding the post of mufti of Egypt and shakykh of al-Azhar University. The regime has powerful leverage on the clerical community through its appointments, control over mosques, payments of salaries, and other favors, mostly distributed by the

Ministry of Awqaf and al-Azhar Affairs. These ulama also have special access to state-owned television and radio.

Finally, Chapters 7 and 8 look at the stand of these various groups of fundamentalists toward some critical issues. Chapter 7 explains their attitude toward foreign policy factors: the United States, Israel, Khumayni's Iran, and Arab states. Chapter 8 evaluates their view of internal and strategic questions including the relative merits of reform and revolution, the use of violence and nonviolence, and the nature of the Islamic state and society they seek to establish. Chapter 9 summarizes the evidence and conclusions.

2 Contemporary History of Fundamentalism in Egypt

The development of Islamic fundamentalist groups in Egypt has not been a succession of triumphs but rather a series of periods of growth cut short by strategic incompetence, limits to public support, and government repression. Thus, while fundamentalism enjoys a base of support in Egypt, it has never gained a position of ideological or political hegemony. On several occasions, the government has destroyed these groups with relative ease. While Egypt's leaders must also be cautious in dealing with the threat of revolutionary Islam – showing respect for the religion and the concerns of believers – they can also overawe the movement when necessary.

In the 1940s and early 1950s, organized fundamentalism was larger, more united, and more threatening to the existing system than it has been at any time since. But the Nasir regime smashed the Muslim Brotherhood in the 1950s and 1960s, producing experiences so traumatic that they made the group timid and subject to government intimidation thereafter. Sadat allowed the Brotherhood to revive in the 1970s, setting off a new wave of fundamentalism that included revolutionary groups which sought to overthrow the government. Sadat repressed the extremists, who gained revenge by assassinating him. The Mubarak regime was able to make a *modus vivendi* with the Brotherhood and moderate opposition parties by permitting them to function as long as they avoided violence and limited their attacks on the authorities. It continued to repress the small revolutionary fundamentalist groups which failed to win any broad following.

THE FALL OF THE MUSLIM BROTHERHOOD

The Muslim Brotherhood has always been the most important Islamic fundamentalist group in Egypt. Founded by Hasan al-Banna in 1929, the Brotherhood grew rapidly throughout the 1930s. It had tens of thousands of members, large arms caches, and a strong base in the police and army. In contrast to this robust movement, the government was a faltering, unpopular monarchy. The Brotherhood's institutions reached throughout Egyptian society, including a section called the Secret Organization which was responsible for military training and terrorist activities. By 1948, the Muslim Brotherhood played a particularly prominent role in raising funds, purchasing weapons, running military training camps, and sending hundreds of volunteers to fight in Palestine. By this time, the Brotherhood's membership had risen to over half a million. Students, workers, civil servants, and the urban poor attended its meetings and enthusiastically echoed its ideology.

While the Brotherhood had always used some violence against the authorities and its critics, the level of confrontation rose considerably in the late 1940s. Under the emergency regulations implemented during the 1948 Palestine war, the government dissolved the organization. In response, a member shot Prime Minister Mahmoud Fahmi Nuqrashi, and the regime retaliated by ordering the assassination of the Brotherhood's charismatic founder and leader, Hasan al-Banna, in February 1949.[1]

A series of attacks and counterattacks followed between the government and the Brotherhood as waves of violence erupted throughout Cairo. Thousands of Muslim Brothers were arrested and sent to detention camps. Nuqrashi's assassin was executed and ten Brotherhood leaders were sentenced to life imprisonment. But King Farouk knew that the Brotherhood had a large following and backed down to avoid an all-out conflict. He appointed a new cabinet which released many of the imprisoned fundamentalists.

When the government launched a campaign against the British military presence in the Suez Canal Zone in 1951, Brotherhood militants did most of the fighting. Once again, as in the 1948 war, the fundamentalists seized a measure of patriotic legitimacy. The organization also established strong links, through Anwar al-Sadat and others, with the clandestine Free Officers group within the army.

When revolution finally came to Egypt in July 1952, it was the Free Officers rather than the Brotherhood that seized control and sent the king into exile. Under Lt Col. Gamal 'Abd al-Nasir, the dominant ideology was populist, Arab nationalist, and socialist, rather than Islamic fundamentalist. Nasir's triumph set the course not only for Egypt but for the whole Arab world. Arab nationalism gained hegemony and political Islam went into eclipse for a quarter-century. Having failed the test in the revolutionary crisis of the monarchy, Egyptian fundamentalism would later suffer from a sense of defeatism, a lack of belief in its ability to take power. In contrast, the nationalist regime planted its roots deep within the army and other institutions, implemented reforms which gave it a mass popular base, and shaped the consciousness of the succeeding generations of Egyptians. These changes brought some counter-reaction, allowing fundamentalism to appeal to some people, but also created vested interests and attitudes which opposed radical Islamic movements.

The future course of events was not completely clear in Nasir's early years in power. The Brotherhood debated how to deal with the new regime – whether to try to persuade Nasir to turn toward Islam or to attempt to overthrow him. Banna's successor, Hasan al-Hudaybi, attempted to stop Nasir from monopolizing power, work with the government, and gradually move the country toward Islam. Another faction, led by Sayyid Qutb, called for a tougher political stand and advocated an attempt to seize power.

In addition to facing a determined military dictatorship, the Brotherhood had several internal weaknesses. After al-Banna's death, there had been no one leader who was strong enough or respected enough to unite the group. It also lacked a structure and discipline capable of making a revolution. It tended to overestimate the intrinsic appeal of fundamentalism to the masses and to underestimate the power of the army and the potential popularity of nationalism.

Nasir accused the Brotherhood of infiltrating the army in a takeover bid, but did not move against it immediately. His main foreign policy initiative was a treaty with Britain in which London would withdraw its forces from the Suez Canal area in exchange for Cairo's respect for British strategic and commercial interests there. This agreement was, in psychological terms, the equivalent of the Camp David accords a quarter-century later. Supreme Guide Hasan al-Hudaybi denounced it in an open letter of August 1954 and demanded the treaty's revocation. Nasir refused, al-Hudaybi was arrested, and the treaty was signed on October 19, 1954.

A week later, this conflict exploded in an event which was a turning point in the history of Egyptian fundamentalism. While Nasir was giving a speech from a balcony in Alexandria, a Muslim Brother fired eight shots at the leader. In the crisis, Nasir took over as head of state and moved quickly to destroy his rivals. Six Brotherhood leaders were subsequently executed; Supreme Guide al-Hudaybi was sentenced to hard labor for life; more than 800 militants were given heavy prison sentences; and as many as 6000 others were imprisoned without trial. The Brotherhood was outlawed and this proud, powerful organization disappeared from the Egyptian political map literally overnight.

Repression alone does not account for the rapidity and totality of the Brotherhood's – and Islamic fundamentalism's – eclipse in the 1950s. Nasir filled the ideological vacuum with an aggressive pan-Arabism, social reforms, mass mobilization, and his own powerful, popular personality. Arab nationalism, in effect, replaced Islamic fundamentalism as a solution for Egypt's woes. The Brotherhood could not compete with Nasir's offer of real reforms, spiritual enthusiasm, and apparent success.

The lesson of the Brotherhood's own fragility was one which its surviving leaders – all of whom were to spend long years in prison – have not forgotten to this day. Underneath the militant rhetoric grew a sense of defeatism in the face of government power, the appeal of nationalism, and the pain of Nasir's torture chambers and detention camps.

Part of the problem has to do with the Brotherhood's leadership. While al-Banna himself had been a charismatic figure, successors have dwelt in his shadow. None of them has had the skills of maneuver and the ambition for power which Nasir – or Khumayni – possessed. Just as the fundamentalists looked back on the seventh century as a golden age, the Brotherhood's chiefs seem to feel they are incapable of matching al-Banna's exploits. And even in al-Banna's lifetime the Brotherhood itself was becoming more of a bureaucracy than a revolutionary vanguard. Its very aspiration to be a mass organization, which required government tolerance to permit legal activities, discouraged radical activity. Those who rose to the top were managers and administrators rather than radical visionaries. Those evincing the latter characteristics were cut down by Nasir's executioners.

During a decade of imprisonment or exile, the Brotherhood's surviving leaders engaged in heated debates which led to several splits. The Brotherhood was in a bind. If it tried to fight the wildly popular Nasir, it could not function openly and would make few inroads among the Egyptian people who virtually worshipped him. At the same time, the regime did not abandon the potent power of religion to its enemies, seeking instead to re-interpret and dominate Islam as a pillar for its own rule. As one Egyptian writer explains, "After the revolution, the number of mosques increased greatly, a number of religious broadcasting stations were set up, the Islamic

Conference and the Islamic Research Council were founded, the law to develop al-Azhar (the historic, prestigious Islamic university) was issued, and religion became a compulsory subject for passing school examinations." Al-Azhar was brought into line with the regime's ideology and was amply rewarded for this cooperation. Leading ulama (clergy) issued decrees supporting government policies. Nasir and his colleagues, including Anwar Sadat, pre-empted the fundamentalists in the field of religion. Fundamentalists could not easily claim that they were fighting for Islam against Nasir's godless secularism. The real issue between the Brotherhood and Nasir was over who would hold power.[2]

THE SECOND ROUND

In 1964, Nasir, at the height of his power and confidence, freed the remaining Brotherhood prisoners in a general amnesty. Nasir, like Sadat a decade later, wanted the fundamentalists to help him counter the Marxist left. Muslim Brothers were returned to government posts they had once held and paid salary arrears for the period of their imprisonment.

During this time, however, Sayyid Qutb, the Brotherhood's leading theoretician, openly challenged Nasir's regime by developing a startling ideological innovation. He suggested that Egypt under Nasir was not at all an Islamic society or country. Rather, it was in a state of "jahiliyyah," the derogatory Qur'anic name for the ignorant, pagan pre-Islamic society. Qutb said the Prophet Muhammad would have described Nasir's system, based on Arab nationalism, as "rotten."[3]

According to this perspective, true Muslims were justified – indeed, commanded as a religious obligation – to reject and overthrow Nasir. If Qutb's innovation had been generally accepted, it would have produced a major change in the history of Islamic thought and Middle East politics. By undermining the strong sense of solidarity traditionally in force among Muslims (the "ummah," comunity of believers) it could have had the same effect that the doctrine of class struggle had produced in the West. Even more immediately, Qutb's doctrine threatened the classic, religiously sanctioned Sunni Muslim tradition of obedience to the ruler and state. In short, this idea provided radical fundamentalism with a revolutionary ideology whose effects would later be felt throughout the Muslim world.

Whether the Brotherhood was actively engaged in subversive efforts remains unclear, but Nasir certainly had reason to doubt its peaceful intentions. In a speech on August 29, 1965, Nasir stated that his security forces had thwarted a Brotherhood plot to kill him and overthrow the regime. As many as 27,000 people were arrested, hundreds were sentenced by a special court, and 26 were tortured to death. Three top leaders – Qutb himself, Yusuf Hawash, and 'Abd al-Fattah Isma'il – were hanged in Cairo on August 29, 1966. Investigations into the army and police uncovered numerous Brotherhood cells. During the trial, there were charges that the movement was aided by Saudi Arabia. The Brotherhood's foreign representative, Sa'id Ramadan, was sentenced in absentia on charges of being a Western agent and went into exile in Switzerland.

The blow administered by Nasir drove the Muslim Brotherhood underground for five more years, until after Nasir's death and Sadat's accession to power in 1970. It is thus important to remember that the organization was excluded from participation in the most important era of political change in modern Egypt, was branded the enemy of the popular revolution, and was twice accused of plotting to kill the country's charismatic leader.

While most Egyptians thought of Nasir as their liberator and as hero of the Arabs, the fundamentalists saw his regime as one of barbarism and brutality. Today, the mainstream of the Brotherhood has tried to rewrite history, claiming that it always supported the revolution and playing down its conflict with Nasir. In contrast, the revolutionary militants – most of them too young to have directly experienced Nasir's repression or appeal – reject all the fruits of the 1952 revolution.

Egypt's humiliating defeat in its 1967 war with Israel, however, undermined the legitimacy and enthusiasm accumulated by Nasir. It called into question the effectiveness of Egypt's government for many who had previously supported the regime. While the other generation might have appreciated the gains brought by the revolution, younger people either took them for granted or felt that little had been achieved. Pan-Arabism had failed to unite the Arabs into one state and had not persuaded them to accept Egyptian leadership. Rather than destroying Israel, the Arabs were routed. Western culture and values seemed destined to displace Egypt's traditional ways, a development many people rejected or found disconcerting. Millions of Egyptians migrating from countryside to city faced traumatic shifts in their lives. In short, there were numerous things wrong with the society. The official ideology seemed unable to explain what was happening, and the government's proposed solutions seemed incapable of dealing with these issues and problems.

As one leading Egyptian magazine put it: The 1967 war marked the "beginning of the withdrawal of the edge of the 'prayer rug' from under the feet of the July [1952] revolution. The success of the revolution was due to the social class that turned to it. After the 1967 defeat, attitudes of the middle class turned to introversion, withdrawal, and silent political protest, which came to form the basis of the political rejectionist religious groups."[4]

SADAT REVIVES THE BROTHERHOOD

When Sadat came to power in October 1970, he was regarded by most of Nasir's senior lieutenants as a weak man who would be easy to control. This was not to be the case. He quickly purged the left when it challenged him. He released the Brothers still being held in camps in May 1971, including Supreme Guide Hasan al-Hudaybi, seeking to use them against the Marxists.[5]

Sadat's promotion of Islam was not merely opportunistic. He had pre-revolutionary ties to the Brotherhood and prized his reputation as a man of Islamic piety, an image he would develop into that of the "believing president." Still, he had also been a member of the tribunals which had earlier smashed the Brotherhood, and its leaders knew that their freedom to function – even their personal freedom from prison – could be quickly withdrawn if they displeased him.[6]

Having apparently learned from its experiences in 1954 and 1965, the Brotherhood supported Sadat from the time of his battle against the left (the May 1971 "Corrective Revolution") until its split with him over the peace initiative toward Israel in 1977. The Brotherhood had its own reasons for opposing the Marxists, whose secularism conflicted with its Islamic orientation. The group was socially and economically conservative. Its leading members tended to be, as one study put it, "primarily found among engineers, doctors, and other professionals, i.e., other elements of the social structure who tend to benefit from a 'capitalist' rather than a 'socialist' economic system."[7] Many businessmen, particularly from among former emigres to the pious Persian Gulf states, supported it. In addition, the Brotherhood itself was still not a legal organization and its leaders hoped to win from Sadat the right to function openly.

Sadat involved Brotherhood leaders in drafting sections of his new constitution.[8] This consultation, however, did not reconcile the Brotherhood to the document's provision that "the principles of the Islamic Shari'ah are a principal source of legislation."[9] They wanted the Shari'ah to be the sole source of Egypt's laws. Moreover, Article 3 stated that the people were the sole source of authority while, to a fundamentalist, only Allah held that power. Although the Constitution was far more favorable to Islam than Nasir's decrees (Islam was virtually ignored in his leftist National Charter of 1962), this issue remained controversial. The demand that all Egypt's laws be based on Islamic law enjoyed a broad popularity among the general public and even elements in the regime. It was constantly debated in the press and Parliament, becoming the main issue and slogan of the Brotherhood throughout the 1970s and 1980s.

While the Brotherhood was willing to live within the rules of the Sadat system, some of those released from prison – and younger people whom they influenced – were unreconstructed revolutionaries. In April 1974, came the first major action of a new generation of Islamic radicals. A small group calling itself the Islamic Liberation Organization unsuccessfully attempted a coup d'etat starting with the seizure of the Military Technical Academy in Heliopolis.

These followers of Salah Sariyyah, a veteran fundamentalist born in Palestine, believed that killing the heretical rulers would unleash a revolution bringing rule by the Shari'ah. They sought to capture weapons in their raid which would be used to wipe out Egypt's political leadership at a gathering where Sadat was to speak that evening. Instead, Sariyyah and his associates were captured and executed. Among the 92 people indicted, there were 16 military cadets and 2 sailors.[10] According to official statements, which might be underestimates, about 30 officers and over 100 enlisted men were discharged from the armed forces for their alleged sympathy toward the fundamentalists' assassination plan.[11]

On March 14, 1976, Sadat took a further step toward a semi-pluralist system by authorizing "platforms" within the single, ruling party – the Arab Socialist Union – as prototypes for a future multi-party structure. To defeat the left and seek to normalize their own position, Brotherhood activists supported Sadat in the 1976 parliamentary elections.[12] In return, the still illegal Brotherhood was allowed to start publishing a journal, *al-Da'wah*, which refrained from calling for revolution, attacking Sadat personally, or defaming the army. It did, however, strongly criticize the regime's failure to deal effectively with education, housing, transport, and inflation.

These continuing problems were further highlighted by the dramatic riots of January 1977 in response to Sadat's efforts to trim the high level of government food subsidies. These events led to a growing sense of national crisis which made fundamentalists more confident and the government less willing to tolerate their activities. While the clerical hierarchy helped the government by supporting it, this loyalty only further alienated radical fundamentalists from the clergy.

The rector of al-Azhar, Dr 'Abd al-Halim Mahmud, broadcast over Radio Cairo his support for the government and appealed to all Muslims to stop the violence. He denounced the riots as "the lowest that humanity could stoop to" and declared they were organized by "the enemy lying in wait to destroy all our aspirations." In contrast, a long editorial in *al-Da'wah* mocked the government for blaming the widespread riots on the Communists. Instead, it said the riots were merely "normal symptoms of a more profound and prevalent disease afflicting various sectors of our people."[13]

The national sense of crisis, the conflict between fundamentalists and clergy, and the government's determination to suppress the revolutionaries were all enhanced by the next development. In July 1977, the former Minister of Awqaf (religious endowments) and al-Azhar Affairs, Husayn al-Dhahabi, was kidnapped and was later murdered. The responsible party was al-Takfir wal-Hijrah, an extremist fundamentalist group which repudiated Egypt's entire social system and even viewed the Muslim clergy as heretics under whose auspices it was unlawful to pray. Thus, it was necessary to remove oneself from normal pursuits in order to prepare for the violent overthrow of the Jahiliyyah society. Al-Dhahabi had publicly criticized the sect and it seized him to demand the release of several previously arrested cadres. Five members, including the leader, Shukri Mustafa, were hanged in March 1978 for the murder. Many others were sentenced to long prison terms.

By this time, there were already two Islamic fundamentalist streams. The Brotherhood, though still illegal, focused its efforts on publications and electoral politics. In practice, it had become a reformist group. In contrast, several tiny sects organized on the college campuses and neighboring communities adopted Qutb's revolutionary ideology and carried out occasional violent attacks.

CONFRONTATION AND ASSASSINATION

The growth of Islamic groups happened at the same time as Egypt was suffering from deepening social, economic, and political problems. These factors, alongside several specific events, intensified the conflict between the fundamentalists and the regime. President Anwar al-Sadat's decision to make peace with Israel may have eased some of Egypt's material difficulties but heightened the fundamentalists' anger and broadened their base of support. The Iranian revolution came to power in February 1979, showing that Islamic fundamentalists could overturn a powerful regime. Khumayni's victory inspired some enthusiasm in Egypt but its impact there should not be overstated. The upheaval in Iran inspired Egyptian fundamentalists by proving that an Islamic revolution was possible, but hardly any of them saw Khumayni as a leader or Iran as a model of what they wanted to accomplish.

The more important factors were the developments in Egypt itself. The emboldened Brotherhood, long active on the Palestine issue, saw Sadat's action toward Israel as a betrayal of Egypt's Islamic duty. It condemned the Camp David agreements of September 17, 1978, denounced the Egyptian–Israeli peace treaty of March 26, 1979, and campaigned against the normalization of relations with Israel in August 1979. In these efforts, it allied itself with the left for the first time.

Sadat responded by publicly warning the Brotherhood on March 10, 1979; suspending *al-Da'wah* twice (April 29 and June 26, 1979); banning political activity in the universities; decreeing that autonomous mosques be brought under the control of the Ministry of Awqaf and al-Azhar Affairs (July 1979); and openly accusing al-Hudaybi's successor as Supreme Guide, 'Umar al-Tilimsani, and his movement of trying to overthrow the regime.[14] In 1980 the government enacted a law, known to opponents as the "Law of Shame," which made intentions to act against the government as well as overt revolutionary acts punishable by the powerful public prosecutor's office.

The government's civilian sector also enjoyed considerable assets in trying to combat or coopt Islamic sentiment. The armed forces, an institution particularly important to keep free of radical oppositionists, began publishing a religiously oriented magazine for soldiers called *al-Mujahid* to woo those wavering between traditionalism and radicalism. Mosque construction on army bases increased and the military even offered to pay the expenses of those soldiers participating in the Hajj and Umrah pilgrimages. The government also launched two Islamic publications of its own, *al-Liwa' al-Islami* ("The Islamic Banner") and *al-Urwah al-Wuthqah* ("The Firm Tie").[15]

As always, the regime also mobilized its own clerical supporters in order to neutralize anti-regime fundamentalists. The Ministry of Awqaf and al-Azhar Affairs had great power in rewarding compliant ulama and punishing dissidents. The mufti (chief religious judge) of Egypt issued a proclamation saying that Sadat's agreement with Israel was in harmony with the Qur'an and the views of the Prophet Muhammad. Men of religion willing to support the regime were paid well and given time on state radio and television, newspaper columns, and publishing subsidies. But ideology was more important than cupidity in shaping the pro-government thinking of the majority of clerics. The Sunni Muslim tradition of backing the authorities – as the lawful rulers and to avoid anarchy – was a decisive factor in the worldview of leading clerics and pious Egyptian Muslims.[16]

Sadat's regime, which had originally employed Islam to combat leftism, now intensified promotion of a moderate version of Islam in order to vitiate the appeal of the fundamentalists. Religion became a compulsory subject in schools, though the grade in that course was not added to the student's average and did not affect promotion. Religion was also required in the university curriculum. Government and pro-government figures called on the Islamic, moderate-dominated al-Azhar University to play a more active role in combating extremism.

In addition to the government, Egyptian secularist intellectuals also decried and opposed the rising tide of fundamentalism. One of them, Zaki Najib Mahmud, commented, "I rub my eyes and think I am living through a nightmare or a frivolous comedy. I had to live to see the fundamentalists' clamor for cutting off the hands of thieves, for stoning the adulterous and similar penalties which run counter to the spirit of our age! Can they really be serious in calling for a return to the glorious past while using the radio and other modern media which did not exist in that past and were created by the modern spirit?"[17] Yet, the relative freedom of Egypt only made it more possible for fundamentalists to propagandize and organize than in more repressive lands. Professor Emanuel Sivan wrote, the "gap between the level of modernity and that of Islamic revival is wider [in Egypt] than in other Arab countries." But the degree of modernity also inspired the turn toward Islam as a reaction against it.[18]

Rather than advocate violent revolution, the majority fundamentalist stream was taking advantage of the pluralist opening provided by Sadat. Two independent Islamic candidates, Shaykh Salah Abu Isma'il and Hasan al-Jamal, were elected to Parliament in 1979.[19] The Brotherhood followed up these opportunities by allying with legal opposition parties, ignoring their secular orientations. An agreement was reached in 1984 between al-Tilimsani and Fu'ad Siraj-al-Din, leader of the Wafd party, that Muslim Brothers would be put onto the Wafd's list in exchange for the votes of their supporters. This advantage was particularly important since Sadat, to limit the opposition, had required any party to win at least 8 per cent of the vote before receiving any parliamentary representation. The Wafd allowed the Brotherhood to retain discipline over its own members as well as to keep its own ideology.[20]

Particularly frightening for Egyptians was the prospect that fundamentalist radicalism could destroy the nation's unity and bring violent disorder. Sectarian strife between Muslims and the Coptic Christian minority (estimated at 10 per cent or more of the population) was especially dangerous. The general response of fundamentalists to the Coptic issue has been that there are no problems, that they respect the Christians, and that Christians would be well-treated in an Islamic state. Clashes, the argument continues, are caused by outsiders seeking to stir up trouble. But such bland assurances could not cancel the fact that fundamentalist groups were often at the forefront of anti-Christian agitation. Large-scale fighting broke out on June 17–19, 1981, triggered by a quarrel between Muslim and Coptic neighbors in the poor Cairo suburb of al-Zawiyyah al-Hamra'. In this event *al-Da'wah* took an extremist line. It claimed the Copts were arrogant and militant, slandering Islam and gathering arms to kill Muslims. In the tense conditions of the time, such statements were dangerous provocations.[21]

When Sadat judged that the Brotherhood had grown too bold in its criticisms and the revolutionary groups too daring in their anti-regime violence, he decided that the fundamentalists must be suppressed. In September 1981, trying to repeat what Nasir had done in 1954, he ordered the arrest of over 1500 people, almost 90 per cent of them Islamic activists (though Christian militants were also rounded up). They included Brotherhood leader al-Tilimsani and the popular Cairo preacher 'Abd al-Hamid Kishk, as well as Brotherhood spokesmen like Salih 'Ashmawi and Muhammad 'Abd al-Qudus.

Protest demonstrations outside Kishk's mosque were broken up by police. The Brotherhood's three chief publications were banned and ten Islamic religious societies were dissolved. The government took control of 40,000 privately owned mosques (most held by their members in the form of religious endowmnents), and announced that only approved preachers would be allowed to deliver sermons in them.

Even more worrisome than the Brotherhood were the autonomous Islamic groups (jam'iyat) which had formed in universities and neighborhoods. Fundamentalists had won elections in many student governments. There were an estimated 7000 known members of their organizations. The government imprisoned 235 commanders of university groups, among them national leader Hilmi al-Jazzar. Sadat said he wished to offer his "young sons, who have been deceived ... an opportunity to think and return [to the fold]."[22]

Alongside the roundups, the government also implemented new regulations designed to weaken fundamentalism at universities. Special campus police units were reintroduced to patrol the grounds. Faculty chairmen and deans were given a free hand in punishing students for "indulging in party politics." It was forbidden to carry weapons on campus and non-students were denied entry. The opening of the academic year was postponed by three weeks to give the university authorities time to prepare.[23]

Thus was the status of Islamic fundamentalism on the eve of the 1981 anniversary celebrations of the October 1973 war. But as President Sadat stood in the reviewing stand that day, he was shot to death by Islamic terrorists of al-Jihad, some of them junior members – and one a lieutenant colonel – of the Egyptian military. Al-Jihad militants in Asyut launched a takeover bid and were quickly crushed, with dozens of casualties on both sides. There were reports of violence elsewhere. Vice-President Husni Mubarak took over and faced the crisis. He stated that the attack was part of a larger plot to kill the country's leaders and install a Khumayni-style Islamic regime but insisted that the number of army men involved in the conspiracy was "extremely small."[24]

Like the failed assassination against Nasir in 1954, the successful killing of Sadat in 1981 was another turning point for the course of fundamentalism in Egypt. Yet rather than signaling the onset of a revolution, as the extremists had hoped, the murder horrified Egyptians and ended the second wave of fundamentalist growth in Egypt. Ironically, however, the replacement of Sadat by Mubarak brought new opportunities for a more moderate, reformist brand of fundamentalism.

MUBARAK TAMES THE OPPOSITION

In addition to repressing the disturbances, Mubarak instituted a new strategy of reconciling the opposition, much of which was also shaken by the crisis and feared complete suppression. Essentially, the result was a reinforced political contract in which the government allowed the critics to function – even consulting with them on occasion – in exchange for their restraint. Mubarak quickly met with Ibrahim Shukri, Khalid Muhyi al-Din, Mustafa Kamil Murad, and Mumtaz Nassar, leaders of the legal opposition parties of the left and right. Mubarak reportedly told them, "The fundamentalists will kill you before they kill me," stressing their common interest in stability and limiting Islamic extremism.[25]

After a thorough investigation and a three-month trial, a military court condemned four assassins and al-Jihad's leader, Mohammed 'Abd al-Salam Faraj, to death in March 1982. Five people were sentenced to life imprisonment, and twelve were given long prison terms. Two others, including the blind Shaykh 'Umar 'Abd al-Rahman who authorized the assassination on the basis of Islamic doctrine, were acquitted.[26]

Mubarak's first years in office were marked by relative social peace. The Camp David accords could be blamed on the late Sadat while his successor could maintain them and reap the benefits. The Brotherhood continued its electoral activities but failed to obtain either its own legalization or the establishment of the Shari'ah as the basis of all laws. The radical groups functioned on campuses and in some communities, carrying out a few terrorist actions, but did not threaten the state's stability.

The terrorist attacks which took place during 1987, though more numerous than in the preceding or succeeding years, illustrate the lack of success for such tactics. The targets of unsuccessful fundamentalist assaults included Makram Muhamad Ahmad, chief editor of the weekly *al Musawwar* and an outspoken critic of fundamentalism, and former Interior Minister Nabawi Isma'il. The new radical group responsible for these attacks, Survivors from [Hell] Fire, was smashed and many of its leaders were captured. There were periodic roundups of extremists and occasional small riots or demonstrations. But more terrorism came from leftist or radical Nasirist groups, supported by Libya, than from the fundamentalists.[27]

A more peaceful Islamic revival did, however, flourish and involved millions of Egyptians. Mosque attendance increased; a growing number of women adopted conservative Islamic fashion in public. This Islamic cultural wave was symbolized in the spring of 1985 by a battle of bumper stickers when drivers began displaying Islamic slogans on their cars. Some described this phenomenon as a kind of rolling plebiscite on the role of religion in society; others suggested the people were responding to threats that cars lacking such stickers would be vandalized. Either way, social developments seemed to suggest rising, if relatively apolitical, Islamic power.

Perhaps the strongest issue for the fundamentalists was the Shari'ah question on which their positions were supported by broad sectors of the Egyptian people. The Parliament had appointed a committee in December 1978 to determine how Egypt's current laws might be made to comply with the Shari'ah. It found that the great majority were already consistent with Islamic law though, for the fundamentalists, this was hardly the point since they wanted the Shari'ah to herald the inauguration of an Islamic state. The committee's task was completed in 1982 and parliament determined that the reform of bringing all laws into accord with Islam must be gradual. This provoked a stormy debate, peaking in 1985, with the opposition making immediate change its main demand. The government, however, never yielded.[28]

On May 5, 1985, parliament defeated the effort to make the Shari'ah the law of the land. Although the constitutional court ruled a 1979 law increasing women's marriage and divorce rights unconstitutional on technical grounds, on the same day, July 1, 1985, parliament passed a virtually identical statute.[29]

Although the fundamentalists lost on both the Shari'ah and women's rights, there was no upsurge in violence or anti-regime activity. In the short run, at least, the growth of Islam seemed to be a classic case of religion reconciling people with the difficult circumstances of their lives. The government thus remained firmly in control, tolerating but not appeasing the Brotherhood and the moderate fundamentalists. Simultaneously, it extended a tough policy of sanctions and repression against radical fundamentalists who engaged in violence. The regime also exercised a great deal of authority over the religious establishment as a whole. Of the approximately 50,000 mosques in Egypt, 7000 were directly controlled by the government and the rest were under its supervision.

To maintain the support of the clerics, the government gave them better financial conditions and paid a fee for those giving the important Friday sermon. Al-Azhar built up its programs for training local clergy and religious teachers. The Ministry of Awqaf and al-Azhar Affairs oversaw institutions to ensure they maintained proper religious practices. In the words of the ministry's director of mosques, Saykh Yusu Mahmud Ahmad, "It supervised what is said in the mosques to guarantee honesty and truth in order to safeguard the truth and integrity of the faith and to protect the country's safety."[30]

While the vast majority of Muslim clergy remained supportive of the system, the Brotherhood was confirmed in its reformist strategy. Feeling that its own greatest achievement was in reestablishing its organization, the Brotherhood was determined to be credible as a peaceful, law-abiding group. Rather than affirming its revolutionary past, the Brotherhood's leaders denounced such activities as myths created by their Nasirist opponents. As Muhammad Abu al-Nasr, the supreme guide of the Brotherhood who had come to office after al-Tilimsani's death, told interviewers in 1987, "For over 30 years, the Free Officers' Movement has been maligning the Brotherhood, portraying its leaders as killers and murderers and filling the press with such lies and distributing free books containing such accusations." But this image was now changing, "The people saw how we operate . . . proving to them that the allegations about us were purely false. In this year's elections, the situation was different . . . Everyone raised the motto, 'The only solution is Islam.'"[31]

The April 1987 elections were indeed an impressive show of the Brotherhood's popularity. The government had clear advantages in publicity, money, and power, and the ruling party won 339 seats with 70 per cent of the vote. But, the "Islamic Alliance" of the Socialist Labor Party, the Liberal Party, and the Brotherhood, won 60 seats with 17 per cent. Most of these voters and members of parliament belonged to the Brotherhood. The Wafd party gained 35 seats with 11 per cent of the vote.[32]

Though some secularist intellectuals found these trends frightening – one suggested they might turn "Egypt into another Lebanon" – the government continued its policy of tolerance plus constraint.[33] It allowed relative freedom of organization and publication, television appearances by opposition clerics (something not permitted their secular opposition colleagues), fundamentalist candidacies and victories for professional association and parliamentary posts, the establishment of medical clinics in mosques (used to recruit people), and travel abroad to Islamic conferences, even in Iran.[34]

As one Brotherhood activist, Ma'mun al-Hudaybi, commented, "It is not wise policy for any state to deny the presence of a large segment of the population that espouses a certain ideology and . . . whose members are cohesively and strongly bound together. Nonrecognition of such an entity cannot in any way be in the state's interest." Far from rejecting this cooperative arrangement, he urged the state to go further, providing a greater incentive for the Brotherhood to use its energy within legal channels. "In every phase we never tired of searching for a way out of our situation because we did not want to remain illegal," he added. If the Brotherhood attacked the government, it also did not use violence and it criticized the radicals who did. Since it had a great deal to lose, the Brotherhood did not even organize demonstrations and remained quiescent despite defeats on its most passionate causes like that of the Shari'ah.[35]

This acquiescence was particularly vital for the Mubarak regime as it faced severe economic problems in the 1980s. Egypt's debt had risen from $3 billion in 1973 to $18 billion in 1981, $24 million in 1985, $44 billion in 1987, and $50 billion by 1988, according to World Bank figures. Annual debt service reached $5.5 billion. Falling oil prices reduced remittances from Egyptians working in the Arab oil-producing countries, Suez Canal revenues, and Arab tourism. In 1986, the Egyptian economy reached a low point. These hardships might have been expected to encourage internal instability and an upsurge of radical activity. Yet the fundamentalists were well under control, and – given its situation – Egypt faced remarkably little internal disorder, despite isolated though frightening outbreaks like the February 1986 Cairo riots.[36]

CONCLUSIONS

Mubarak could congratulate himself on the relative success of his Islamic policy at helping to preserve peace at home. While the trend toward Muslim practices among the general populace was evident, much of this was a non-political return to traditions. The radicals remained small in number and their violence was contained by the authorities. Their ideologies were too far out of Egyptian Islam's mainstream to have mass appeal.

Egypt's history has taught the Brotherhood leaders that their organization could survive and prosper if it adopted a reformist ideology. Challenging the government was a losing proposition. Men who had spent many years in terrible prisons had no wish to return there. The younger revolutionaries and radicals saw this conclusion as a betrayal. But fiery ideologues preaching new interpretations of Islam gained few followers and those resorting to violence were quickly imprisoned or executed. The growth of observance of Islam among the populace seemed to reconcile the masses with the status quo rather than radicalize them.

Nasir and Sadat had enjoyed similar periods when Islamic organizations were apparently crushed or tamed. While these groups had never seemed likely to overthrow the regime, they did cause it considerable trouble. They attempted to kill Nasir and did kill Sadat. Given Egypt's enormous problems – and the inevitable search of many young people for alternatives – Mubarak and Egypt's foreign friends cannot take the current situation for granted. Still, the difficulty in overturning the army, challenging the government, and defeating the popularity of Egyptian or pan-Arab nationalism has imbued the older generation of Muslim Brotherhood leaders with caution. Officers and members of the ruling elite have a deep, abiding mistrust of the Brotherhood which makes them determined to limit its power while willing, if necessary, to repress it again.

An examination of the ideology and divisions among these Islamic forces allows us better to understand their strategy and objectives as well as to gain some capacity for predicting their behavior. The situation of these fundamentalists also tells us a great deal about Egypt's contemporary society and its prospects.

3 The Muslim Brotherhood: Ideology and Program

The repression that the Muslim Brothers suffered in the past – including a period of almost two decades when it was totally outlawed – has affected its attitudes toward the government, revolution, violence, and the ideology of the revolutionary fundamentalists. The Brothers have been successful at reestablishing their structure and maintaining their freedom only at the government's sufferance, and their leaders are well aware of this. The relationship between the movement and the national leaders – Sadat, then Mubarak – has had a profound effect on the Brotherhood's thinking. It now claims status as a legal, reform-oriented group trying to improve society rather than seize power.

The modern period for the Brotherhood began in 1971. Sadat released hundreds of imprisoned leaders of the group, including 'Umar al-Tilimsani, its future leader. Sadat met the organization's delegation at the Ganaklis rest house and offered them an alliance which finally culminated with his issuance of a full pardon to all imprisoned members in July 1975. *Al-Da'wah* was allowed to resume publication the following year.[1]

For its part, the Brotherhood rewrote its own history, downplaying the conflict with Nasir, denying the 1954 assassination attempt, and even claiming credit for the coup against the monarchy. "The June 23 [1952] revolution was our revolution," claimed Brotherhood leader Muhammad al-Ma'mun al-Hudaybi. "We were one of its major forces ... If you review the Muslim Brotherhood's history, you will find that all the principles of the revolution were taken from our heritage. They [Nasir and the Free Officers] did not apply them and deviated from them. This is our main reason for our dispute with them." Hudaybi even claimed that the Brotherhood was an advocate of a democracy betrayed by the Nasirists. "Let us take the principle of a sound parliamentary life, for example. This is one of our basic demands. Have we achieved such a thing 40 years later?" Any mention of the Secret Organization, which handled terrorism and military training in the 1940s and 1950s, made the revived Brotherhood's leaders extremely uncomfortable. Its violence and apparent revolutionary activities during that earlier period, according to al-Hudaybi, were merely intended to fight British colonialism and occupation. "Every popular movement in Egypt or anywhere else had its own secret organization at one time or another," he explained.[2]

Even after the shock of Sadat's trip to Jerusalem and the Camp David accords, the Brotherhood did not abandon this new moderate posture in practice, though its rhetoric became stridently radical. As the Egyptian magazine *Ruz al-Yusuf* recalled, the Brotherhood's leader, 'Umar al-Tilimsani "did not pursue an extremist policy against Sadat or revolt against him. Al-Tilimsani even called on the Arab states not to ostracize Sadat. Some Muslim Brothers considered this stand as less than was necessary to oppose peace with Israel. Al-Tilimsani said he opposed the peace treaty from a religious basis (i.e., Islam rejects the occupation of Muslim land by non-Muslims). But al-Tilimsani launched no attacks on Sadat. No violence was allowed."[3]

The leading Egyptian scholar of modern fundamentalism, Professor Saad Eddin Ibrahim, summarizes the Brotherhood's operational ideology. When Sadat finally allowed the organization to revive, "its remaining leaders had made the strategic decision to discard violence. The decision was preceded by heated debates among the membership inside and outside Nasir's prisons. [Some] younger members never accepted the new strategy of 'non-violence' and became the founders of the new jama'at and jam'iyat as well as a number of relatively apolitical Islamic reform groups."[4] When the new, radical groups began using terrorism and operating independently of the Brotherhood, Ibrahim wrote, "The Muslim Brotherhood's leadership has detached itself from other Islamic groups which engage in violent confrontations . . . With this tactical caveat, which is reiterated in nearly all issues of *al-Da'wah*, the Muslim Brotherhood has not spared any occasion to highlight the corrupt practices of the regime, often without mentioning Sadat by name."[5]

AL-TILIMSANI'S POLICY

The leader in this process from militancy to moderation was 'Umar al-Tilimsani, a lawyer by training, a member of the Brotherhood since the early 1930s, and a close associate of founder Hasan al-Banna. Imprisoned in the 1940s and again from 1954 to 1971, he became Supreme Guide in 1973. He died in May 1986 at the age of 81 and, though the Brotherhood was still a "dissolved organization," he was given a large funeral attended by many national political figures.[6]

Al-Tilimsani openly and frequently talked about the Brotherhood's new moderate approach. Although he disagreed with the slogan "No religion in politics and no politics in religion," al-Tilimsani always stressed the group's need for official recognition and acceptance. He praised Mubarak as a leader who was bringing more freedom, and described him as "a very good, intelligent, clear man who knows what he wants." It is not surprising that the radicals accused the Brotherhood of selling out to the regime.[7]

Nonetheless, the Brotherhood continued to have a large number of complaints about the government's conduct of policy, the extent of corruption, and the shape of Egyptian society. Foremost among these was the regime's unwillingness to legalize the organization, whose uncertain status was thus a constant threat whenever the rulers deemed its behavior unsatisfactory. The Brotherhood was quite willing to use legal channels but timid in challenging the government. If the government were not to legalize the Brotherhood, warned Mustafa Mashur, a top leader, "We will file a suit in court . . . and with God's help we will try to win it." The Brotherhood's official organ, *al-Da'wah*, remained banned after the events of 1981 and the group had to operate through its unofficial control of the *Al-Liwa' al-Islam* magazine.[8]

Al-Tilimsani both repeated this complaint and defended himself from accusations of appeasing the rulers: "The regime has not given us back our legal status and we have not ceased from calling for the restoration of our rights, but we receive no answer. Some opposition groups accuse us of collaboration with the regime, but they are blind. We are directed in our opposition and our actions by the teachings of Allah."[9]

Al-Tilimsani denied that the Brotherhood had ever used terrorism, saying that al-Banna had condemned it (though the group clearly carried out assassinations in the 1940s and 1950s).

> From the reign of King Farouk [1936–1952] until today, Egyptian governments have closed the doors to us that have been open to everyone else, as though we were not Egyptian citizens. The organization cannot legally exist. Its magazine was suspended . . . Religious gatherings and the call for such gatherings are forbidden. Security men continue to pursue the Brotherhood day after day. The elections came and the door was closed to the candidacy of independents. Before this there was the Political Parties Law which

completely isolated the Brotherhood . . . However, it was necessary for us to participate in the elections, so we saw the Wafd as the party closest to us, especially after [party leader] Fu'ad Siraj-al-Din condemned secularism and affirmed support for article 2 of the constitution. In addition, the Wafd itself has not killed or tortured any members of the Brotherhood, nor does it pursue them or confiscate their money and possessions.[10]

Al-Tilimsani was defending the Brotherhood's growing cooperation with the Wafd. The populist, secular-oriented Wafd had dominated the political scene (though its electoral success was often foiled by the palace) during the monarchy but had quickly been eliminated by Nasir. In political and ideological terms, the Brotherhood and Wafd were quite different but they found each other useful in a formal electoral alliance in 1984. As al-Tilimsani explained, "The Wafd is a legal conduit and the Brotherhood has a popular base, so what is wrong with them coordinating in this area to bring about good?"[11]

Indeed these electoral maneuvers were extremely successful. They allowed the Brotherhood to circumvent its non-legality by using other parties as fronts for its influence. The Brotherhood yielded none of its independence or main positions in these alliances while forcing the party politicians to make concessions for its support. As an Egyptian publication concluded, "Perhaps the greatest manifestation of victory for the Muslim Brotherhood is that all parties without exception, have placed at the top of their platforms the application of Islamic Law, whereas they had all previously considered this demand to be 'reactionary,' regressive, and a mixing of religion with politics and politics with religion."[12]

GENERAL STRATEGY AND ELECTORAL POLITICS

The strategic goal of the Muslim Brotherhood in the 1970s and 1980s was to rebuild its structure and reestablish its influence. Even its greatest Egyptian critics acknowledge that "The Muslim Brotherhood has not generally thought in any clearly defined way about taking power or forming a government." Instead, al-Tilimsani and other leaders defined its role as a "watchman" or "guardian" ensuring that the government did not stray from Islam and its laws. In short, it constituted itself as an Islamic pressure group.[13]

In the 1984 elections, the Brotherhood provided the Wafd with the "Islamic vote." The party won 58 of the 488 seats with 15 per cent of the vote. Although alignment with the fundamentalists cost the Wafd some Coptic and secular support, the results were satisfactory. The Brotherhood now held eight seats in the People's Assembly and found dozens of other members sympathetic to some of its positions. As one leader put it, "The Brotherhood was the popular base of the Wafd and the Wafd represented a political window for the Brotherhood. Both sides benefited . . . We gain more than we lose from our presence in these parties."[14] The group also did particularly well in elections for leadership of professional organizations – lawyers, journalists, engineers – and university student unions. In each case, the government took many measures to fix the elections in order to minimize such advances.[15]

The Brotherhood's real preference was to have its own party, a demand repeatedly stated by al-Tilimsani and other leaders, but the authorities refused to yield any ground on this point. Not only did the Mubarak regime want to limit the Brotherhood's strength and keep it dependent on the government's good will, it was also reluctant to have a real test of fundamentalism's popularity, much less to allow one party to claim a monopoly on Islam.[16]

Brotherhood leader Salah Shadi gave further expression to the reason for wanting a party and the basis for the organization's self-restraint. "We are forbidden to talk about the Brotherhood's ideology. Otherwise, we would be accused of reviving a disbanded group, and the penalty for this charge is three years in prison . . . If we had a 'party,' the Brotherhood's 'quality' would restrain the [radical] groups' 'quantity.'" This argument, a major point in the Brotherhood's appeal to the government for tolerance and concessions, is that allowing a legal fundamentalist party would lessen the support and participation in the revolutionary terrorist groups. Asked, "What road will you follow?" even if the government does not change its policy, Shadi quickly responded, "The legal road."[17]

The Brotherhood's commitment to this course is illustrated by one incident. Whan al-Tilimsani was dying, its leaders submitted an urgent request to the Interior Ministry asking for permission to hold a general assembly to select a new Supreme Guide. The government rejected the plea on the basis that an illegal organization could not have a legal meeting. The Brotherhood gave in and called a small private gathering for this purpose.[18]

Friction over each side's relative power plagued the alliance with the Wafd, however, and the Brotherhood broke with it, joining the small Liberal Party in 1986. Given the relatively greater size of the Brotherhood over the Liberals (even compared to the Brotherhood/ Wafd balance), these new partners were dominated even more by their Islamic colleagues. The Brotherhood's faction was led by Salah Abu Isma'il (who became the party's vice-president) and Yusuf al-Badri. The Liberals were forced to abandon their earlier acceptance of the Egypt–Israel Camp David accords, change the party's name (dropping the word "Socialist"), and give the Brotherhood predominant influence over the party newspaper and 50 per cent of the organizational posts.[19]

The Brotherhood's willingness to "punish" the Wafd by marching out with its supporters only increased the group's leverage within the opposition. As one Arab writer said, "No one can dispute ... that the Muslim Brotherhood, its illegality under the law notwithstanding, has come to represent a considerable weight in the political theatre in Egypt and is a force that has its own popularity and supporters who follow it wherever it goes ... [The Muslim Brotherhood has] firmly established itself."[20]

In the 1987 elections, the Brotherhood led an Islamic Alliance including the Liberals and the Socialist Labor parties, whose platform called for economic reforms, building private-sector industry and agriculture, more democracy, less corruption, and applying the Shari'ah. The Muslim Brothers proved indefatigable campaigners, producing a large number of posters, registering people through the mosques it controlled, and turning out voters for their candidates. The Alliance won 60 seats of which the Brotherhood held 36. An *al-Ahram* election analysis concluded that the Brothers brought the opposition over 420,000 votes, more than one-third of the Alliance's support and about 8 per cent of the total ballots.[21]

This achievement – which again might be undercounted in the official results – was impressive but also serves as a reminder that the Brotherhood's base of support is limited. For its part, the Brotherhood was also not eager to enter the government unless it could implement some of its principal objectives. It would not, al-Tilimsani explained, "participate in any ministry unless the first article in the regulations of that ministry is application of Islamic law." Moreover, in July 1987 the Brotherhood expressed its continued deference to the regime by joining the ruling National Democratic Party in voting for President Mubarak's nomination to a second six-year presidential term. Only the Wafd opposed it.[22]

The Brotherhood continued to demand more political rights through legal channels and the government still gave little ground. One Brotherhood leader threatened in 1988, "The election law was designed to keep the Muslim Brotherhood out of the elections ... The Muslim Brothers will take the society's program to the Committee for Political Parties and request its approval. If the committee does not approve, a lawsuit will be filed against the Committee for Political Parties."[23] This was not exactly a call to Holy War against the Mubarak regime.

The Brotherhood also built a strong institutional base which gave it wealth, prestige, and a great deal to lose in any confrontation with the government. Its supporters won positions in the doctors', journalists', and lawyers' associations and in university clubs. Islamic banks and investment companies with links to it provided interest-free financial services. A range of medical, social, and charitable organizations extended its network throughout Egyptian society.

After two decades of effort, the Brotherhood had done well to reestablish itself and carve out an impressive niche within Egyptian politics. The current generation of its leaders, at least, was committed to peaceful, legal efforts. They knew first-hand the costs of unbridled militancy and the difficulty of making an Islamic revolution. Al-Tilimsani and his colleages thus revised Brotherhood ideology in order to make the organization into a pressure or lobbying group. Its priority was to make the Shari'ah the basis of national law ("the Qur'an is our Constitution!" was one oft-repeated slogan).

Al-Tilimsani's successor, Muhammad Ahmad Abu al-Nasr, was equally adamant yet equally conciliatory over the Shari'ah issue. While attacking the authorities for not implementing the Shari'ah, he added, "As Muslims, the [government] officials are not really against implementation of the Islamic Shari'ah; it is just that there are pressures here and there to delay its implementation. In the end, however, only what is right prevails; everything else disappears." He continued, "All we ask is that the authorities declare that they agree to implement the Islamic Shari'ah. The actual implementation could then begin gradually and quietly until full implementation ... is achieved. To give you some examples, under Islam alcoholic drinks were banned in three stages and slavery in several stages."[24] This view implies great patience and a belief in the good will – and proper Islamic thinking – of government officials, an attitude the radicals would never accept.

ATTITUDE TOWARD RADICALS, VIOLENCE AND DEMONSTRATIONS

The Brotherhood views revolutionary groups as offshoots of its movement and ideology that have mistakenly taken up violence. The problem of revolutionary groups is blamed on both the government's errors in being tough with the young people and its restrictions on the Brotherhood. One Brotherhood leader attributed the radicals' misjudgments "to the passion of youth. We all go through this phase at first."[25]

Al-Tilimsani noted that the revolutionary groups al-Jihad and al-Takfir wal-Hijra had called the Brotherhood infidels and claimed it had renounced jihad. Al-Tilimsani explained, albeit somewhat disingenuously, that his movement's ideology was different because, "Our religion forbids violence ... If I permit killing another person who differs with me, then I also permit my own killing in return." In further denying that the Brotherhood is a violent organization, al-Tilimsani added, "If there had been a desire for violence and political assassination in the Muslim Brotherhood, the extremist youth would have joined us, and would not have found the need to join other groups." 'Isam al-Din al-Aryan, former leader of the Islamic Group at the University of Cairo and now a Brotherhood leader, says that there are two kinds of Islamic opposition groups; those having foreign connections who seek to overthrow the government, and the Brotherhood which seeks "to introduce reforms and change the regime by legal means."[26]

These protestations seem somewhat ironic as history, or perhaps reflect the costly experience of the Brotherhood's past violence. The killing of Prime Minister al-Nuqrashi had brought the retaliatory murder of al-Banna; the attempt on Nasir's life was terribly punished. Yet the government has attributed no act of terrorism or violence to the Brotherhood since 1981, a sign that the leadership is practicing what it preaches.

The Brotherhood and similarly minded Islamic activists also argue that the radical groups would wither if the Shari'ah were adopted as the basis of Egypt's laws. One commentator claims, "All the officials have acknowledged the necessity of this application and have admitted, including the ruling party deputies, that application is a popular demand, although neither ... have set an immediate time for its attainment. Delay, in my opinion, means a wider gap between the growing Islamic current and the rulers which gives the malicious foreign forces – and they are many – a chance to split the ranks and make things more difficult."[27]

While the Brotherhood does not like to discuss the subject, the basis for the radicals' terrorism and revolutionary activity derives from the thought of one of its own former leaders. Sayyid Qutb was first to declare it permissible to wage war (jihad) on nominally Muslim societies which, by abandoning the religion's precepts, could be considered comparable to pre-Islamic society (jahiliyyah). And it was the then Supreme Guide of the Brotherhood, al-Hudaybi, who strongly criticized these themes of Qutb in his own book, *Preachers, Not Judges*, and won the day for a more moderate faction.[28]

The Brotherhood continues to reject these central elements in the radicals' ideology. For example, a leading Brotherhood figure, Muhammad Kamal 'Abd al-Aziz, attacked the radical groups by saying, "A Muslim has no right to accuse another of infidelity, regardless of his ideology, unless the latter openly declares his infidelity, in which case he will answer to the state and the law and not to any individual or group." Brotherhood leader Abu al-Nasr commented, "The Muslim Brotherhood does not believe in renouncing a ruler, a subject, or anyone who upholds the two vows of Islam [to God and the prophet]."[29]

Equally impressive is the Brotherhood's refusal to engage in demonstrations – even for causes its supports – which might bring the authorities' anger. When there were attempts to organize a mass demonstration in Cairo favoring establishing the Shari'ah as the basis for all legislation, the Brotherhood denounced the idea. Muslim Brotherhood member of parliament Muhammad Matrawi explained that his group only used legal, parliamentary methods and Egypt was not ready for demonstrations.[30]

The problem of violence in Brotherhood theory was particularly brought to the fore when al-Tilimsani died and was replaced as Supreme Guide by Muhammad Hamid Abu al-Nasr. Nasr claimed that, as a young man, he had been the first person in Egypt to pledge allegiance to the organization's founder, Hasan al-Banna. He had taken the Brotherhood's ritual oath over a Qur'an and a gun – a symbolism not precisely pacifist in its implications. Over 50 years later, Abu al-Nasr reinterpreted this event: "The presence of the Qur'an alongside the pistol did not signify murder and assassination. Rather, it was a reference to protection of the truth by force."[31]

There is a generational aspect to the gap between the Brothers and the revolutionary groups. Though the Brotherhood has many younger members, its leadership is chosen in a traditionalist manner by the long service and age of the individuals. The radicals engage in a more modernist style by having young, charismatic individuals direct them. There are also some differences in recruitment patterns, with the Brotherhood attracting low-level government employees, shop owners, and less-educated people, as well as a cadre of successful businessmen and professionals. The radicals draw their supporters from people with some university training but who are likely to be either still students or unemployed graduates.

It is clear, however, that while the Brotherhood views the revolutionaries as badly guided people fighting for a relatively good cause, it also sees them as competitors. The most vivid example of this conflict was in Asyut, the stronghold of Islamic fundamentalist movements in Egypt. In 1987, the Brotherhood won a parliament seat there by a wide majority. But when the Brotherhood became more active at the local university, claiming the name of the Islamic Group there, supporters of al-Jihad disrupted some of its meetings and there were violent clashes. The Brotherhood's parliamentary representative and president of the faculty club, Dr Muhammad al-Sayyid Habib, called the radicals "a small group of young zealots . . . There is heat and excitability and the young people have limitless zeal, impatience, rashness, and energy, without reasonable, mature, balanced leaders . . . We find that when they leave the university they turn to the matters of life and view its requirements differently . . . The loud voice always gets the attention; but in the long run, the calm way is the one that allows reason and compassion and is in keeping with the nature of these people. It is also the true way, the way of the Prophet." In short, the Brotherhood has a patronizing attitude toward the young radicals. They did not learn the lesson of the government's power and the difficulty of staging a revolution that the Brotherhood leaders grasped in the 1950s (and had time to think about while sitting in prison during much of the 1960s and some of the 1970s). The extremists were seen as young and hotheaded, failing to understand that Islam does not flourish under compulsion.[32]

The question of whether the Brotherhood has become an organization of sincere reformers or whether it acts merely out of caution and fear of the authorities remains open. The distinction may matter little if the regime continues to be able to intimidate the Brotherhood or to contain it with concessions allowing it to function. There have been real changes in Brotherhood ideology toward a more moderate position though this situation could be altered in extreme circumstances or when a new generation of leaders takes over in the future.

INTERNAL FACTIONS

In the 1980s, the two main Brotherhood factions were led by Mustafa Mashhur and Salah Shadi. Both men were veteran members of the movement, originally recruited by its founder. Mashhur had been sentenced to 10 years in 1954 and had subsequently lived in exile in Munich. He returned to Egypt but then left in September 1981 when he learned of Sadat's impending roundups, and spent five more years in West Germany before returning. Some writers suggested that Mashhur took the harder line and that Shadi was an especially vocal advocate of the Brotherhood having its own party rather than joining existing ones. But personalities, rather than ideology, seemed to divide these groups.

When al-Tilimsani died on May 21, 1986, the man chosen to succeed him was a compromise candidate: Muhammad Ahmad Abu al-Nasr, a 73-year-old veteran of the movement and the senior member of the National Guidance Committee. He rose gradually in positions of responsibility from a branch chief in his home town of Manfalut, to the al-Jihad office in three larger towns, headed the Asyut area (the most intensely fundamentalist region in Egypt), and then was supervisor for all Upper Egypt. He was on the committee responsible for obtaining arms for the Brotherhood force in Palestine in 1948, then a member of the guidance committee for Upper Egypt. He was one of the three Brotherhood officials who maintained liaison with the leaders of the 1952 coup (the other two were executed by Nasir). Abu al-Nasr was sentenced to 25 years of hard labor by the regime and was imprisoned from 1954 to 1972. In the election, Abu al-Nasr was particularly supported by the other ex-prisoners from the Nasir era.[33]

One reason Shadi was not chosen provides an interesting perspective on the contemporary Brotherhood's attitude toward violence. Some members of the Guidance Council rejected Shadi because he had been a member of the Brotherhood's Secret Organization during the pre-Nasir period, an association that would link his name to the regime's suspicion that the Brotherhood was planning terrorism and revolution. As one leader commented, that connection might allow the organization's enemies to attack it. Shadi was a police officer who, like Abu al-Nasr, had been personally recruited by al-Banna. On one occasion, Shadi recounted, he saw the Special Organization's head defy al-Banna. Thus, Shadi implied, he had become especially conscious of the danger that a violent underground branch might seek to take over the Brotherhood.[34]

Abu al-Nasr's success, however, did not mark the end of factional conflict. The fact that a number of members of the Brotherhood's leadership continued to live in self-imposed exile (Munich being the main center) meant that intrigues, albeit unsuccessful ones, were likely to continue. What is most telling is the absence of an active internal lobby insisting that the Brotherhood should follow the example of the radical groups in taking up arms against the regime. The Brotherhood never protested as radicals were arrested (an estimated 2500 from late 1985 through 1986, according to Interior Ministry figures). Nor did it take any active role during the February 1986 Central Security Unit riots. All factions, at least for the time being, accept the justifications of reformism propounded by al-Tilimsani, though there are certainly groups among the younger recruits who have sympathy toward the jama'at.[35]

CONCLUSIONS

If the Brotherhood's beloved founder, Hasan al-Banna, laid down the organization's broad guidelines and original revolutionary aims, al-Tilimsani and his colleagues created a new ideology for the group. It eschewed violence and revolutionary activity – the Brotherhood has no military force like the old Special Organization of the earlier era – in favor of legal and reformist efforts. Criticism of Egypt's government and society is still sharp, but is also constrained by a fear of persecution. The very gains made by the Brotherhood, including its lucrative links with Islamic investment companies, give it a stake in the stability of the existing system. While it hoped to win over the radical activists, the Brotherhood has also come to see them as competitors for the Islamic activists and public. On a number of critical matters, the Brotherhood has supported Mubarak's government.[36]

The path taken by the revolutionary groups – in their criticism of Egyptian politics, society, and of the Muslim Brotherhood itself – was very different. The Brotherhood's Supreme Guide Abu al-Nasr, explained, "The general atmosphere [at present] is not conducive to the establishment of an Islamic state . . . The most important thing is to work for the implementation of the Islamic Shari'ah and to try to persuade the authorities to abolish the freedom-restricting laws ... Everything can be done on [the basis of the Shari'ah] from education to the methods of government. Islam should govern all aspects of activity. That is what we ask for."[37] Thus, while militant, the Brotherhood has become more of a reformist rather than a revolutionary group.

4 The Jama'at

This chapter considers the structure and ideology of the jama'at, the Islamic fundamentalist groups which seek to institute an Islamic government by violent revolution. While a number of their leaders were former Brotherhood members, these groups differed with the Muslim Brotherhood because they rejected any compromise with the existing structures. Their ideology is carefully examined since it is so much at odds with the Islam understood and practiced by most Egyptian Muslims and thus constrains these groups' popularity.

While the jama'at are the most dangerous threat to Egypt's stability they have been quite unsuccessful in building a broad base or preparing for a serious insurgency. The jama'at generally operate underground, are usually small, and have charismatic leaders. In some ways, they resemble Western cults in their high-pressure recruitment methods and attempts to regulate every aspect of their members' lives. One must be careful to distinguish between the "jama'at" and the "jam'iyat." The latter are groups which operate openly to propagandize and encourage Islamic behavior in neighborhoods (where they often congregate around specific mosques) and university campuses. The jam'iyat may serve as recruiting pools for the jama'at and there are sometimes organic links between them, particularly in the case of al-Jihad. The jama'at can be seen as a vanguard of dedicated professional revolutionaries while the jam'iyat form a pool of sympathizers. Nonetheless, given the different methods of operation, degree of commitment, and other factors, the distinction between these groups is an important one.

It is interesting to note that each of the four main jama'at (it is estimated that there may be several dozen such groups in Egypt) that have emerged sprang into public attention by a major act of terrorism. In each case, the leaders and main activists were arrested and executed. These events were:

- the 1974 attack on a military school by the Islamic Liberation Organization, led by Salah Sariyah;
- the 1977 kidnapping and murder of the former minister of awqat by al-Takfir wal-Hijrah, led by Shukri Mustafa;
- the 1981 assassination of Sadat by al-Jihad, led by Muhammad 'Abd al-Salam Faraj; and

- the 1987 attacks on prominent Egyptian figures by the Survivors from [Hell] Fire.

In the first and last instances, the small groups involved seem to have been destroyed by the ensuing repression. While al-Takfir wal-Hijra went into eclipse, al-Jihad survived by switching to a long-term strategy of building up its organization and a network of jam'iyat.

Nonetheless, there has been a constant round of small-scale terrorist activities coupled with roundups of militants by the police. Some clashes were initiated by jama'at attacks, some by the authorities. In Aswan in April 1986, for example, police fought with demonstrators who had been trying to take over a mosque. That same month, four officers and 29 civilians were arrested and accused of stealing ammunition from the military, raising money through robberies, and planning to overthrow the government. They were linked with al-Jihad. In October, 1986, the police uncovered a plan to take over a radio station in Alexandria and three groups were found to have caches of bombs and weapons. A small Iran-backed group, al-Tahrir al-Islami, was also broken up. According to the Ministry of the Interior, during the last five months of 1986 and January 1987, 377 members of radical groups were arrested. In the summer of 1987, the Survivors of [Hell] Fire tried to kill the editor of *al-Musawwar*, Makram Muhammad Ahmad, and two former ministers of the interior, Hassan abu Basha and Nabawi Isma'il. Thousands were arrested in the aftermath.

Saad Eddin Ibrahim, who interviewed several dozen imprisoned members of the Islamic Liberation Organization and al-Takfir wal-Hijrah, reached a number of conclusions about the jama'at's ideology and composition. They all held a comprehensive philosophy calling for, "The rebuilding of a new social order based on Islam which provides a complete vision of what society should be on earth and what it will be in heaven, an historic analysis, a view of friends and enemies, a set of acceptable tactics, and a strategy for waging, the radicals claimed, revolution." While Arab regimes claimed that they were already putting Islam into effect, they actually were suppressing Islam. It was the religious duty of true Muslims (i.e., the members of the jama'at) to wage jihad to bring about an Islamic government which would produce an Islamic society.[1]

GENERAL IDEOLOGY

Beyond these general principles, however, the jama'at often held conflicting views. Perhaps the strangest was the Islamic Liberation Organization, also known as the Technical Military Organization from its attack against the technical military academy. It was fundamentalist in the narrowest sense, claiming that the sole sources of Islamic law are the Qur'an and the Sunna, rejecting Ijma' (consensus), Qiyyas (analogical reason), the revered first four caliphs, and the founders of the main schools of legal interpretation. In short, its members placed themselves outside the Sunni Muslim tradition of Egyptian Muslims.[2]

The Islamic Liberation Organization's tactics grew out of its ideology. It differentiated between the political system and the society: Egypt's leaders were bad and the people wanted true Islam. Thus, if a few individuals at the top could be removed, the masses would respond by rising up in revolt. "All that the religious Egyptians need is a sincere Muslim leadership," the group argued. Its position was parallel to that of 19th-century European terrorists who believed a small group could – through assassinations and other acts of "propaganda of the deed" – spark a revolution.[3]

When people did not respond to this call for rebellion, the revolutionaries began to criticize the masses as well. This attitude is more typical of al-Takfir wal-Hijrah. It argued that since the society as well as the government was corrupt, true Muslims had to withdraw from it. The group's name expresses its ideology: one must make a "hijrah" (migration out of society, as Muhammad did when he left Mecca for Medina) because of having seen society as being in a state of unbelief, "takfir." In this sense, al-Takfir wal-Hijrah's plan corresponds to utopian groups in the West. It sought first to migrate in order to create a miniature, ideal society of its own and only at some later stage return to try to transform the existing society. Al-Takfir's confrontation with the authorities was apparently opposed by the group's leader who considered the armed clash as premature.

Finally came al-Jihad, which tried to combine revolutionary violence with disciplined organization. This approach, similar to the history of Communist parties, is the most dangerous. Long, patient work to build a mass base, however, can also lower the immediate level of violence and terrorism. Rather than an integral part of a revolutionary strategy, the assassination of Sadat was a quick reaction to the massive arrests of a few months earlier. Khalid al-

Islambuli, whose brother was one of those imprisoned, was the major advocate of this action, but al-Jihad's later activities showed the return to a pattern of slower development in building a cadre organization.

Although many of these groups' views are too eccentric for all but a tiny minority of Muslims in Egypt, there is also substantive room for debate over many matters within the context of mainstream Islam. Some examples of the revolutionary style of interpretation can be seen in the thought of al-Islambuli, the young army lieutenant who was the key architect of Sadat's assassination. In al-Islambuli's case, one might argue that his unfamiliarity with traditional Islam – he graduated from a French missionary school – was partly responsible for his heterodox analysis. Yet he drew on a portion of the Islamic tradition to justify his radical views. For example, he was fond of quoting *hadiths* (traditional stories on the deeds and sayings of the prophet Muhammad) which seemed to indicate support for revolution: "Who kills to raise the word of God is exalted because he is in the path of God"; "Who kills to raise the word of God is exalted and if he dies in doing so then he is a martyr." Islambuli argued that the Shari'ah, jihad, and martyrdom were three stages necessary for establishing an Islamic state (the Muslim Brotherhood stressed only the first in the 1970s and 1980s). He also talked frequently about the "jahiliyyah of the 20th century," the regression from Islam in Egypt, a concept that the Brotherhood (and certainly the official clergy) did not accept.[4]

AL-JIHAD'S IDEOLOGY

By far the most important theoretician within the jama'at was Muhammad 'abd al-Salam Faraj, the al-Jihad leader, who was executed for the assassination of Sadat. Like Islambuli, Faraj accentuated the parts of Islamic doctrine and literature which served his purpose. Thus, he wrote, "'Forgiveness,' 'modesty,' 'clemency,' 'avoidance,' and 'patience,' which some interpreters [of the Qur'an] say amount to a total of 124 [mentions], all these are nullified by the [verse in which] God addressed the Muslims by saying, 'After the months of *haram* [the three months of pilgrimage, in which fighting is forbidden], besiege and seize and disable and kill all the idolaters, wherever you find them.'"[5]

Faraj's book, *Al-Faridah al-Gha'ibah* ("The Neglected Duty"), argued that the Islamic duty most often ignored is that of jihad, incumbent on all good Muslims. Jihad had to be waged also against those who pretended to be Muslims – the rulers, leaders, and clergy of Egypt – as well as non-Muslims. In short, Faraj claimed for the radicals the right of excommunication, an idea foreign to the theory (if not, at times, the practice) of Muslims over the centuries. A member of the official clergy or even of the Muslim Brotherhood would say that all Egyptians who claim to be Muslims or who come from Muslim families are, in fact, Muslims. The radicals argued that only those living according to Islamic law (by their interpretation) could claim that status. By such arguments, the revolutionaries could intensify the commitment of their cadre but also – since they wrote off millions of Egyptians as *de facto* non-believers – would find it harder to build a mass base or engage the sympathies of the masses. The mainstream clergy and the Muslim Brotherhood argued that the average Egyptian Muslim had only to reform, rather than revolutionize, his behavior.

Faraj and his young followers were contemptuous of the moderation, gradualism, and introspection favored by the official clergy. Those opposing the interpretation of "jihad" as a call for violent revolution, wrote Faraj, "say . . . that they are in the stage of 'jihad of the self,' they have not yet reached the stage of 'jihad against others.'" Faraj's response was that jihad is an obligation for all Muslims. Learning has a role in trying to uproot sin, but Islam cannot be limited to good works, devotion, and piety. God has decreed that the Muslims must fight the unbelievers "and God will torment them by your hands, and He will humiliate them and make you triumph over them." Al-Jihad had contempt for those who claim that "politics distracts the heart from the remembrance of God." Its doctrine was that jihad is essentially political and to wage it "is the apex of piety in Islam."[6]

Al-Jihad challenged not only the theory of the mainstream Muslim or reformist fundamentalist groups but all their existing institutions as well. The existing mosques were rejected because they were not based on proper piety and are subordinate to the government. The mosques and awqaf (foundations whose income is directed for religious purposes) were considered so compromised that al-Takfir kidnapped and murdered the scholar who had been the government minister charged with their oversight. Television, radio, and the educational system – essential to official Islam's effort to persuade the people toward greater religiosity – were all aberrant because of their involvement with the state and should, therefore, be boycotted.

Thus, the jama'at conclude that the society is in a state of jahiliyyah so corrupt that no legal means can be used to deal with these problems. Instead, violence (which is rationalized as jihad) is justified to right these wrongs. Since the jama'at represent true Islam – in accord with the preachings of the Prophet Muhammad and supported by Allah – it must triumph even though the odds against it seem enormous. Thus, in one package, the revolutionaries have a justification for their actions and a prediction of ultimate victory.

The attitudes of the extremists are articulated very well by 'Umar 'abd al-Rahman, al-Jihad's leading clerical advisor who issued the formal legal opinion sanctioning the killing of Sadat.[7] He espouses the view that outside powers are trying to destroy Islam: "Muslims . . . are being assailed by bondage and by the West." He quotes the Prophet Muhammad on the threat posed by non-Muslims and the ultimate victory of the believers: When Muhammad said, "The nations are about to rally against you and descend upon you just as diners descend upon their meal," the Muslims were afraid since they were outnumbered. The real problem, Muhammad told them, was that the Muslims were confused and defeatist. Their greatest weakness was a reluctance to die for their faith. 'Abd al-Rahman concludes, "That is why we believe that an aversion to death when one is fighting for God's cause is nothing but a departure from Islam." Both Faraj and 'Abd al-Rahman blame all the Muslims' problems – ranging from Egypt's defeat in the 1967 war with Israel to economic and political weakness – on the people's refusal to return to Islam, wage jihad and become martyrs if necessary.

'Abd al-Rahman's interviewer, however, asked a question which would also be raised by mainstream and even by Brotherhood clerics: How could 'Abd al-Rahman justify violating the Qur'anic verse that "whoever killed a human being, except as a punishment for murder or other wicked crimes, should be looked upon as though he had killed all mankind." After Sadat's assassination, al-Jihad killed four police officers, 62 soldiers and 21 civilians, and wounded 237 people. "How can the group accept that?"

'Abd al-Rahman, like other radicals, at first inaccurately claimed that the government initiated the violence. This response is a sign of how difficult it is to justify attacks on fellow Muslims even in the revolutionaries' ideology. Al-Jihad, he claimed, had nothing to do with waging an armed revolution. Its activities consisted of merely holding "public lectures" in mosques to provide "lessons on the faith

... to enlighten the minds of young people and instill the principles of Islam into their hearts." In carrying out such education work and preaching, al-Jihad aimed "to fight against Communism, and ... against [Sadat's] surrendering to the Jews." The violence in Asyut only "began when the government surrounded the mosque where we were delivering a lecture ... It was right for us to fight the government because [it is] an oppressive and unjust regime that does not rule in accordance with what God has ordained. Those men of the regime are also the tools with which it inflicts its damage. Without those men the regime can do nothing. That is why that clash in which people were killed and wounded was inevitable."

The interviewer pressed him further on this touchy point of waging jihad against fellow Muslims, asking what was the theological precept that justified such an action. 'Abd al-Rahman tried to limit al-Jihad's culpability and make as narrow as possible the ranks of those enemies he seeks to excommunicate as Muslims: "It is a formal legal opinion by Ibn Taymiyah which says, 'If the enemy hides behind Muslims and uses them as a shield, it becomes the duty of Muslims to kill those who were [so] used.'" He assured his interlocutor that such action was justified even in killing Muslim children. If blameless, those so slain would be rewarded in the world to come. He complained about government harassment of campus groups, including the killing of one activist who was putting up posters. "I believe that the clash between us and the government will continue because there is no way we can talk with each other."

Again, it is worth noting that there is a tremendous gap between the Islamic theory – in which there is much talk of martyrdom, holy war, and the total destruction of Islam's enemies – and the political ideology of the jama'at in which each act of violence must be extensively justified as defensive, used only as a last resort, and in which even the regime's police and soldiers must be portrayed as victims of an anti-Muslim leadership.

Any hint of collaboration with the regime must be strictly rejected. Here there is an implied criticism of the Brotherhood and 'Abd al-Rahman protests a great deal about how even the most basic activities of al-Jihad – preaching, teaching, publication of its views – are carried out against the government's wishes. "We are committed to the duty of fighting for the cause of God. Like praying, fasting and giving alms, fighting for the cause of God is also a duty imposed on us by God so that we might win His pleasure and earn a place in Heaven. We believe that no Muslim at this stage can rely on political maneuvers to correct Muslims' conditions as long as it is clear that fighting for God's cause is a duty."

These ideas are almost precisely the same as those put forward by Qutb and Faraj, showing that there is an essential unity to the ideas, though not on strategy and details, among the jama'at leaders. But once one knows what they are against -- jahiliyyah – and the strategy they propose to bring a revolution – jihad – the question of what is going to be put in place of the current system remains. The jama'at have a simple answer: the proper reign of Islam. They still find it easier to describe what this is not than what this actually means in practice. Implicitly, they claim themselves to be the bearers of Allah's ideas. In 'Abd al-Rahman's words:

> We are not . . . the bearers of our own or other people's ideas. We do not believe in democratic ideas, nor do we believe in natural law or the ideas of the French Revolution, which some people are calling for. We do not believe in the principles of the Bolshevik Revolution, which many have followed, nor do we believe in material[ist] capitalism which controls the destinies of believers. But we do believe in the way of the followers and adherents of the prophetic tradition. To us the Qur'an and the prophetic tradition are the authentic premises for our ideas and our way of life and death. This confirms what was said by our prophet Muhammad, "Two things I have bequeathed you: The Qur'an and my tradition. If you adhere to them, you will not stray."

Thus, they are "fundamentalists" because they argue that their view is the accurate and correct one propounded by the Qur'an and the "tradition" (i.e., the "sunnah" from which the main branch of Islam – Sunni – takes it name). Since all authority comes from Allah, all systems of thought that place sovereignty in human hands – Western liberal or Marxist thought – are unacceptable. Capitalism, a system which places material goods and processes as the arbiters of society, is un-Islamic, as is Communism, which places centralized planning and a ruling ideology at the head of the system. Both of these systems are seen as idol-worshipping, setting up humans and human ideas rather than Islam – Allah's ideas – as supreme.

While Faraj and 'Abd al-Rahman were key figures in establishing the jama'ats' theory (and a good deal of their practice as well), the undoubted father of the new ideology was a man who died a decade before their appearance, Sayyid Qutb.

SAYYID QUTB

Perhaps the most interesting thing about Sayyid Qutb's background, which he shares with other leading figures in the jama'at including Sariyah, Shikri Mustafa, and al-Islambuli, was his apartness from the whole central system of Egyptian Islam – the Islamic school system, al-Azhar, and the clerical hierarchy. He attended a secular school, became a civil servant and an expert on education. His main interest was literary work. Only late in life did he become attracted to Islamic fundamentalism and join the Muslim Brotherhood. It might be said, then, that Qutb's self-education made him more able to think independently about the problems of Islam in present-day Egypt while, at the same time, made him more likely to deviate from accepted thought and practice.[8]

Qutb was born in 1906 and grew up in the Asyut area. His father was a secular nationalist activist and Qutb originally followed these ideas. He worked for 16 years in the Ministry of Education, where his reform efforts were frustrated within the bureaucracy. An unhappy romantic incident made him a lifelong bachelor. While working in the civil service, he kept up his literary career. Partly to get him out of the way after his harsh criticisms of the monarchy, he was sent in 1949 to the United States on an "educational mission" which lasted two and a half years. On the way to the New World, he was seized with a powerful longing for Islam and became extremely religious. America horrified him and, on his return to Egypt in 1951, he joined the Brotherhood at the age of 45. Almost immediately, he became a leading figure in the movement and was elected to its leadership council in 1952, meeting regularly during the early years of the revolution with Nasir and the regime's other leading figures. He soon quarreled, however, with the regime for refusing to become an Islamic government.[9]

Qutb was sentenced to 25 years imprisonment in 1954 and was jailed for a decade. During the very same years that other Egyptians were celebrating as great deeds the nationalization of the Suez Canal Company, Nasir's defiance of the West, and his bids to lead the Arabs, Qutb was experiencing the regime's torture chambers and brutality. What others were finding a thrilling experience of progress, he felt it to be a terrible experience of barbarism and, thus, of jahiliyyah. Out of this experience came his book, *Ma'alim fi al-tariq* ("Signposts Along the Way"), which would become the main text for the jama'at. Qutb was released from prison in 1964, due to the intercession of President 'Abd al-Salam Arif of Iraq, but was rearrested a few months later, condemned to death for treason, and executed with two other Brothers in 1966. The prosecution in his trial used the book to argue that Qutb was a traitor who was planning a coup d'etat; both pro-regime clerics and Brotherhood critics held that it proved that Qutb was a heretic.

In this work, Qutb adapted the idea of jahiliyyah to apply to contemporary Egypt: "The world is living today in jahiliyyah. In every order other than the Islamic order people worship one another. It is within the Muslim scheme alone that all the people will be liberated from worshiping one another by worshiping God alone, to be inspired by Him and to obey Him alone." His doctrine was an attack on Egyptian and Arab nationalism, socialism, and Nasir's regime which, in his view, incorporated all these erroneous ideas.[10]

Qutb thought that jahiliyyah was everywhere and called for a rebirth of Islam, an idea that made his opponents compare him to the Protestants who sought to totally revise the Christianity of their day. Qutb wrote, "How must this Islamic resurrection begin? A vanguard must resolve to set it in motion in the midst of the jahiliyyah that now reigns over the entire earth. That vanguard must be able to decide when to withdraw from and when to seek contact with the jahiliyyah that surrounds it."[11] From the first two sentences arises the self-proclaimed mission of the jama'at and from the third comes their quarrels over the proper tactics for reaching that goal.

Since the only legitimate sovereignty comes from Allah, the kind of regime usually accepted as Islamic – a God-fearing, observant one – was inadequate. What was needed was an Islamic government. While in this broad conception Qutb paralleled what Ayatollah Khumayni was formulating about the same time in his own way, Qutb never spoke of the clergy as being the vanguard and future rulers. After all, al-Banna himself and Qutb were not clerics. The clergy in Egypt were by and large staunch supporters of the regime, and their own Sunni tradition was quite different from Khumayni's Shi'ite one.

THE CRITIQUE OF JAHILIYYAH

The jahiliyyah theorists draw on classical Islamic thinkers and texts. Among the advocates' favorite quotations is one from the medieval scholar Ibn Taymiyah, who said: "Any group that departs from the clear and established Islamic canon laws such as prayers, fasting, and the prohibition of usury and corruption must – according to the consensus of the Muslim Ulama – be fought even if they proclaim that 'There is no god but Allah and Muhammad is his prophet.'" They also cite a Qur'anic verse, "God does not forgive polytheism, less than that He forgives to whomsoever he will." And there are also certain sayings attributed to Muhammad (hadith): "I have been ordered to fight people until they believe there is no god but God and I am His prophet. If they do so their lives and property are safe, and God will judge them."

The concept of the contemporary jahiliyyah is the core idea which separates the revolutionaries from the doctrine of both the official clergy and the Brotherhood. Its critics included the Brotherhood's former Supreme Guide, Hasan al-Hudaybi, in his book entitled *Preachers Not Judges*. A typical critique of Qutb's thought, which deserves to be quoted at length, goes as follows: "This [kind of] thinking does not arise from Islam, but rather is very close . . . to the thinking of the Kharijites who violated the consensus of the Muslims in [seventh-century] Islam and whose act of violation was one of the causes of the great strife [which helped to destroy the caliphate]. Egypt, with all its mosques and scholars, the role al-Azhar plays within it, and these tremendous numbers of people who have gone on the regular and off-season pilgrimage each year, negates the charge" that jihad needs to be waged against that society "and makes it a matter to which one must not pay attention." People can be considered to have abandoned Islam only on clearcut evidence of extreme acts. "Apostasy in Islam of necessity consists of a well-known repudiation of religion, for instance the repudiation of prayer or the tithe; the commission of sins does not remove one from the shelter of faith or stamp him with apostasy. The existence of corruption in the society does not mean that the society is infidel. These are all obvious points which are to be taken for granted among Muslim jurists and the scholarly public."[12]

In other words, to call Egypt a pagan country was an insult to all of its Muslim people, ignoring the great achievements of its mosques and clerics while distorting Islamic doctrine. One did not leave Islam by sinning but only by deliberate defection or by rejecting the most basic duties of a Muslim.

The views of Qutb are not only outside of Egyptian Islam, they are antithetical toward it:

> A very large part of this thinking is not the fruit of a natural growth

in Egypt but is basically a plant that has been imported. There are many parties and many interests encouraging its infiltration into Egypt. For example, had it not been for a relative vacuum in scholars and proselytizers, this thinking would not have found territory over which to roam at will. For example, some people have tried to inflate the magnitude of existing forms of corruption in order to conclude by stating that the corruption which has become widespread can be solved only by violence. For example, some economic circumstances have been a cause of isolation among young people and the infiltration of despair into their spirits, which has thrown them into the embrace of extremism and the desire for violence. Therefore, these religious groups have snatched them up.[13]

The doctrine of jahiliyyah seems to imply, says one shocked Egyptian writer, that the coming of Islam and of Muhammad never happened and a revolution as complete as the one Muhammad wrought in the seventh century is needed to create an acceptable society.[14] It is not easy – in fact, for a Muslim it is sacrilegious – to accept the tossing out of 1300 years of Islamic history and the casting of new, often unknown, figures as the new Muhammad of our age.

Thus, writes another observer from the Brotherhood, "The presence of some kind of deviation from a sound concept does not compel us to reject the sound concept itself." In other words, because Egypt is not a perfect Islamic society, that does not mean that it is a pagan one. The best countermeasure was to allow other, more orthodox clergy, even from the Brotherhood, to explain their errors to the fundamentalist youths in prison. "Young people need to know exactly where things that touch their religion stand: whether they represent a mistake, a sin, an injustice, or infidelity." Thus, if the Brotherhood was granted more freedom, it could better combat the false notion of jahiliyyah. "Not all those who oppose Islam are infidels, but those who oppose certain things in Islam are infidels. This is what is truly lacking in youth: a sensible attitude by which to pass proper judgment based on awareness rather than conception."[15]

Thus, on both political and theological grounds, those rejecting the doctrine of jahiliyyah have a strong argument. By its very nature, arguing that Egypt has abandoned Islam is not an argument which most Egyptians will find persuasive.

MOTIVES

Leaders of the Brotherhood praise the young jama'at activists for seeking Islam though they criticize the form in which they find it. Brotherhood Supreme Guide Muhammad Hamid Abu al-Nasr also suggests that the reason for the false ideas are the lack of a proper version of fundamentalism among Egypt's young people:

> We are deprived of contact with the youth to explain to them the rules of Islam. Young people form judgments based on what they understand, so if the Brotherhood develops an entity it can play a role in helping them understand Islam and jurisprudence in Islam. We welcome any new ideas so long as they are within the compass of the call. In the absence of a guide or an advisor or a teacher, how can the youth come up with anything new? By having a group able to regulate their movements, to listen to and analyze their points of view and to add to or take away from such views until the right opinion is achieved . . . Take, for example, the group that advocates change by force. We are against it and indeed believe in "call unto the way of the Lord with wisdom and fair exhortation," and, therefore, we reject any kind of radicalism or terrorism. When the Brotherhood attains its legal status, these thoughts can be controlled and unified along a straight, right path.[16]

Those recruited to the jama'at are, on average, younger than Brotherhood members. Some of their reasons for joining are typical of the decisions made by young people to affiliate with radical organizations: a craving for action or adventure, dreams of heroism, impulsiveness, boredom, idealism, rebellion, and a search for purity. Like other cult-style or terrorist groups, the jama'at force their acolytes to go through successive stages of membership as their commitment and knowledge – or, to put it another way, the brainwashing process – develops. Candidate members must pass tests of their loyalty to become full members.

Personal frustration, particularly the inability to find a job, and the cultural shock of moving from countryside to city are important factors in the choice to join. Recruits are often spotted by members as those most fervent in their prayers at mosques; and the jam'iyat are also fertile recruitment grounds. Efforts are made to separate the new participants, psychologically and sometimes physically, from their families and society. Only the revolutionary group is portrayed as a decent institution, all others (including rival jama'at) are virtueless; television and radio are dismissed as corrupt. Thus, the member should take his attitudes only from the leaders. Charismatic individuals set down what is right or wrong for the members, though a leadership council may also have some decision-making authority.

Inside the group, morale can be high and a willingness to devote one's life, or even to die, for the cause may reach a peak. "Their elan and purpose were derived from a fundamental Qur'anic tenet calling on all Muslims to observe the principle of 'enjoining the good and prohibiting the evil,'" writes the Egyptian scholar Hamied Ansari. To outsiders, even pious Egyptian Muslims, the jama'at may seem like fringe and heretical groups. Al-Tilimsani and other Brotherhood leaders suggested in earlier days that they were pawns of the government set up to counter the Brotherhood.[17]

A useful typology is to differentiate between revolutionary groups trying to overthrow their own government and "liberation" groups seeking to destroy what they perceive as foreign rulers. For those in the first category, the goal is to destroy the world of their fathers. Those in the second category are carrying on the mission of their fathers. The jama'at prefer to see themselves as being in the latter category, which would make their task much easier. They want the great majority to support political and social change against an evil, non-Islamic government. But most Egyptian Muslims identify enough with the regime or society, even if they see plenty of room for reform and improvement, that they view the radicals as being in the first category: as a threatening, "out-group" rather than as embodying their own aspirations. Similarly, the people tend to see the jama'at's ideology as that of heterodox rather than as zealously orthodox Muslims. In contrast, Syrian Sunni fundamentalists – who fight against a radical Alawite regime – or Lebanese Shi'ite fundamentalists – who battle Sunni Muslims, Lebanese Christians, and Israeli Jews – have a far greater claim on their compatriots' loyalty and support.

Both the jama'at's and Brotherhood's followers think that they are pursuing their highest Islamic duty which is, in turn, the highest duty of humanity itself. In the words of Saad Eddin Ibrahim they are:

> convinced that such adherence to the purest sources will deliver them, their society, and the world from all the ills of our time – from the world's decadence, corruption, weakness, poverty and humiliation – in other words, purity of religious practice is believed to be the road to total salvation. It will enable the faithful to

establish a perfect social order on earth – an order that is virtuous, just, human, compassionate, free, strong, and prosperous. It is an order that is believed to be far superior to both Communism and capitalism. For the Islamic order balances the interests of the individual with the welfare of the community. It balances the material of the "hereafter" in preparation for Heaven: "You do for your world, as if you would live forever; and for the hereafter as if you would die tomorrow." Adherence to the purest sources of Islam, the Holy Qur'an and Sunnah, furthermore ensures the faithful Paradise or Heaven when all humans are resurrected in the Day of Judgment.[18]

One of Ibrahim's interviewees, a young man whose death sentence for attempting to overthrow Sadat had been commuted to life imprisonment, followed the pattern typical of the jama'at activists. He was the eldest son of a middle class family who studied engineering at university. The shock of the 1967 defeat led him to a personal crisis from which he found deliverance in reading the Qur'an. It was literally a "born-again" experience. At the university mosque he met a student who told him that Zionism, Communism, and capitalism were all enemies of the Qur'an. He read about the Muslim Brotherhood, joined the Islamic Association (jam'iyat) and became one of its leaders. He then became involved in underground conspiracies.[19]

Rajab Madkur, a former member of al-Takfir wal-Hijrah who broke with the group, provides a passionate repudiation of those who repudiate (takfir) Egyptian society. But the very intensity of his anger reveals the power of the jama'at over its members.

How many legitimate rights have been lost, how many people's honor has been victimized, how much inviolable blood has been shed, how many sins have been committed, how many relationships have been severed, how many husbands have lost their wives and had their children go homeless, how many fathers and mothers have gone about vagrantly in the country in search of their children and failed to find them, how many devoted Muslims have had the charges of apostasy unfairly and inimically applied to them! Yes, God has made it my destiny to review this thinking in the light of the Qur'an and the sayings and doings of the prophet, and here I am, considering the vastness of the distance between the position the prophet of God . . . held and the true nature of this group.[20]

THE ISLAMIC LIBERATION ORGANIZATION AND AL-TAKFIR WAL-HIJRAH

Salah Sariyah, leader of the Islamic Liberation Organization, was a Palestinian born near Haifa. He lived in Jordan until the Jordanian army defeated the PLO in September 1970 and then went on to Iraq and Cairo. He was involved in several fringe radical parties and established his own cells in Egypt, where most of his recruits were students at the universities of Cairo, Alexandria, al-Azhar, and the Technical Military Academy. The Islamic Liberation Organization was destroyed by government repression after its 1974 putsch attempt.

Others, with more mainstream Egyptian fundamentalist credentials, were organizing al-Takfir wal-Hijrah at about the same time. The name generally given this group reveals a great deal about its ideology. "Takfir" means to repudiate, and the group began by repudiating all the institutions of the existing Egyptian society as jahiliyyah. The Brotherhood rejected this idea as heresy. "Hijrah" means to migrate and refers specifically to the Prophet Muhammad's decision to leave impious Mecca for Medina, where he built an Islamic society, gathered his forces, and returned to conquer his former home a few years later. The group intended to do the same thing in Egypt. In contrast to the Islamic Liberation Organization, which thought only the government was pagan and thus that a single act of rebellion might lead the (truly Islamic) masses to rise up against it, al-Takfir saw the need for social as well as political revolution. Other jama'at, most notably, al-Jihad, took a broader view on the possibility that one might make a personal, spiritual "hijrah" while remaining at home to fight the existing institutions. Al-Takfir's members generally referred to their group as the Society of Muslims, a name carrying the implication that they were the only ones worthy of that status.[21]

Al-Takfir's founder was Shukri Mustafa, a young Brotherhood activist influenced by Qutb's work, who had been imprisoned during the second wave of arrests in 1965. Mustafa was a member of the generation between that of the Brotherhood leaders and those who would be recruited to the jama'at in the 1970s. Soon after being released from prison in 1971, Mustafa broke with the Brotherhood's more moderate line and began recruiting followers of his own. He called on supporters to refuse to pray in mosques, reject service in the army, and never take a government job. The downfall of Islam, in

Mustafa's view, began when Muslims stopped dealing directly with the Qur'an and accepted as clerical intermediaries the great medieval scholars who formed the schools of Islamic jurisprudence. These men, who interposed themselves between the believers and Allah, were heavily responsible for the rebirth of jahiliyyah.

His wrath was particulary focused on the state-backed clerics. For centuries, as Kepel summarized Mustafa's views, the history of the clerics "has been the story of the ulama's complicity with the princes." It is interesting to note that Mustafa, like Qutb, was certainly a "laymen" in these terms and had little formal Islamic training. As in Qutb's work, the parallels to Protestantism are strong. Equally, it is not surprising that the kidnapping and murder of a leading official cleric was the deed for which the group became famous and which doomed it.[22] Mustafa's view, it should be noted, was the exact opposite of Khumayni's, which sees the clergy as the repository of pure Islam and the rightful rulers of an Islamic state.

The Islamic Liberation Organization and al-Takfir wal-Hijrah are mainly of historic interest. Repression following their main terrorist deeds – the attack on the Technical Military Academy and the murder of the former minister of awqaf, respectively – largely destroyed them.

AL-JIHAD

A number of survivors from these two earlier groups joined al-Jihad.[23] It was left to this third organization both to carry out a far more successful attack and to build an organization more capable of surviving the ensuing storm.

While al-Jihad has recruited hundreds of members around the country, it has failed to break out of its cult status and become a mass organization. Thus, 'Umar 'Abd al-Rahman complained, "Although we are embarked on the course of fighting for the cause of God, and that involves suffering and being true to God, we have found no one who will listen or pay attention to us. And we have been wondering until now why it is that no one yet has written about us or recognized us. Unfortunately, we understand why. The media are ignoring us because they tend to flatter the government, and this is contemptible."[24]

The organization began in the mid-1970s as a jam'iyat at the University of Asyut, which had 130,000 students, and where it demanded that the university administration separate males and females and forbid art and sports activities. After a period of little growth, al-Jihad formed three subcommittees: indoctrination and training (propaganda), "readiness" (military training, stockpiling weapons and explosives), and economics (finances, buying supplies and weapons). Plans were made for assassinating leaders, seizing government buildings and broadcasting centers, and taking control of Asyut as a base from which to advance on other cities. Those involved in these plots were arrested in 1979.[25]

Muhammad 'Abd al-Salam Faraj was a student at the College of Engineering at the University of Cairo where he was involved in Islamic and anti-leftist activities. After graduating, he worked as an engineer for a company in Alexandria and joined al-Jihad in 1978. When most of the organization's leaders were arrested in 1979, he reconstituted it and wrote his book on jihad as an ideological platform. He claimed, "The rulers of this era are apostates from Islam." He found a number of able recruits, particularly Karam Zahdi, leader of the Islamic Society at al-Minya, and other jam'iyat activists. It was estimated that 85 per cent of al-Jihad's members were students and that most came from poor families and rural areas. Some soldiers, though a relatively small number, also joined.[26]

The principal blow against al-Jihad was the crackdown after some of its members assassinated Sadat. Around 300 activists were arrested and charged with seeking to overthrow the government by force. Almost all of them were between the ages of 20 and 28 years old and most were medical, law, or pharmacy students at either the universities of Asyut or al-Minya.

Given al-Jihad's spectacular act in killing Sadat, the official clergy and the Brotherhood leaders extensively criticized its ideology, particularly as it was embodied in Faraj's book, *The Neglected Duty*. Building on Qutb's concept of the state and society as "jahiliyyah," Faraj amplified the duty of Muslims to wage jihad against these institutions. He claimed that Muhammad threatened the tribe of Quraysh with violence unless it gave up its false gods. The pro-regime mufti of Egypt, however, interpreted this passage as Muhammad offering to sanctify them, to bestow on them the gift of Islam. These are sharply contrasting philosophies of religion. In the mufti's view, Allah is calling on the people to purify themselves from sin by adhering to the true religion. According to the mufti, "There is no compulsion in Islam." Allah does not force people to accept his word.[27]

Al-Jihad not only had an ideological interpretation of Islam, but also had a strategic theory far superior to that of its two predecessors. Because of the need to devise ways of surviving under the conditions of illegal operation, al-Jihad's operational methods seem similar to those of Lenin. It organizes students and others within the jam'iyat, agitates through mosques wherever possible, and feeds recruits into underground cells. This allows the organization to be far more durable than those purely secret groups which are easily broken when their small ring of leaders is rounded up. In short, al-Jihad is engaged in a protracted struggle against the regime. Even if conditions at present restrict the group's appeal, it can train and strengthen its cadre and await more propitious circumstances.

SURVIVORS FROM [HELL] FIRE

New jama'at have formed in Egypt which impatiently demanded more immediate revolutionary action. The Survivors from [Hell] Fire (perhaps better translated as "Those Spared from Hell") was an offshoot of al-Jihad with an estimated 30–70 members. Since it viewed the regime as an "infidel" one, the group decided it was permissible to confiscate government funds and to kill officials who did not observe Islamic law. It forbade praying in mosques because they were built with government financing. The Survivors' leader, 'Abd al-Qawi Muhammad Kazim, a construction equipment operator, ordered the assassinations of two former interior ministers (Hasan Abu Basha, Nabawi Isma'il) involved in anti-fundamentalist repression, and a newspaper editor (Makram Muhammad Ahmad of *al-Musawwar*) who was outspokenly critical of the Islamic extremists. These attacks were staged, without murdering the intended victims, in May, June, and August 1987. In the subsequent roundups, most of the members were killed, as was Kazim, or captured by the police. Another leader was Dr Majdi al-Safti (born 1959), a pediatrician.

There are also some other sects, which might be called more "traditional" fundamentalist groups, that demand the rebuilding of the caliphate, have distinctly mystical ideologies, or are led by men who claim to be the "mahdi," the Islamic messiah who heralds the end of days.[28] Al-Jihad remains the pre-eminent group, and trumpets the need to wage violent conflict with the authorities.

RIVALRY AMONG THE JAMA'AT

While the jama'at are all against the government, mainstream clergy, and the Muslim Brotherhood, they spend a great deal of energy fighting each other. To cite two examples, al-Jihad found it difficult to obtain agreement even between its Cairo and Asyut branches. Al-Takfir's critical confrontation with the authorities began when it used violence against other groups and some of its own dissidents. Ideological disagreements even among the different jama'at are quite sharp. Faraj, for example, strongly criticized al-Takfir:

> As for those who would refrain from jihad, the al-Takfir group, it follows that they are in a stage of weakness. They call for isolation from society, in holy flight from it, in hope of obtaining power. They then seek to return as warriors to found the Islamic state. In the view of the Jihad organization, their opinions amount to mere escapades that stray from the path to the establishment of the Islamic state. Suppose they say the path to setting up the Islamic state is first holy flight to another country, the establishment of a state there, then a later return as conquerors. As one of their representatives says: "that he will move to the mountain, then return to confront Pharaoh, as did Moses, and afterwards God will split the ground beneath Pharaoh and his soldiers." Yet all these antics led to nothing more than abandoning the sole, correct and legitimate means of establishing the Islamic state![29]

Attempts to merge al-Takfir and al-Jihad in the 1970s failed due to ideological differences and personality clashes. Leaders and followers in the two groups often accused each other of being infidels.[30] Al-Takfir used violence against supporters of the Islamic Liberation Organization and other sects. It is not surprising that organizations whose existence is based on the belief they possess absolute truth (while considering all other Islamic thinkers and institutions as being in error), find it difficult to compromise.

The jama'at are also extremely antagonistic toward the Brotherhood, which they accuse of using Islam to further its leaders' own personal ambitions and of helping to strengthen the hated regime and system. For example, a writer favoring al-Jihad claimed the Brothers' "tactics . . . conflict with their effort to reach power, not to mention conflicting with the Islamic values they promote." The Brotherhood supported economic policies which exploited the poor and Egypt's problems; failed to take "decisive positions against the Zionist and

American presences in Egypt" but made this issue a low priority to avoid conflict with the regime; restrained young people's energies "on the pretext that they should 'wait for the right conditions'"; depended on "Arab states that fund the organization" (presumably Saudi Arabia); and nurtured retrogressive, personalist reform views of Islam. In short, the writer concludes, the Brotherhood seemed to be gaining strength but the very methods (gradualism, reformism) fostering their success also made them less likely to achieve a revolutionary takeover.[31]

CONCLUSIONS

All the jama'at agree on certain ideological points. They reject the state and society as being un-Islamic and in a state of unbelief (jahiliyyah), and argue that it is an essential duty of Moslems to fight against it (jihad) and to lead a revolution to create a new, Islamic society. On these points they differ from both Islam as it is interpreted by the overwhelming majority of Egyptians and from the current ideology of the Muslim Brotherhood. If the Muslim Brotherhood can be equated to the chastened, increasingly reformist Marxist parties in Europe, the jama'at are parallel to tiny, noisy Maoist or Trotskyist sects which claim to return to the pure source of their doctrine.

There were also ideological and strategic differences among the groups. The Islamic Liberation Organization thought a single act of insurrection would mobilize the people behind it, al-Takfir sought to withdraw from Egyptian society to build up a proper Islamic system, al-Jihad tried to organize a vanguard revolutionary movement, and the Survivors from [Hell] Fire considered al-Jihad to be too slow in initiating violence. But the deeper division is between charismatic leaders who were incapable of submitting to another's authority and among groups claiming they possessed absolute truth unwilling to compromise with each other. Such rigidity does not make it easy to create a successful revolutionary movement.

Of course, Islam has a powerful resonance in Egypt as the well-spring of popular identity and worldview. But while the jama'at can appeal to some of the youth and claim to embody proper Islam, other factors such as their strange beliefs, demand for fealty to the point of martyrdom, and inner disputes over strategy and tactics weaken their ability to build a mass-based revolutionary movement.

Also contributing to this strong limit on the jama'ats' appeal is the fact that the vast majority of clerics and average citizens do not view themselves as being in a state of jahiliyyah. In the final analysis, the jama'at are not "fundamentalists" in the sense that they return to an earlier version of Islam. Their ideology draws on some past Islamic theology to make drastic revisions of Islam as it is understood by most Egyptians.

5 The Radical Jam'iyat

This chapter examines two types of radical, but not currently revolutionary, groups – the jam'iyat and the associations built around charismatic preachers. The jama'at have remained small and underground, and have suffered from severe repression. If radical fundamentalism is to revolutionize Egyptian society, the impetus will have to come from the organizations which reach a much wider audience on campuses, in neighborhoods, or around individual charismatic preachers. Many extremists engaged in terrorism were shaped and radicalized in the jam'iyat; al-Jihad began life as such a student organization.[1] Thus, understanding the ideology and behavior of the jam'iyat is critical to assessing the role of religious fundamentalism in Egyptian society.

JAM'IYAT ON UNIVERSITY CAMPUSES

Like the Muslim Brotherhood and the jama'at, the jam'iyat were fostered by the fundamentalist prisoners released in the early 1970s. The first jam'iyat-style group is said to have been founded at Qasr al-'Ayni hospital in 1970 by doctors and interns who had been influenced by Muslim Brotherhood prisoners they were treating. The study groups formed at the hospital soon spread to the medical faculties of Cairo, Ayn Shams, and al-Azhar universities and elsewhere. These early groups also met with al-Azhar faculty members who were close to the Brotherhood and studied al-Banna rather than Qutb.[2]

The government allowed student fundamentalist groups to form and even gave them some support during the mid-1970s to combat the growing strength of Marxist organizations on campus. The fundamentalists expanded quickly between 1975 and 1979 but this very success proved their undoing as the jam'iyat emerged as a greater threat to the regime than the leftists they were supposed to counter. Some of them praised Iran's Islamic revolution, demonstrated against Sadat's trip to Israel, began preparations for armed struggle, disrupted the universities, or threatened an uprising if the Shari'ah was not made the basis of Egypt's laws. Most of the leaders and cadre of the revolutionary fundamentalist groups al-Jihad and al-Takfir came out of the jam'iyat during this period. The General Union of Egyptian Students, under fundamentalist control, denounced Sadat's peace agreement with Israel.[3]

An Egyptian analysis of the jam'iyat's growth at that time found them "led by young men of unusual intelligence" and attracting university students and skilled workers. In Cairo, members were said to have penetrated such sensitive sectors as the water, electricity, arms, printing, and oil industries; the ranks of transport workers and army technicians; and academic, scientific, and technical circles.[4]

Consequently, the jam'iyat were one of the main targets of Sadat's crackdown in 1979. Sadat criticized the jam'iyat, blaming them for violence and Christian–Muslim clashes. Hundreds of their leaders and activists were arrested and the campus groups were dissolved. The government repealed the more liberal 1976 by-laws governing student activity and organizations, replacing them with tougher statutes. It also dismissed elected student councils, invalidated the regulations of university student unions, abolished the General Federation of Egyptian Students, and confiscated its funds. University guards were returned to the campuses and ordered to intervene against student political activities. The regime's agents tried to fix student elections. The government promised to do more for students, particularly in the area of housing, to reduce the jam'iyats' following. But all these measures did not destroy the movement. There was another round of unrest and roundups in September 1981. One of those arrested was a jam'iyat leader at Asyut whose brother, Khalid al-Islambuli, organized the assassination of Sadat as an act of revenge.

Both the more moderate views of al-Hudaybi and the revolutionary ideas of Qutb influenced the jam'iyat. But if one is searching for an ideological and historic model for these campus and community groups, it can best be found in the writings of the Muslim Brotherhood's founder, al-Banna, and that organization's militant activities in the 1930s and 1940s. The campus groups were more willing to undertake coercive, even violent, action than was the contemporary Brotherhood. While some of the leaders and activists of the pre-1979 wave of jam'iyat eventually joined the jama'at, others went into the Muslim Brotherhood, organized independent neighborhood Islamic associations, or became inactive.

After the Mubarak government allowed a gradual return of the student group's rights, a second wave of jam'iyat arose on the campuses in the 1980s. In February 1985, the Egyptian University

Student Federation was reestablished and held its first national meeting the following month. A wide variety of local groups were revived or founded at this time.[5]

THE JAM'IYAT'S APPEAL

Jam'iyat, often called "societies for the defense and interpretation of the Holy Qur'an," use the slogan of "The Model Islamic Nation." The two names reveal some important points about the jam'iyat. First, they seek to deepen participants' knowledge and commitment to Islam. Second, they try to function as miniature Islamic societies which show how a proper, pious Muslim polity should work. This second point has potentially conflicting implications. On one hand, by forming mini-utopias, these groups' energies are attracted away from revolutionary action; on the other hand, a sizeable body of able, active Egyptians are put outside the norms of the national society. This can be a first step in "resocializing" them into a very different worldview which leads to the rejection of society altogether, the path followed by the jama'at.

A key to the campus groups' popularity has been their ability to deal with the psychological and material needs of their members. Students and adolescents often seek a sense of personal identity, security, and a feeling of belonging to a group. Participation in jam'iyat offer all these rewards. By embracing Islam, young Egyptians also rebel against the perceived laxity of their parents and of Egyptian society. But it is a relatively "safe" rebellion since they are affirming – rather than rejecting – their culture's traditional roots and most prized values. This is why Islamic fundamentalism is more popular than Marxism or the leftist nationalist creed called "Nasirism" today. Moreover, while their ethos is traditional, the students are responding to problems caused by modernity: anomie, career pressures, big city life, and new roles for women, for example, for which their upbringing and ideas have usually not prepared them. In a sense, while fundamentalism appears as a rejection of modern life, it is also a way of adapting to it. Islam provides an anchor in a sea of frightening, confusing change.

Life for Egyptian students is not easy. Courses of study are narrow, preventing students from acquiring a liberal education at the same time as they learn technical skills. Thus, many fundamentalists are people who have been highly educated as engineers or agronomists, yet suffer a spiritual vacuum due to their ignorance of history, sociology, or political science. Conditions are terrible, with overcrowded lecture halls and laboratories in which it may be hard to hear or even see the teacher. Rote learning discourages creativity and flexibility. To pass the exams, one must buy the professors' manual and pay for intensive tutoring from teachers who themselves are underpaid. On top of all this, the graduating student has poor prospects for obtaining a job in his chosen field, much less one that pays a decent salary. In short, students have good reason to feel oppressed and dissatisfied and they have a real need to seek alternatives in the jam'iyat.

The jam'iyat are also, in practice, mutual support societies responding to these real student problems. On campus the jam'iyat relieve the pressure on students by supplying low-cost "Islamic" clothes, textbooks, and lecture notes at 80 per cent discounts, providing a bus service for female students, and fulfilling other needs. They have sought to introduce "the Islamic way" on campuses, opposing dance parties, jazz concerts, films, and even chaperoned excursions, Western types of entertainment, and sometimes science teachings they deem contrary to Islam. Some tried to pressure Muslim students to drop social relations with Christians. In 1979, the local group in Asyut succeeded in segregating the sexes so that females were assigned to separate lecture halls. Some female students protested but to no avail.[6] Others presumably felt more secure in this "protected" environment.

Assessing the jam'iyat's accomplishments on campus, a critic complained, "They have denied fundamental rights to university students, especially regarding the mixing of male and female students. They have used violence against those who disagreed with them (i.e., beating any male student caught talking with a female student) . . . They began to use direct force, such as attacking video stores which they believed were selling indecent films (i.e., anything other than news or Qur'an – particularly kissing or sex). They have used weapons, including knives and cleavers, in confronting the police." The government estimated that over 300 violent incidents took place at various universities in 1986 alone.[7]

While these groups have been action-oriented, they engaged in only meager attempts at developing an ideology. Discussions in that direction usually moved quickly to questions of narrow and short-range tactics. The young doctor 'Isam al-Din al-'Aryan suggested, in a 1980 article, that Egyptian nationalism had promoted Westernization and thus prevented the fulfillment of its own goal of expelling foreign influence. As a response, he suggests that women wear veils, men have untrimmed beards and white jalabiyahs (long white robes), that people marry at an early age, and that they attend public prayers on the 'Idd al-Fitr and 'Idd al-Adha holidays. This symbolism is insufficient, he admits, because Islam must encompass all life activities, but he offers no strategy and complains that many militants become inactive after graduation. The jam'iyat usually paraphrase either the Muslim Brotherhood's ideas or the jama'at's ideas. Qutb's thoughts are particularly popular. Islam is usually presented as the only way to liberation. The jam'iyat usually do not denounce everything as jahiliyyah. Their spirit seems closer to a long tradition of movements advocating a return to strict Islamic observance rather than to a revolutionary praxis.[8]

Each jam'iyat cell is headed by a commander or amir. An effort to link them together in a national organization headed by a general commander was stopped by the government repression of 1979. Today these groups are very decentralized and the government would probably act harshly against any new effort at unification. The authority of each local leader – and the ideological position of that jam'iyat – varies, depending on his ability and the organization's cohesiveness. The main centers of campus activity are Alexandria, Asyut, Tanta, Ayn Shams, and Cairo. While the jam'iyat are a minority among the students, they have a certain advantage since they are well-organized, attract a larger portion of the most active students, and claim to represent proper Islamic piety.

ISLAMIC ACTION IN ASYUT

Asyut is a traditional fundamentalist stronghold for jama'at, jam'iyat, and the Muslim Brotherhood. The situation in Asyut does not provide a typical picture of jam'iyat operations since it is by far their strongest and most radical locale. But events in Asyut indicate the direction other groups would like to take. The student organization there calls itself the Islamic Group, but is often referred to as al-Jihad by its critics, who wish to link it to the jama'at of that name. In the late 1970s, male and female students mingled freely on campus but, through the jam'iyat's efforts, classes and cafeterias were segregated according to sex and it is now rare to see men and women speaking to one another. Knives were sometimes used against students or even teachers seen talking to members of the opposite sex. About thirty jam'iyat adherents destroyed the instruments of students preparing to play music at a graduation party. The police reportedly stood by and did not interfere. The jam'iyat has not only won wide student support but has also gained backing from many faculty members.[9]

Dr Muhammad al-Sayyid Habib, chairman of the faculty club at Asyut and a Muslim Brotherhood member of parliament, discounted the jam'iyat's influence. "They have become people with a loud voice, but they do not have a strong effect. Ask everyone about that." When Habib tried to give a pro-Muslim Brotherhood lecture at the beginning of the academic year, however, "I was surprised by a group consisting of about thirty people from al-Jihad standing in barricades at the door to the auditorium and preventing the lecture from being held. I told them, that is not compatible with the teachings of Islam."[10]

Habib's view shows the competition between the Brotherhood and the jam'iyat – though some campus groups at Asyut and elsewhere are closer to the Brotherhood. The Brotherhood views the more radical students as naive and impractical. The jam'iyat considers the Brotherhood to be collaborators with the government.

Ruz al-Yusuf, a secularist, Nasirist periodical critical of the fundamentalists, gave a higher assessment of their power claiming that "Islamic groups consolidated their grip on the University of Asyut ... keeping students and administration in a state of fear." They wanted "prayer, abstinence and study, and see no benefit or need for parties and music." When a policeman shot and killed a jam'iyat member who was putting up posters, the group's leaders held a one-week study strike and memorial prayer services at a local mosque. The jam'iyat accused the security services of trying to discourage people from attending it.[11]

Members of Islamic organizations in Asyut claim they use violence only in self-defense: "We in the Islamic group protect ourselves and we protect the male and female students at the university from themselves and from Satan, since the university is a place for knowledge and Jihad, and not for dancing, music and singing." They claim to respect Christian students, as long as they keep within the proper bounds. It seems clear, however, that the presence of large numbers of Copts spurs the jam'iyat to greater action and that the presence of strong fundamentalist groups – as in Asyut – usually coincides with a relatively high proportion of Christians in the area.[12]

STUDENT ELECTIONS

The fundamentalists' showing at student elections in a wide range of universities and faculties has been impressive, particularly given government-inspired moves by administrators to remove their candidates from the ballots. Jam'iyat candidates were usually evicted from the lists for alleged lack of previous campus activity. But those so removed included some of the most energetic student activists including the president of the social committee of the Ayn Shams University Student Union.

The Ayn Shams' jam'iyat held a conference involving thousands of students to protest this purge. It called for ending the university administration's deletion of fundamentalists from the ballot, removing student by-laws imposed after Sadat's repression of the jam'iyat, abolishing the campus police, and forbidding Interior Ministry interference in school affairs. It called on faculty members to support the Islamic students' positions so that the university would be run by university officials rather than by the government and its security forces.[13]

The Ayn Shams University administration even forbade the wearing of jalabiyahs and the niqab (the full veil) for women. This step was taken to weaken the solidarity and lessen the visible presence of the jam'iyat, though the ostensible grounds were regulations against improper clothing. Garb deemed immodest was also banned.[14]

The results of the 1986–7 elections at Cairo University showed how well the Islamic student groups could do even in the face of the discrimination mounted against them. They won most of the seats at the following faculties of Cairo University:

Faculty	Seats won
College of Medicine	71 of 72
College of Dentistry	35 of 47
College of Pharmacy	45 of 47
College of Engineering	60 of 60
College of Sciences	47 of 48
College of Agriculture	41 of 48
College of Education	24 of 48
College of Law	40 of 48
College of Business	43 of 48[15]

REASONS FOR JAM'IYAT'S GROWTH

There are several reasons for the growth of the jam'iyat. First, the jam'iyat stress a defensive, rather than a revolutionary, orientation in order to appeal to reformists and to moderate Muslims. There is relatively little ideological thinking among these groups, which stress action more than theory. Kepel suggests that ideology might have been deliberately eschewed to avoid splits over doctrine. One of their main slogans is "the Islamic religion is in danger" and the protection of Islam is attractive to students raised in that tradition. Hysteria is whipped up over alleged foreign and regime conspiracies or threats from Coptic Christians. Jam'iyat can claim to be supporting proper behavior and a moral society against foreign, atheistic, and destabilizing innovations. While the jam'iyat have their own interpretation of Islam – distinct from prevailing views – it is far less idiosyncratic than that of the jama'at. And while jam'iyat members might wear the badges of Islam – beards and traditional dress – they are much less politicized than the jama'at cadre. As Kepel puts it, they "were recruited on a minimalist Islamicist basis" in which indoctrination "lacked the intensity" of groups like al-Takfir.[16]

Second, they propose building a model Muslim community rather than the more dangerous and controversial goal of overthrowing the state. Both the constructive and utopian aspects of this program appeal to idealistic students who are seeking some direction and solutions to the deep problems of daily existence and cultural shock that they face in their own lives.

Third, the opposition to the jam'iyat among students is weak and divided. Many students are passive and uninvolved in politics. Support for the regime, though appealing to those wishing to build their careers, seems opportunistic and ignores grievances (including student complaints) about government policies. Outspoken pro-secular forces are not organized and in some ways lack legitimacy since such views seem tied to Western values and opposed to deep-rooted Egyptian and Muslim norms. The Marxist and Nasirist left are in retreat. They are more directly targeted by government pressure and their ideology requires more of an intellectual leap for Egyptians than does Islamic fundamentalism. The students' background does not prepare them for becoming Marxists and they can no longer idealize Nasir, given all his failures. It is also easy to overstate the modernizing, Westernizing, or liberalizing affect of Egyptian universities. Colleges are underfunded and their buildings are in a sad state of deterioration. Courses are overcrowded and discourage creativity by stressing rote memorization of facts. The scientific, engineering, and professional faculties usually provide a narrow technical training. Thus, while students absorb Western technology, they learn little about democratic, secular, or humanistic ideology.

Finally, as suggested earlier, the jam'iyat try to cope with the students' real problems. They comfort those from rural backgrounds who find it difficult to adjust, providing them with a sense of community. They protect female students who may face harassment or who are not used to the freedom provided on the campuses. Textbooks or class notes are sold at low cost, giving poor students a way of surviving in the university environment where they must buy books and lecture notes to supplement the teachers' incomes. Study halls are held in mosques to facilitate learning. Bus routes are organized for commuting female students who otherwise have to face the overcrowded and unchaperoned public transportation system. An observer who assumes that support for the jam'iyat comes only from ideological extremism or traditionalist obscurantism would miss the basis of their appeal.

The jam'iyat's activities have concentrated on establishing an Islamic order on the campuses. The critical question here is whether the jam'iyat are committed mainly to dealing with student and university issues or to overthrowing the Egyptian state and social system. To date, they have devoted far more effort to the former than to the latter goal.

As in all student movements, the theory is that all this campus organizing will gradually extend outwards as students graduate or seek to affect those living around them. The latter objective is pursued through marches, rallies, and public prayer meetings. The last-mentioned activity was one of the most effective for these groups in the late 1970s. Large prayer meetings were held in October 1978 to mark the Islamic 'Idd al-Fitr and 'Idd al-Adha holidays in Cairo's Abidin Square and Alexandria University stadium. In addition, the jam'iyat continue to distribute propaganda through seminars, lectures, posters, and pamphlets, calling for the application of the Shari'ah.

One of the best perspectives on the views of jam'iyat campus leaders is provided by an interview with 'Usama Rushdi, leader of the Asyut group.[17] Rushdi lists his main objectives as the segregation of the sexes in university lectures, cafeterias, and buses; forbidding musical performances and other "un-Islamic" forms of entertainment; and encouraging prayer and piety. In these respects, the movement is like other puritanical waves of reform which have arisen periodically within Islam. The obsession with feminine purity – Rushdi emphasizes the prohibition against women exposing themselves immodestly and says his group treats women students as if they were sisters – is both a reflection of the psychological stresses in Muslim society and a rejection of Westernization.

Rushdi's claim that he does not condone violence against those who do not accept his views may seem self-serving, but the bulk of jam'iyat activities have been more peaceful than their critics at *Ruz al-Yusuf* imply. Certainly, they fall far short of the terrorism of al-Jihad or al-Takfir. The killing of one student by police was so disconcerting to the jam'iyat that it continued to be constantly mentioned by them years later. While some of their members are no doubt likely to become recruits for revolutionary groups in the future, the jam'iyat as a whole are not engaged in such activities.

What remains unresolved are such questions as the groups' view of waging jihad against the jahiliyyah society. They take an intermediate position on this issue. Rushdi, for example, says there is no reason to have any other political groups at the university because most of the students prefer God's ideology to that of anyone else. He opposes nationalism and socialism, wants an Islamic nation and the return of the Caliphate, and calls Nasir's era a "black period." Yet the concept of "jahiliyyah" society is rarely, if ever, invoked. The essential doctrine and strategy of the jam'iyat is based on the idea that reform can succeed. There are two ways, however, in which the jam'iyat do not accept the Muslim Brotherhood's legalism. First, they eschew parliamentary politics, preferring organization and mobilization. Second, they are quite willing to use intimidation in a systematic way to achieve their goals. While the jam'iyat accept some ideas from the jama'at thinkers, in both theory and practice, they have been a more militant and activist version of the Muslim Brotherhood. Thus, while hundreds of future revolutionaries and scores of terrorists are likely to emerge from the university groups, the jam'iyat themselves are likely to remain preoccupied with campus politics.

COMMUNITY-BASED JAM'IYAT

The points made about campus-based jam'iyat generally apply to community-based ones as well in terms of their programmatic and ideological similarities. The neighborhood groups, however, are small and more scattered. They flourish particularly in poor urban areas inhabited by immigrants from the countryside and neglected by the regime. These neighborhood groups refuse to register with the Ministry of Social Affairs. A number have been started by students or ex-students in the deprived areas where they live. In Asyut, for example, Kepel notes that "an entire universe of poverty-stricken students is packed into" an area around the campus, "cut off from their family milieu and highly receptive to any voices that . . . promise an improvement in their conditions."[18]

In the neighborhoods, they promote low-cost clinics and Islamic private schools. Many of these fundamentalist groups are friendly to the Brotherhood though they remain independent. They are interested in grassroots organization rather than seizing state power. In the district of Al-Minya, 150 miles south of Cairo, Ali 'Abd al-Rahman led a local group which had taken over some of the functions of government. It enforced an Islamic ban on alcohol, in one case burning a truckload of beer. As a campaign against corruption, its members "destroyed 'pornographic' video tapes, disciplined unchaperoned young men and women, and flogged drunks loitering in the street."[19]

It is possible that the jam'iyat linked to revolutionary groups will try to turn whole areas into fundamentalist "liberated zones" from which government activity is barred. In the Cairo neighborhood of Ayn Shams, also a prime area of student activity, militants tried to forbid music and dancing. One suspected police informer was flogged and a high-ranking police plainclothes man was murdered. In August 1988, five people were killed by police in violent demonstrations. Police raids on mosques to arrest radicals often angered ordinary people who resented the authorities or thought such attacks on places of worship to be impious. In times of crisis or unrest, the jam'iyat might mobilize their areas into places of massive riots beyond the uncoordinated upheavals Egypt has experienced in the past. Such uprisings could destabilize the country.

Muhammad al-Maraghi, president of the Islamic Dawn Association (Jam'iyat Fajr al-Islam) of Alexandria, claimed his group was involved with reformist rather than revolutionary activity. "Anybody can see our political decisions by referring to the rules of the Qur'an and the Prophet's traditions . . . We tell them: If Islamic groups are subjected to the will of certain authorities, these authorities can control and contain them instead of oppressing them."[20] In other words, where the government mismanages or ignores problems, local groups will act but they do not seek an unwinnable test of wills with the regime. On the other hand, the danger that these groups will stir up Christian–Muslim clashes in mixed neighborhoods, as happened several times in the 1980s, is extremely worrisome.

The jam'iyat in Asyut have a strong neighborhood, as well as campus, presence. Its Shari'ah Society mosque held the five daily prayers and a worship meeting on Friday which included a "News and Commentary" discussion. As an Egyptian journalist summarized it, the main point of the latter was to suggest that "if the Islamic caliphate still existed, what happened would not have happened." One of the leaders gave a lecture on Monday. The group even used video showings to attract and persuade people. Around 800 people attended Friday prayers in the mosque with about 200 more standing outside. About 90 per cent of the crowd seemed to be under the age of 25.[21]

Ahmad 'Abd al-Salam, a doctor who supported pro-government and opposition secular parties (and says he almost became a Nasirist) before choosing to be a fundamentalist leader said of the Asyut Islamic Group, "Our aim is to establish an Islamic state [but] we reject application of the Shari'ah through the People's Assembly." Since the Shari'ah is God's law, it does not need approval by Egypt's parliament. This view is a direct criticism of the Muslim Brotherhood, which is also strong in Asyut. The jam'iyat have clashed several times with the Brotherhood. "Force is compulsory," al-Salam continued, "Our people need force more than any other. We believe that we must rally the people around our ideas and try to pressure the government for reform. If this doesn't happen, what is left but force?" When asked why jam'iyat members badly beat two students who were standing with women, he repeats, "Force is the means of last resort." The jam'iyat are willing to organize within the society but not to participate in the political system: "We refuse to enter the People's Assembly, although we will enter federations and unions because they are service and pressure groups."[22]

The government has increasingly made a distinction between jam'iyat using non-violent – and sometimes high pressure – methods and those pursuing revolutionary goals. The Muslim Brotherhood has also sought to work with the community and Islamic groups in the professions – doctors, pharmacists, journalists, and a Federation of Islamic Associations – which have sprung up and gained influence in their sectors. In the words of Brotherhood leader al-Tilimsani, "As for the Islamic association ... there will be no quarreling groups among them, nor among the Muslim Brothers ... I see that the government is allowing complete freedom to the Islamic associations, each on its own, and that whoever breaks the law, the judiciary would handle this judgment fairly."

CHARISMATIC PREACHERS

The Iranian revolution probably would not have succeeded – and certainly would not have taken the turn it did – without the presence of the overwhelming charisma of its leader, Ayatollah Ruhollah Khumayni. By both doctrine and structure, Iran's variety of Shi'ite Islam is much more likely to produce such figures than is the Sunni Islam of Egypt. The Egyptian government has far more control over the Islamic clerical hierarchy than did the Shah's Iran, while the Shi'ite ulama had a greater degree of doctrinal latitude than do their Sunni counterparts. Nonetheless, the prospects for an Islamic fundamentalist upheaval in Egypt rest in no small part on the movement's ability to produce such a person.

At least on a limited scale, all the leaders of the jama'at have been charismatic men. But their success has been on a quasi-cult level. They attract small groups of followers whose obedience to the leader's commands is enhanced by their isolation from other influences. Some preachers in Egypt have large followings for their fundamentalist-type messages. They operate in a manner analogous to popular Christian fundamentalist ministers in the United States, but they depend on drawing thousands of people to services and the sales of tape cassettes. The mass media is closed to clerics who are critical of the government. There is, however, something of a catch for these opposition clerics: to function openly they must be cautious lest the government arrest them or close down their mosques.

The two best examples of this type of preacher are Shaykh Kishk and Hafiz Salamah. A third man, Salah Abu Isma'il, is the most visible as the leader of the Muslim Brotherhood faction in political parties and parliament. Isma'il's case shows how a potential charismatic leader is tempered by involvement in legal and electoral activities.

An Arab magazine aptly expresses the difference between the authority of an official leader of Egyptian Islam, the shaykh (head) of al-Azhar, and the popularity of Kishk: "The difference between

Shaykh Kishk and Shaykh al-Azhar is the difference between popular Islam (Islam of the streets) and official Islam, or between Islam of the masses and Islam of the government. Kishk expresses the anger of the people, whereas Shaykh al-Azhar expresses the wishes and programs of the government."[23]

At the heart of Kishk's appeal is his truly remarkable ability as a speaker. In his Friday sermons, Kishk is the consummate demagogue: modulating his voice to create the maximum excitement in his audience, pouring sarcasm on the targets of his criticism, mixing in literary illusions and (not always accurate) references to science to give his arguments an aura of modernity. He denounces corruption, mistreatment of the poor, government incompetence, and immoral behavior. Each performance is persuasive or frightening, depending on the listener's inclinations. Yet the heat of Kishk's words is matched by the vagueness of his program. Egypt is rotten and corrupt; Egypt must be made into an Islamic society, he argues, but never explains how this is to be done. While Kishk is potentially a revolutionary firebrand, he is more immediately a revivalist who exhilarates followers but does not necessarily move them to action.[24]

Still, Kishk does have some potential power. He condemned Sadat as "traitorous to fundamental Islamic principles" and during a period of Muslim–Christian tension in September 1981, a fiery Kishk sermon provoked his followers to leave the mosque and attack a church opposite it. This was one of the main events that led Sadat to order massive arrests and, in turn, led to his murder.[25]

Kishk ridicules both the revolutionary Jama'at leader – "a pubescent boy who has read three words or a few pages of Ibn Taimiyya or Ibn 'Abd al-Wahhab and can pose as a guardian of the faith!" – and the Muslim Brotherhood – which submits the Shari'ah to parliament "that they might approve or reject God!" Yet, as Kepel puts it, "While the 'star of Islamic preaching' offers a merciless analysis of the . . . state, stigmatizing it in terms of great violence, he is less than eloquent when it comes to any plan of action to overthrow that state and to establish the Muslim society in its place. But it is toward just such a prospect that his sermons lead."[26]

Another populist preacher, Hafiz Salamah, had been willing to go further than Kishk in confronting the regime. He became a hero for leading resistance to the Israelis in his native Suez during the 1973 war. He had thousands of followers through his leadership of the Jam'iyat al-Hidaya al-Islamiyyah (Islamic Guidance Society).

In June 1985, the 70-year-old Salamah tried to use his privately funded al-Nur mosque in Cairo's crowded al-Abbasiyah quarter to launch a campaign of demonstrations to demand implementation of the Shari'ah. He called for a march from the mosque to Abdin palace to demand that Mubarak apply Islamic law. The Interior Minister refused permission for the demonstration, warning that mercenary elements might infiltrate the protest and lead to violence. Salamah complied with the order temporarily and cancelled the plan.[27]

When Salamah tried to revive his campaign, however, the government, through the Ministry of Awqaf, responded by taking over the mosque and firing Salamah from his post as its imam (leader). When he tried to issue another message of defiance from his pulpit, the electricity was cut off to his microphone. Salamah's followers stopped two government-appointed clerics from taking over the podium. Police then closed the mosque and later drove away supporters of Salamah who tried to pray in a nearby vacant lot. Salamah himself was arrested on July 14 with a group of fundamentalists – including blind Shaykh 'Umar 'Abd al-Rahmän, who had encouraged al-Jihad's killing of Sadat – and was charged with sedition. President Mubarak warned that the government would not tolerate extremist action which threatened the country's stability. Salamah was then released in mid-August to make the pilgrimage to Mecca. The authorities had given him a carefully calibrated warning. The preachers' option of functioning freely would not be foreclosed, but the alternative would be arrest if he exceeded permissible bounds.[28]

While the authorities take action when militants employ violence, Islamic preachers also have a wide measure of latitude to say things which no secular opponent of the government would dare to match. Although 'Abd al-Rahman clearly issued a fatwah (an Islamic legal option) used by al-Jihad to justify its murder of Sadat, for example, he was found not guilty by the court trying the assassins. A supporter wrote of 'Abd al-Rahman, "He spoke the truth whenever he had a chance. Is advocating the cause of God considered an attempt to overthrow the government?" The judges were also convinced that "issuing a fatwah does not constitute instigation."[29]

As a politician, Salah Abu Isma'il is more careful to work within the system and to show flexibility, or opportunism, as required. When the Muslim Brotherhood was being persecuted in the 1960s, he reportedly called it "a group of people who had lost their way" and rejoined only after the government allowed it to function again. Isma'il then became a tough critic of Sadat but also played a centrist role in the Brotherhood. He led the group's alignment with the Wafd party and entered parliament in May 1984. When partnership with the Wafd proved unsatisfactory, he resigned from the party's membership after eight months, later leading the Brotherhood faction into the Liberal party. He criticized the regime for "non-Islamic" conduct but restrained his attacks. As one of the Brotherhood's younger generation – he was born in 1934 – Isma'il's style hints the group's future direction will be militant rather than revolutionary. He could become a leader of the Brotherhood in his own right and the most important fundamentalist in Egyptian politics.[30]

Contrary to jama'at leaders, the main figures in the jam'iyat or independent mosques have not been ideological innovators. Government weakness during an economic or foreign policy crisis could some day turn charismatic preachers into revolutionary leaders and jam'iyat into jama'at. But this would require major changes from current conditions, including their willingness to sacrifice personal and organizational privileges. While the Egyptian Sunni hierarchy is more divided than the Iranian Shi'ite clergy, the centers which do exist – most notably al-Azhar – are subject to a great deal of government control.

6 Popular Islam and Official Ulama

The Egyptian state has many religious assets to counter fundamentalism and uses the powerful religious institutions to strengthen itself. For centuries, Egypt's rulers have worked closely with the religious establishment. In Iran, the Shi'ite clergy was a largely independent body with a past record of having an adversarial relationship toward the monarchy. Sunni Egypt has no such tradition or structure.

The establishment ulama in Egypt have their own ideology which is as coherent as those of their fundamentalist rivals. Saad Eddin Ibrahim provides a succinct definition of this worldview: "Establishment Islam emphasizes beliefs, worship, and rituals, while it generally remains silent on matters of politics. If pressed, it cannot but acknowledge the virtues of implementing Shari'ah, although suggesting a 'gradualist' path, often qualified with a statement of 'preconditions' that must first be fulfilled." As a group, young and educated Egyptians had less regard for establishment Islam as uninspiring or backward.[1]

The ulama's professional interests and their desire to protect their status clash with the competing claims of the mostly lay fundamentalists to be the proper interpreters of Islam. Having spent years in the study of the Islamic texts and theologies, the ulama are genuinely shocked at the impudence and ignorance of their challengers. The clergy are also disturbed by the fundamentalists' original, even heretical, formulations.

The establishment ulama, however, are no mere puppets of the government. They have their own opinions and approach to Islam which are as well-rooted in history as those of the radicals and revolutionaries. Indeed, the mainstream ulama correspond far closer in practice to the actual life of Egyptians in modern times than do the new fundamentalists. Compared to the majority of Muslims, who act in response to norms and lessons gained during over thirteen centuries of Islamic history, the fundamentalists invalidate most Islamic thought since the seventh century. But it was during those intermediate centuries that Islam made its peace with the reality of realpolitik. It survived so well by accommodating to the compromises required in ruling large societies, the adjustments called for by modern industrial states, and even the vagaries of human nature.

And there is no shortage of verses in the Qur'an and other Islamic texts which can be used to justify the ulama's personalistic, conservative approach to religion. As one Qur'anic verse puts it, "Allah does not change a people's lot unless they change what is in their hearts."

In its confrontation with the fundamentalists, the government has criticized the mainstream clerics for providing insufficient guidance for the younger generation. The ulama, in turn, claim the regime has failed to set a good example and has been too harsh toward the militants. The clerics suggest that they can deal effectively with the issue if the politicians only give them more money and strengthen their prerogatives.

This chapter discusses the regime's leverage over "official" Islam, the attitudes of officials of al-Azhar and other establishment institutions, and the average Egyptian's attitudes toward religion.

AL-AZHAR AND STATE CONTROL OVER RELIGION

There are three institutions which form the basis of the establishment clergy and the foundation for ulama–state cooperation: al-Azhar University, the Ministry of Awqaf and al-Azhar Affairs, and the religious court system headed by the mufti of Egypt. Al-Azhar, the great religious university founded in 970 and famous throughout the Islamic world, is a pillar of mainstream Islam. It trains Islamic judges, preachers and teachers who take up positions throughout the country and abroad. The head of the school, the shaykh al-Azhar, is appointed by the government which also subsidizes its operations. The power of government helped to increase the prestige and wealth of al-Azhar and its leading officials while the support of al-Azhar gave the regime greater legitimacy. In recent decades, however, these links with the rulers, instances of corruption, and decrees seemingly at odds with traditional Islamic practices eroded respect for al-Azhar. At the same time, the overall weakening of Islam itself in Egypt in the face of change and Western influence has undermined al-Azhar's position among the general public.

The Ministry of Awqaf and al-Azhar Affairs is the main government agency dealing with Islam. In cooperation with al-Azhar, it controls some 10,000 state mosques, the hiring of preachers, millions of dollars in subsidies, many hours of television and radio time, and hundreds of state religious schools. As Ibrahim summarizes it, the "activities of establishment Islam have grown as rapidly as those of 'activist Islam.' Between 1970 and 1985, the state-supported mosques have more than doubled their number of religious educational institutions and their student intake has more than tripled ... The number of radio and television hours of religious programs have quadrupled during this period. There is now a radio station which is exclusively devoted to such programs; religious broadcasting accounts for nearly one-quarter of the hours of all other radio and television channels." In addition, al-Azhar and other establishment institutions have increased their number of publications by 400 per cent.[2]

Much of the fundamentalist movement, as has already been noted, is led by lay people who are often contemptuous of clerics. Other radicals are friendly toward that minority of ulama whom they consider to be honest and pious, while antagonistic to those who are seen as pro-government supporters of un-Islamic reforms. Many fundamentalists see al-Azhar as both the author and the victim of a decline of Islam in Egypt. It is a victim insofar as the government has forced al-Azhar to issue fatwas backing the regime's actions and ideology. Such decrees declare certain practices or ideas acceptable to Islam. But al-Azhar is the culprit insofar as it has willingly accepted this role.[3]

This close relationship between al-Azhar and Egypt's rulers began under the monarchy and accelerated during the Nasir era when the government gained a firm grip over the institution. It forced establishment ulama to support socialist measures and pan-Arab policies. A 1961 law undermined al-Azhar's thousand-year-old autonomy. New faculties were added in secular subjects like medicine, agriculture, and commerce to the historic curriculum of religion, Islamic law, and Arabic. The ulama were unhappy about losing their special status in this reform but could do nothing against Nasir.[4]

In the 1970s, Sadat loosened the reins a bit, but his pressure for fatwas supporting peace with Israel, permitting government fundraising schemes which involved the payment of interest, and accepting the expansion of women's rights put the leaders of al-Azhar in a dilemma. Some ulama backed reforms in the Personal Status Law at that time but later, in the more relaxed atmosphere of the Mubarak period, reversed themselves. Partly through the activity of such clerics, the law was amended in 1985 to reduce women's rights. They also supported adoption of the Shari'ah for the basis of all Egypt's laws.

Fundamentalists claim the government and establishment ulama "misuse" Islam for their own purposes. But the latter two groups can also cite numerous precedents defending their more conservative interpretation of Islam, a view of religion which will also be acceptable to many or most Egyptian Muslims. Thus, Sadat's Prime Minister 'Abd-al-Aziz Hijazi defended his new personal wealth in 1974 by noting that the Qur'an endorses the social hierarchy: "Some of you We [God] have placed over others in rank." The following year, the shaykh of al-Azhar, 'Abd-al-Halim Mahmud, wrote a book arguing that Islam endorsed the idea of private property and that someone who died deprived of his property is a martyr. Others criticized such pronouncements, attributing them to the wealth of Mahmud and of other al-Azhar officials. The regime then came to the shaykh's defense, calling him the "living symbol" of all Muslims and warning that attacks on him exceeded permissible bounds.[5]

The mufti of Egypt is the chief clerical jurist who issues decrees interpreting Islamic law. But he also recognizes the overall dominance of state authority. Mufti 'Abd al-Latif Hamzah, for example, said that he could decide in capital punishment cases only when secular courts fail to reach a decision. Even then, his judgement would not be binding. He also argued that the mufti and the shaykh of al-Azhar should not interfere with politics. On women's rights he took an intermediate position: they may work outside the home if they dress and act in accord with Islamic law and avoid unnecessary contact with men.[6]

Yet the establishment ulama believe, like the fundamentalists, that Islam is a complete system which should be the foundation of Egyptian society. Dr al-Tayyib al-Najjar, former president of al-Azhar University, put it this way: "The canonical law of Islam involves more than just prescribed legal amounts of punishments and modes of worship; it is a total way of life." He also wants the Shari'ah enforced as law. "The gradual application of Islamic law is legitimate, and its favorable consequences are guaranteed." In contrast to the radicals, al-Najjar stressed gradualism but his ideal goals were similar.

"It is a mistake," he continued, "to think that the provisions of Islamic law cover merely the required modes of worship, that is prayer, alms giving, fasting and the pilgrimage, or the prescribed legal punishments for certain crimes such as adultery, theft, drunkenness, libel, and highway robbery. The provisions of Islamic law are not restricted to those matters. They cover all transactions that are required in life and necessary for people's happiness, security and stability. They also deal with people's personal, social and political affairs."[7]

THE DEBATE WITH THE RADICALS

The radicals reserve a special hatred for the ulama they perceive as state employees, bureaucrats, formalists, hypocrites, and opportunists who are perverting Islam and profiting from this betrayal. In interviews with Saad Eddin Ibrahim, revolutionary fundamentalists described ulama like Mahmud as "parrots of the pulpit," stooges of the government, or "religious mercenaries."[8]

Shukri Mustafa, the leader of al-Takfir, blamed Egypt's descent into jahiliyyah on the ulama who had condoned the evil practice of politicians. He cited Mahmud Shaltut, a Nasir-era shaykh of al-Azhar, and the popular preacher Muhammad Mutawalli al-Sha'rawi – who said that certain kinds of bank arrangements and Treasury bonds permitted what Mustafa claimed was the payment of interest – and Shaykh Su'ad Jalal who declared that beer did not fall under the Islamic prohibition of alcohol. Other fundamentalists see al-Azhar as serving the goals of the "infidel regime." Shaykh Kishk ridiculed Azhar, claiming, "There are Azhar graduates today who cannot even read the Qur'an with the text in front of them!" He ridiculed some of the shaykhs of al-Azhar for having received degrees in France or West Germany and claimed that one of them had even majored in secular philosophy. Since the Nasirist reforms of 1961, he complained, "the leadership of al-Azhar has ceased to render any service to Islam." Kishk's criticism has some basis in fact. The number of students failing in the study of the Qur'an at al-Azhar has steadily increased, partly due to the decline in the traditional elementary schools which largely concentrated on memorization of the Qur'an.[9]

Kishk wanted to reform the ulama into playing a proper role as independent men of religion who advise and warn the prince about God's will. For the revolutionaries, however, the ulama are irredeemable sinners. This attitude is not surprising since the leaders of the jama'at are themselves laymen who take the interpretation of Islam into their own hands. They point out that Islam holds that it needs no clergy to intervene between the individual believer and God. Some of the jam'iyat seem to have more respect for the ulama, though they choose the ones they believe to merit respect.

One of the revolutionaries' main arguments is that when the rulers do not follow Islamic laws and behavior, the good Muslim must wage jihad to overthrow them. The mufti responded for the establishment ulama. He quoted the Prophet Muhammad as saying that you may hate and deny your rulers while still being innocent, but if you consent and follow them in your heart then you are a sinner. He interpreted this to mean that the subject is only corrupted if he, too, joins in a ruler's wrongful actions. The ruler cannot be expected to be a perfect Muslim and Islam does not permit disobedience or the killing of a Muslim ruler as long as he is loyal to Islam and allows prayer. In other words, rebellion is permitted only if the ruler becomes an apostate or suppresses the practice of Islam. Charging the ruler with unbelief for deviating from a few rules has no basis in the Qur'an or Sunnah. Finally, in the mufti's opinion, "Jihad is not a struggle against others, but rather is a continuing struggle to purify oneself from sin and Satan and to adhere to goodness and piety and faith." This idea is far more typical of historic Sunni belief than are the harsher ideas of the revolutionaries.[10]

In fact, more traditionally minded Muslims even charge that fundamentalists are responsible for many of Islam's current problems. The militants' invocation of Islam can be, in the words of Muhammad's son-in-law, Caliph 'Ali ibn Abu Talib, "The use of a true statement intended to perpetrate evil." The radicals are said to be too harsh and divisive. One writer, Dr Mustafa Mahmud, complains so eloquently that he is worth quoting at length as representing the views of many mainstream Muslims:

> Today, we see Islam being forced into even more significant and more extensive civil strife. We see Muslims killing other Muslims everywhere. We see people proclaiming there is no god but Allah and slaughtering each other in Lebanon, Iraq, Iran, Syria, Libya and every Arab country. Here they want to kill each other under the banner of the canonical law of Islam and in its name...
>
> In the past [the Caliph] 'Umar ibn al-Khattab did not cut off thieves' hands when there was famine. The Prophet [Muhammad] did not cut off anyone's hand in times of war... The canonical law of Islam involves more than just prescribed legal punishments. It involves justice, mercy, knowledge and work... We are a nation that does not read and does not reason. Instead, we think of demonstrations, cheers and marches to demand the application of Islamic law. But what is Islamic law? It is all of that. Islamic law

involves knowledge, work, justice, mercy and good morals. It involves more than just prescribed legal punishments which are nothing more than a device imposed by the canonical law of Islam to provide security and protection for the Muslim community. However, the canonical law of Islam as a whole [also] ... involves law for general mercy and love and regulations for the growth and development of Islamic society.

Didn't our prophet, Muhammad ... tell Muslims, "Pardon each other and dispense with those prescribed punishments?" The prophet said, "The punishment will have to be enforced in those matters that are brought to my attention." The prophet advised Muslims to settle their disputes and to forgive each other. He advised them to accept compensation and not to let him know about the offense, because if he is informed about those offenses, the prescribed legal punishment will have to be carried out. The prophet said that because he does not like to enforce legal punishments. He prefers forgiveness and mercy between litigants.

This is Islam: the religion of tolerance, mercy, affection and forgiveness. Islam is the true religion that does not resort to violence unless all opportunities for reform have been exhausted. It is the religion that was revealed as a divine act of mercy.

But violence, terrorism, coups, strikes, demonstrations, airplane hijackings and car bombings are the work of cunning politicians and people with ulterior motives. They are the work of capricious troublemakers, criminals and people who toy with people's minds ... We are opposed to people like that because they will not lead us into salvation. They will rather lead us straight into hell.[11]

In addition to this analysis, a number of other factors persuaded the establishment ulama to support the government's effort to constrain or punish the militants. They were genuinely shocked by some of the revolutionaries' actions, including al-Takfir's murder of a leading mainstream cleric who had been both a dean at al-Azhar and the minister of awqaf. They disagreed with the extremists' ideology and were outraged that these young men – ridiculed even by Shaykh Kishk as ignorant – wanted to usurp the ulama's prerogative of interpreting Islam and its law. They were frightened of the anarchy and upheaval threatened by Sadat's assassination. They also acted to defend their own privileges and the social stability in which they so strongly believed.

"The Shari'ah is not implemented through car stickers, nor is Islam served by demonstrations and marches," the shaykh al-Azhar stated. He, too, favored the implementation of the Shari'ah as the basis of Egypt's laws but had more confidence in gradualism and proper channels. "The People's Assembly has begun to amend existing laws and adapt them to the Shari'ah. Much time, money and work are being invested in this . . . Serious work is being done and the results are satisfactory . . . If the legislative procedure is delayed, the way to improve it is not though shameful methods which damage the country's reputation, security and stability." Other ulama also criticized the charismatic preacher Hafiz Salamah for advocating demonstrations for the Shari'ah.[12]

The revolutionary and radical groups claim they advocate and embody true Islam. They appropriate for themselves the title of being the only true Muslims. These tiny movements assert that they provide understanding of the correct priority and provide the only accurate reading for the Qur'an, the Sunnah, and the history of the Muslims and of Egypt. Other Egyptian Muslims do not have to accept these assertions and many see such behavior as arrogant and misleading. The vast majority of the clergy derides these arguments. As one commentator notes, the revolutionaries seem to be at war with the mass of Egyptians rather than waging a struggle on their behalf: "Having declared the entire society 'atheistic' . . . they hold it permissible to take the property and lives of its members."[13]

HOW SHOULD AL-AZHAR COUNTER EXTREMISM?

Criticism of al-Azhar and the mainstream clergy does not come only from radicals. The government demands that they do more to counter the militants' misreading of Islam by providing Egypt's youth with a proper Islamic education. During periods of massive government roundups of radicals, the state pressed mainstream ulama, al-Azhar officials, and even charismatic preachers like Kishk (himself a strong critic of the government) into supporting these tough measures.

The most notable example of this bickering between regime and al-Azhar began with the comments of the military prosecutor in the al-Takfir case. "The youth are no longer educated in religion," he complained, and so fall prey to charlatans. He suggested that religious education be made mandatory from the pre-school to university levels and complained about the low quality of al-Azhar graduates. The angry shaykhs of al-Azhar countered by saying that the rulers had been insufficiently religious and had thus set a bad example for the younger generation. If the government wanted Azhar to do better, the regime had to be willing to give it more assets to do so and to improve pay and conditions for clerics and religious teachers.[14]

The shaykh al-Azhar condemned the jama'at's violence as intended to "disrupt elections, divert people from the exercise of their rights, and to preoccupy the authorities." He also rejected the revolutionaries' behavior by citing well-known Qur'anic passages opposing the use of compulsion in matters of religion in explaining that conversion to Islam must be voluntary. Defending al-Azhar, he introduced a patriotic theme, noting that the university is an important factor in Egypt's vanguard position in the Arab world, adding that Egypt has been among the chief protectors of Islam.[15]

After Sadat's assassination, the government even brought leading mainstream and Muslim Brotherhood clerics into the prisons for highly publicized and televised talks to revolutionary fundamentalists. But these elders concluded that both sides were trying to use them. The militants wanted an excuse to get out of jail and thus claimed they had seen the light even before the dialogue began; the government wished to claim that the prodigals had recognized the error of their ways and had returned to the fold.[16]

The mainstream ulama have also been constrained by their reluctance to state that there is one proper line for Muslims to take. When the Mubarak government demanded that al-Azhar denounce Sadat's killers as heretics, this pressure was resented. Precisely because they oppose the revolutionaries' notion that people can be "excommunicated" as Muslims, mainstream ulama were reluctant to take any step implying they had the right to determine who was a real Muslim.

The strength of Islam as the underlying philosophy of Egyptian society and the general direction of its preaching can also move people in a radical manner. "Many leaders of religious opinion in our country," complains an Egyptian writer, "appear on the television screen and in front of the microphones repeating many of these ideas." The government, of course, never allows preachers on radio or television to advocate revolution or to say that society is in a state of jahiliyyah. But each sermon may reinforce the idea that Islam is the answer, an idea likely to appeal to people who face seemingly insurmountable problems. For young people particularly, the pressures of life, the difficulties of finding a job (or the need to hold several jobs), the terrible condition of housing, and a range of other problems might lead them to embrace radical fundamentalism.[17]

THE MAINSTREAM CLERGY AND THE SHARI'AH

While the mainstream leaders generally support the government's positions against the revolutionaries and radicals, they also want the Shari'ah to be invoked as the basis of Egyptian law. The Shari'ah itself is by no means a revolutionary body of law. All factions agree that the majority of Egyptian law already coincides with it, and the Islamic code is a strong protector of private property and of the existing social hierarchy. The attitude of the Brotherhood, many of whose members are trying to preserve their social and economic positions against a corrosive modernity, reinforces this "defensive" aspect of the Shari'ah.

The mainstream clergy argue, however, that such steps would help undercut extremism. Thus, in February 1985, the leading official cleric 'Ali Jadd al-Haqq stated, in a well-worded mixture of support for the Shari'ah and backing for official channels, "The People's Assembly represents the people and . . . the people are eager to see the Holy Law applied . . . The country is perfectly prepared for the application of the Shari'ah . . . without delay."[18]

The fact that the regime was unwilling to comply and repeatedly stalled this proposal in parliament created some friction but no serious conflict between the regime and the clergy. As one close student of al-Azhar notes, as long as the ulama do not conspire against the regime and "express their opposition to various policies and laws in acceptable ways and with a certain etiquette, they are left to themselves to a remarkable degree, while from the clergy's standpoint, we should not forget that there are also government policies that the Azhar can sincerely support."[19]

THE POPULAR, MODERATE ISLAMIC REVIVAL

Islam is both a religion and a set of principles directing the daily activities of society and the individual. It provides not just general guidelines but, as Ibrahim puts it, "a set of comprehensive principles for the regulation of all aspects of life – from the interpersonal to the international."[20] At the same time, Islam, like other religions and ideologies, has both a pure form which exists mostly in theory and a realized form which compromises with the realities of this world. The revolutionary and radical fundamentalists want to impose their notion of Islam – as projected backward onto the seventh century – upon contemporary Egypt. Yet there are many more Egyptian Muslims who seek to practice Islam in the more moderate fashion in which it has existed in previous decades. In short, the battle between fundamentalism and the practice of mainstream ulama and Egyptians may be likened to a conflict between Islamic theology and Muslim history.

Many Egyptians are less interested in Islam than were their parents' generation, others oppose the erosion of their faith by modernism and Westernism, or even seek to revitalize it by adapting to these elements. Some of them are mystics, some argue that the individual must first perfect himself, and some claim that people's behavior must be improved through preaching and peaceful persuasion. Such are the views of the mainstream clergy and of the majority of Egyptian Muslims. None of these very common ideas are revolutionary although most of them seek to strengthen Islam. If this is "fundamentalism," its activists are quite moderate and peaceful in word and action.[21]

Thus, a mainstream cleric like the popular television preacher Shaykh Muhammad Mutawali al-Sha'rawi uses his government-sanctioned access to the media – on which he appears every week and daily during the holy month of Ramadan – to criticize dancing and most music as prohibited by Islam.[22] This very kind of entertainment appears on the same television stations as al-Sha'rawi. Islamic preachers may persuade individual viewers to refuse to watch or even to demand that such programing be barred. Of course, this kind of sermon creates an atmosphere in which campus jam'iyat break up concerts. But one might equally well ask how Middle East music and belly-dancing developed over centuries in Muslim societies – coexisting with the ulama and high levels of Islamic practice and piety – if these things are antithetical to Islam. It is even more interesting to note that al-Sha'rawi was harshly criticized by revolutionary fundamentalists who claimed that he was a government apologist who rationalized even the payment of interest as acceptable under Islam.

Part of the problem is that Egyptians consider themselves good Muslims without necessarily always obeying the shaykhs of al-Azhar – much less revolutionary fundamentalists – just as the mass of

Christians and Jews act toward their equivalent spiritual guides. Al-Azhar produces publications, urges censorship, organizes religion courses in the school system, and undertakes a wide range of other actions which most individuals ignore. This ineffectiveness may anger both revolutionary fundamentalists and a government which feels that al-Azhar's failures breed such people, but also signals that the general population is not eager for a rigid interpretation of their own religion.

Often, as one scholar notes, "It is the believers' own perception of his role obligations, and his conformity to them, that pose the challenge to the ulama." Citizens try to evade – if not too publicly – the Ramadan fast. "Most Egyptians do not pray regularly, and many pray rarely. Most Egyptians are not mobilized in any religiously significant way. Those who are active in Muslim religious pursuits are divided among a number of quite different orientations." Local customs, which people think of as Islamic, often flourish despite their conflict with the ulama's interpretation of Islam. The commercialization of Ramadan, for example, has been compared with the similar phenomenon in regard to Christmas. While observers have focused particularly on increased observance and fundamentalism, there is a great deal more apathy or nominal observance associated with Egyptians' attitude to Islam.[23]

In the face of terrible economic pressures and a lifestyle under challenge from imported products and ideas, Egyptians may turn back to Islam as a personal anchor and as an expression of their roots. This preference for "traditionalism," however, does not mean a turn toward a radical fundamentalism which is very much at odds with traditional Egyptian practice.[24]

To encourage moderate trends in Islam the state allows or finances a wider range of activities and organizations including charitable societies, Islamic youth organizations, the General Society for the Preservation of the Glorious Qur'an, and the Islamic Studies Society which provides courses to university students.

In Egypt, small groups of private citizens frequently get together to build mosques, which sometimes include health clinics and other social services. The government began by subsidizing these mosques and tried to use this money as leverage to take them over through the supervision of the Ministry of Awqaf. Sadat sought to nationalize all private mosques and though he failed the government role was increased. He also established the Supreme Islamic Council consisting of officials from al-Azhar, the Ministry of Awqaf, and others to ensure proper Islamic instruction in religion courses. Independent mosques which refuse such financial aid tend to be newer and smaller. A mosque like that of Salamah's, which refuses state assistance, is able to remain outspokenly critical, but the government showed its willingness to seize that mosque to force Salamah to tone down his attacks. During the 1970s and 1980s, the government reorganized the growing Sufi orders, subsidized groups involved in mosque construction, and increased religious education. As a reward for its support, al-Azhar received added control over all these endeavors.

Thus, al-Azhar and the other ulama are in a conflicting situation. On the one hand, the closer they are to the government, the more power, money, and access to publicity they gain. On the other hand, this same proximity makes it harder for them to appeal to those alienated by the regime or the system. The radicals blame al-Azhar for the decline of Islam and attack the ulama as puppets of the regime; the government criticizes al-Azhar as ineffective in properly socializing the country's youth.

For their part, the ulama say that the government should do more to set a good example and to deal with problems which create radical fundamentalism. They are outraged that untrained young radicals presume to declare the true nature of Islam in ways that deviate from accepted practices. These ulama may be less in touch with the utopian society which allegedly existed in seventh-century Mecca, but they are far more cognizant of the historic problems of Islam in dealing with less spiritually enlightened rulers and people. These clerics have their own interpretation of Islam – and of what is fundamental in that religion – which may not appeal directly to the populace but is still much closer to its own understanding on these issues.

In summary, then, there are four distinct categories of Islamic groups. Each of them has its own claim on what constitutes a proper approach to Islam. Each has its different attitude toward the existing Egyptian system and a strategy for making the society more Islamic:

- The mainstream ulama claim that the existing structure provides an opportunity to make improvements by more vigorous preaching, religious education, and individual self-improvement.
- The Muslim Brotherhood organizes to win votes and to lobby parliament to enact the Shari'ah as the basis of legislation.
- The jam'iyat and some charismatic preachers use campus and

communities to organize their own Islamic communities, denouncing the ulama as puppets of the government and criticizing the Brotherhood as too willing to compromise.
- The revolutionary jama'at reject the system altogether, go underground, and denounce everyone (including each other), claiming that only violence can bring about an Islamic state.

The first group most closely coincides with the attitudes of Egyptians in their millions, the second has hundreds of thousands of voters or members, the third can count on several tens of thousands of activists, while the final category's supporters stand at a few thousands.

7 Attitudes toward Foreign Policy Issues

The fundamentalists view the outside world in a negative fashion. There are enemies everywhere who seek to corrupt and destroy Islam with an almost satanic determination. In particular, they have identified four forces as foes of Islam, each also allegedly determined to block the fundamentalists' triumph: Crusaders (i.e., Christians and the West), the Jews (Israel and an international Jewish conspiracy), Communism, and secularism.

These forces are profoundly evil and no compromise can be made with them. Egypt is under a cultural, economic, and political assault by increasingly powerful foreign ways which represent this demonic quartet. Modernization and Westernization is seen as a danger to Islam's survival and Egypt's sovereignty.

While agreeing on these basic points, the Muslim Brotherhood and the more radical fundamentalists have a slightly different assessment on the priority of these threats. The Brotherhood blames these external factors for all the problems of Egyptian society. Since the internal system itself is not the main barrier to building an Islamic society – Egyptians are essentially victims of foreign forces – the Brotherhood can thus follow a program of reformism at home and make deals with the local power structure.

In contrast, while the revolutionary groups hate these four enemies as much as does the Muslim Brotherhood, they are less immediately concerned about them. For these militants, Egypt's rulers and its system are agents of the foreign demonic forces. Thus, the first, and main priority must be to fight against the internal jahiliyyah, represented by Egypt's government and the mainstream ulama who support it. This debate parallels disputes among Third World Marxist groups in which the "left" sees the main enemy as the domestic bourgeoisie while the "right" calls for a national united front against imperialism.

In general, while Egyptian fundamentalists spend a great deal of time and energy denouncing the external enemies and their multiple conspiracies, they seem to admit implicitly that there is not much they can do. After all, the creation of an Islamic society is a precondition for deflecting the attack. The main emphasis of both the jama'at and the Brotherhood is to limit the extent to which perfidious influences penetrate into Egyptian society. There are two other underlying consequences of their view. First, since the evil forces originate from outside Egypt, they (or those who rule as their puppets within the country) are alien to the society which is itself blameless. Thus, the fundamentalists do not make a deep or thorough analysis of Egypt's shortcomings beyond the accusation that it has departed from Islam. Any examination of possible shortcomings of Islam itself is, of course, unthinkable for them.

Second, while all fundamentalists reject Egyptian and Arab nationalism, the idea that foreign (non-Arab, non-Egyptian) influences are the great threat runs parallel to the conclusions that a nationalist would reach. This line of approach, with some significant exceptions noted below, makes the fundamentalist argument more palatable to a wider audience.

Yet the inward-looking nature of fundamentalist and Egyptian nationalist ideas in Egypt also runs parallel. Perhaps the most famous anecdote of modern Egyptian political history is one told by Nasir. During the 1948 Palestine war, Nasir recounted, one of his brother officers who was dying on the battlefield told him, "The real struggle is at home." Nasir overthrew the monarchy in 1952 and only after consolidating power and dealing with internal issues turned his main attention to the Arab–Israeli conflict and the nature of Egypt's "superpower" relationships. Underlying even Nasir's pan-Arabism is an isolationism whose appeal in Egypt's political culture may be traced to its geographic separateness, territorial compactness, and long history as a civilization.

Since the fundamentalists seek to limit and exclude Western cultural and political influence, they oppose any Egyptian alliance with the United States and favor an anti-American line. Their objection is not so much to specific policies pursued by the United States but rather to that country's identity as a non-Muslim nation whose interests are seen as inevitably at odds with Islam. To make matters worse, the United States has tremendous cultural influence on Egypt. In the fundamentalist's lexicon, America is the world capitol of Crusader imperialism, the main pillar for Egypt's un-Islamic rulers, and the principal source for a corrupting, pornographic/materialist culture.

The fundamentalists' hatred of Communism implies their equal disdain for the USSR. Marxism is even more explicitly materialist as a philosophy than the Western worldview. While the fundamentalists think that industrial capitalism is too unbridled, they are strong defenders of private property. Moreover, it should be remembered that Nasir was an ally of the Soviet Union when he was suppressing Muslim Brotherhood. Indeed, the fundamentalists remember well that the speech in which he denounced a treasonous plot by the Brotherhood – which led to the execution of Sayyid Qutb – was made in Moscow. Like the revolutionaries in Iran, the Egyptian fundamentalists favor a policy of "neither East nor West."

Fundamentalists also advocate Israel's destruction and reject any peace with the Jewish state. As in the case of the United States, the basis for the antagonism stems not so much from Israel's specific policies as from the fundamentalist's view of that country as an agent of Jewish (hence, anti-Muslim) power which inevitably is antithetical to Islam. Fundamentalists also say that the sole way to destroy Israel is through jihad and thus imply that only an Islamic Egypt can accomplish this task which secular regimes have failed to fulfill.

One of the main targets of the U.S.–USSR–Israeli conspiracy is thought to be the fundamentalist movement itself. Thus these foreign, anti-Islamic forces are held responsible for the Egyptian government's actions against the Brotherhood. One Muslim Brotherhood writer says the rulers' 1948 and 1954 crackdowns were instigated by the West and Israel, while the 1965 repression is attributed to Moscow's orders. The subheadings of one *al-Da'wah* article show this thesis: "Moshe Dayan declares in America, Israel does not fear Arab states but [does fear] the Muslim Brotherhood"; "Ambassadors for Western Countries Made the Liquidation Decision [to destroy the Brotherhood] and Egypt's Prime Minister Nuqrashi Implemented It"; "Abdel Nasir Stood on the Kremlin Steps and Declared a War of Extermination Against the Brotherhood to Satisfy the Atheist State [the USSR]."[1]

While fundamentalists' dread and clearly reject these enemies, their attitude toward Iran is ambivalent. They certainly appreciate Khumayni for having achieved the first Islamic revolution, but find it difficult to have warm feelings toward a Shi'ite, Persian state. Egyptian fundamentalists are almost anti-clerical in many respects, while Iran is virtually run by the Shi'a clergy (*mujtahids*). Egyptians consider their own brand of Islam, and of fundamentalism, to be superior. They are certainly not willing to become Tehran's followers. The fact that Iran was at war with Arab Iraq and the question of whether Khumayni's revolution has accomplished very much at home further encouraged Egyptian fundamentalists to avoid over-identification with Iran. Those openly praising Tehran are extremely marginal even within the fundamentalist community.

Finally, the fundamentalists reject Pan-Arabism and Arab nationalism as a competing ideology to Islamic and pan-Islamic ideas. Islam, not secular nationalism – the tool of their arch-enemy Nasir – should be the ruling idea. Some leaders, most notably Kishk, have insisted on a fusion of Arab nationalism and Islam. But even those attacking Arab nationalism are less fervent in doing so than are their counterparts in Lebanon or Iraq, where the issue is intensified by inter-communal conflicts. The Brotherhood has important historical ties with Saudi Arabia which still has some sentimental appeal as an old-style "fundamentalist" state because of the strictness of the Saudi variety of Islam. In general, however, Egyptian fundamentalists are somewhat provincial. Their main concern is with events inside Egypt. The main exceptions here were the rhetorical support for the Afghan struggle against the Soviets and for the Palestinians. Yet this isolationist orientation is by no means in conflict with Egyptian patriotism. While the revolutionary groups are anti-patriotic – the system is too corrupt to merit any loyalty – less extreme groups evince an identification with Egypt.

STAGES OF EGYPTIAN FOREIGN POLICY

The positions Egyptian Islamic fundamentalists take toward regional or international issues occur within the context of Egyptian foreign policy, whose evolution can be briefly summarized as follows:

- *1952–5* – Nasir's isolationism in the immediate aftermath of his revolution. Nasir tried to convince the Americans and the British of his moderation and put his priorities on consolidation of power at home. His foreign policy was aimed almost entirely at persuading the British to pull their troops out of Suez and he put a low emphasis on the Arab–Israeli conflict.
- *1955–70* – Nasir's Soviet-aligned pan-Arabism. Although non-alignment remained his slogan, it was essentially a cover for Nasir's strong pro-USSR tilt. He bought arms from the Soviet bloc (1955), nationalized the Suez Canal company and withstood the Anglo–French–Israeli attack (1956). Regionally, Nasir became the leading force for pan-Arabism and tried to make Egypt the main power in the Arab world. He created a radical Arab

bloc, merged Egypt with Syria (1958–61), and tried to subvert other Arab states. Egypt intervened militarily in the Yemen civil war. A growing emphasis on the Arab–Israeli conflict peaked with Nasir's provocation and Egypt's humiliating defeat in the 1967 war followed by the costly War of Attrition (1967–70).

- *1971–7* – Sadat's non-alignment increasingly moved toward a balance between both superpowers. The 1972 expulsion of Soviet advisors marked a decisive change in Egypt–Soviet relations, provoked partly by resentment at the large Soviet presence and Egypt's huge debt to Moscow. Regionally, he de-emphasized pan-Arabism and radicalism, improving relations with more conservative Arab states. Sadat used the 1973 war to turn to the United States as a mediator in gaining two disengagement agreements with Israel.
- *1977–81* – Sadat's alignment with the United States paved the way for a compromise peace with Israel. He visited Israel in 1977 and negotiated the Camp David peace accords with Israel in 1978. Egypt was condemned and isolated in the Arab world, expelled from Arab counsels, and cut off from Arab aid. Cairo obtained large amounts of U.S. assistance. At home, this policy coincided with a less statist economic orientation, the open-door policy.
- *1981–90* – Mubarak moved toward slightly more non-alignment. While retaining a strong pro-United States tilt, he was somewhat more even-handed than Sadat; Egypt gradually re-entered the Arab world. The 1987 Amman Arab summit allowed states to reestablish relations with Cairo. The 1989 summit brought Egypt back into the Arab League. Egypt helped Iraq in its war with Iran, opposed Syrian ambitions, and pressed the Palestine Liberation Organization (PLO) toward moderation and peace with Israel.

While the fundamentalists disliked Sadat's policy and alignment with the United States – just as they criticized Nasir's pan-Arab nationalism and alliance with the USSR – the more recent orientation provoked a more passionate response in the 1980s. Mubarak's maintenance of good relations with the United States and the peace with Israel met with the fundamentalists' disfavor. But this antagonism was more muted among moderate fundamentalists who appreciated the relative freedom Mubarak gave them.

The fundamentalists' contemporary de-emphasis on international issues in practice is due to a number of factors. Foreign problems are good agitational issues and it is easier to criticize the United States or Israel than to attack Egypt's government or army. But fundamentalists also recognize that they can do little as long as they are out of power. Thus, complaints about Egypt's social and economic problems and calls for Islamic practices (particularly application of the Shari'ah) are more immediate priorities. Even in their terrorist attacks, the revolutionary fundamentalists rarely targeted foreigners in contrast to their radical leftist counterparts.[2]

Beyond this, however, there are additonal reasons for the fundamentalists' domestic priorities. Even when "foreign" issues are invoked they are portrayed mainly in an insular framework. Thus, the evil forces in the world are seen as plotters against Islam – in other words, against the triumph of Muslim values and fundamentalist forces within Egypt. The most important crime of imperialists, Zionists, and Communists is that they are assaulting Egypt's culture, controlling Egypt's economy, directing Egypt's government, and so on. It is their alleged internal threat rather than their foreign behavior which creates the conflict. Despite all the talk about global issues, this is one more sign of a strong isolationist aspect to Egyptian fundamentalism. If the outside world is so threatening – so corrosive to a proper Islamic society – then a wall must be built to keep out foreign cultures and influences.

This point is of central importance in understanding the fundamentalists' ideology in regard to the regional and international scene. Egyptian fundamentalists are overwhelmingly concerned with their own country. They gave lip service to promoting a regionwide turn toward Islam, they talked to some extent about the Afghans' struggle against the Soviet occupation, and they talked a great deal about supporting the Palestinians as the Brotherhood did so avidly back in 1948 with their volunteer fighters. Yet in their overall ideology, these points take second place.

THE FUNDAMENTALISTS AND THE UNITED STATES

Fundamentalists are more concerned about the U.S. role within Egypt than they are toward its regional policy. They see the United States as posing the greatest danger for Islam and the most salient threat to Egypt's sovereignty. America is clearly the most important Western presence in Egypt, with the greatest political, cultural, and economic influence there. The radical fundamentalists seek to arouse the public by declaring the rulers to be U.S. puppets. Such propaganda tries to undermine popular loyalty to the government as a self-respecting Egyptian, Arab, or Muslim regime. Hence, while the fundamentalists' fear and hatred of the United States may be sincere, promoting anti-American emotions is also a very useful political strategy. The popular appeal of American culture and the positive attitudes toward the United States held by many Egyptians limit the utility of this tactic. Yet this very willingness of Egyptians to consume or copy American culture makes its appeal seem all the more frightening and insidious to the fundamentalists.

To fundamentalists, the United States is a cultural threat because of its massive output of films, music, literature, ideas, clothing, and other items which compose most of the Western culture exported to the Third World. In this context, the Brothers criticize such American television programs shown in Egypt as "Dallas" and "Dynasty" and U.S.-made films whose very popularity, they say, causes a decline in moral values. "We are not against some entertainment," said one Brotherhood member of parliament, "But we want the television to respect our moral ideas, especially because this is the television of the state. We will compel the state to change its ways. Day by day, we will pressure [it]."[3]

While such critiques may seem exaggerated or even amusing to some observers, they are only the tip of a profound conviction that the United States is engaged in an all-encompassing, purposeful conspiracy to weaken Islam. If Westernization is seen as a serious threat to Egypt's sovereignty and way of life, anti-Americanism becomes a matter of self-defense. Even if the United States has no intention or consciousness of combating Islam, the fact that Egyptians become more Westernized out of their own volition does undermine traditional beliefs and lifestyles.

Sayyid Qutb, the most important single architect of Islamic radical ideology in Egypt, saw these efforts as part of a centuries-long battle: "At the beginning the enemies of the Muslim community [in Muhammad's time] did not fight openly with arms but tried to fight the community in its belief through intrigue, spreading ambiguities, creating suspicions. They do likewise today. They have plotted and they go on plotting against this nation. Hundreds and thousands have infiltrated the Muslim world, and they still do in the guise of orientalists. The pupils of the latter fill today the positions of intellectual life of the countries whose people call themselves Muslim."[4]

While rejecting American materialism, Qutb also ridiculed the idea of development altogether. Egypt may be unable to catch up with the West but the race itself is not worthwhile. Vying with the West in material progress, he continues, will neither succeed for several centuries nor is it appropriate. What Muslims should want is Islam within an Islamic society.

A particular reason for a fixation on the United States is that it threatens the victory of Islamic fundamentalism in two ways: indirectly, by undermining Islam with its thought and culture; directly, by opposing the pious forces and supporting the current rulers. In confronting this danger, the fundamentalists often feel weak and frightened. The infiltration has been so seductively persuasive as to infect almost everyone and everything. "We must build up the Islamic idea now," Qutb noted, "but the difficulty is that we think in terms which are Western in essence and inimical to Islam."[5] In short, the virus of Westernism has already penetrated the Islamic community itself. The struggle against this phenomenon is a central part of the battle against secularism, the mainstream clergy, and other forces opposed by the fundamentalists.

Presumed U.S. hostility is also a direct threat. The fundamentalists are absolutely convinced that the United States is involved in all sorts of plots against them, ordering the Mubarak regime to destroy them, planning to weaken the Islamic world and even to destroy Islam itself. Such beliefs are too ideologically rooted to be defeated by rational argument or by U.S. behavior and policies. Those who assume America's hostility, conspiracy, and satanic evil will simply interpret any events as demonstrations of these theses.

These views are not merely held by a radical fringe. For example, 'Ali Jadd al-Haqq, the shaykh of al-Azhar and perhaps the most important pro-regime cleric, held ideas similar to those of Qutb on this matter. "Since the clash arose between the East and West, colonialism has been trying to penetrate in order to dominate. The twentieth century has witnessed the end of colonial military power, but some influence still exists . . . and modern means of communication help them."[6]

The fundamentalists argue that Western imperialism exists and poses a tremendous threat. Leftists and nationalists from a broad variety of standpoints would make a similar argument. But while the latter groups attribute the West's perfidy to economic greed or strategic ambition, the fundamentalists claim it is theologically rooted. In contrast to the latter groups, which see the West's target as being Egypt's national independence or treasure, fundamentalists are more likely to believe that the main menace is aimed at Egypt's religion and way of life. Qutb expresses this concept clearly: "Those who believe that the financial influence of the Jews in the USA and elsewhere is what directs the West in its materialistic and imperialistic approach, or that Anglo-Saxon hypocrisy, or the struggle between East and West, are the main factors, ignore a real factor to be added to all these, Western blood carries the spirit of the Crusades within itself. It fills the subconscious of the West."[7]

Britain dominated Egypt for about 70 years, roughly from the 1880s to the 1950s, and the United States is often seen as its successor. The fact that London's influence was indirect – Egypt was independent from 1922 but British officials and troops on the scene helped direct the country's government and choose its leaders – makes Egyptian fundamentalists see Washington as acting in a similar manner. U.S. aid, like nineteenth-century European loans, are perceived as elements of control rather than as a mixture of strategic interest and well-motivated assistance. The American ambassador, like the British high commissioner, may be considered to pull the strings that motivate Egypt's president and prime minister.

"Not long ago," commented Brotherhood leader Salah Shadi, "we were confronting the British hand-to-hand or face-to-face. Today, we are facing enemies that accede to the wishes of America and Great Britain ... The influencing forces that move in the Middle East harbor traditional enmity toward the Islamic concept. They do not accept Islam as a political system and they attack [it] any way they can." While Britain once backed Arab states opposing Nasir in the 1950s (Jordan, Iraq), America is now seen as the mainstay of Arab rulers trying to prevent the triumph of fundamentalism. Once England decided, now America dictates "who would be prime minister." The United States seeks "local collaborators" to stop the rise of the Muslim Brotherhood.[8] This argument also helps rationalize the fundamentalists' failure to gain power. It explains the gap between the fundamentalists' expectation that all good Muslims should support them and the reality of their limited base of support.

An *al-Da'wah* editorial sums up the overall perception of America in words incorporating all these concepts, including some borrowed from leftist analyses:

The United States is the leader of the international crusade and neo-colonialism. The Muslim World in general and the Arab region in particular are considered a prime target for American designs because of their energy resources, strategic location, and tremendous markets. The United States would not permit competition from any rival in its quest to monopolize the pillage of Islamic wealth. It may allow other partners a small share so long as they enhance the strategic objectives of the American imperialist crusade against Islam and the Muslims ... The United States implements its scheme through both its own CIA and client Muslim rulers who sold out their religion, country, nation, and honor. The price for selling out is for these client rulers to stay in the seats of power ... They have been instruments for the American Zionist designs to consolidate Israeli aggression in Palestine. The latest chapter of this American game is to concoct a false peace among the Arabs and the Jews. The American intention is to get the Arabs to shift their hostility away from Israel to a hostility toward the Soviets. True they are all enemies ... But to frighten Arab rulers by an impending Soviet threat is only a trick to make them accept a false peace with the Jews, the arch-enemies of God, his Prophet, and the faithful. How naive our rulers would be if they swallow the bait.[9]

The use of the words "Muslim" and "Islamic" signal that the author here is a fundamentalist, but the essential thrust of the argument is a Third World radicalism repeated in almost exactly the same words by a wide variety of nationalists and leftists.

Alignment with the United States as American Control

Since the fundamentalists view Western influence and contacts with suspicion, they argue that Egypt's alignment with the United States means that Sadat and Mubarak were American puppets and that Egypt had become a U.S. colony. Fundamentalist publications constantly develop elaborate conspiracy theories to show how the United States tries to control Egypt or which attribute the actions of Egypt's rulers to pressure or manipulation from Washington. A proper Islamic state should follow a policy of negative non-alignment – i.e., suspicion and a confrontational stance toward both superpowers – as Khumayni's Iran advocates. As previously noted, the Brotherhood defines non-alignment not so much as equidistance but rather as disengagement. Egypt must align itself only with the Muslim world. The Brotherhood's 1987 election progam called for ending military cooperation with the United States.

Thus, the mere fact that a ruler has good relations with the United States or is praised by Americans, undermines his position among the fundamentalists. When a young Islamic militant was told that Americans had liked Sadat and regretted his death, he replied, "They should like him. He served their interests, and the interests of the Jews. Why Sadat even offered to divert the waters of the Nile into Israel, as if the Nile were his father's property!"[10]

The Third World overtones in the fundamentalist approach are vague but appeal particularly among jam'iyat intellectuals. Ibrahim suggests that these organizations see Egypt – in what might be dubbed a sort of Islamic Nasirism – as having "a divine mission in forming and leading ... an alliance of all Muslims against the ... archenemies of the faith."[11] Dr 'Asim Fahim, a Cairo University teacher and jam'iyat leader, commented, "The Third World should have its own economic common market. All differences among Arabs should be eliminated so there can be a general framework for dealings among Muslims." Yet Egyptian self-sufficiency is a more immediate and serious goal. "Everyone in the labor force can contribute provided we get rid of the saying: 'We cannot survive without the United States.' Before that we used to say: 'We cannot live without the USSR' ... Was Egypt at the brink of death before the two superpowers came into existence? I say: Of course not. We must trust in God."[12]

If the general goal of the West is the destruction of Islam, the immediate target is the elimination of the fundamentalists who are Islam's champions. A supporter of al-Jihad claimed, "The Anglo-American campaign against Muslim nations, peoples or groups is a campaign ... that deliberately and immorally confuses between the duty to defend oneself, which is the duty to fight for the cause of God, and terrorism, which is blatant aggression against nations, peoples and groups. That is why we are calling for a holy war to resist this terrorism." The United States is a real source of terrorism, "telling the government and agencies, 'Be careful of the Islamic radicals.' So we are harassed, driven out of our homes and thrown in prison."[13] Since the Muslims are victims of the United States, they are merely defending themselves from this aggression. It is easy for them to justify their own acts of terrorism as merely self-defense in the service of God.

Not only is force necessary, it is also efficacious. As al-Jihad argues, it is unacceptable to "leave the affairs of Muslims in Palestine, Eritrea, the Philippines, or Afghanistan to the enemies of Muslims at international conferences which are planned by America and Russia. If we believe that we are entitled to something, we must have the power to seize that right from those who usurped it. That is what fighting for the cause of God is all about. There is no other way. Look for example how the use of force made the United States and France leave Lebanon. One person drove his mined car through a multitude of army soldiers and destroyed them. It seems that this is the only method the United States can understand."[14]

If the conflict is a battle to the death between good and evil – between the followers of God and the minions of the devil – then any tactics can be justified. Thus, "it is legitimate for Muslims to hold American or other citizens as hostages if the objective is to apply pressure to an aggressor state so that some Islamic demands can be achieved. However, these hostages may not be killed, and that is confirmed by what God Almighty said 'Whoever killed a human being, except as a punishment for murder or other wicked crimes, should be looked upon as though he had killed all mankind.'" Iran's act of holding American diplomats as hostages is a good model. "Iran used that as a tool to exert pressure so that funds which had been frozen by American banks could be released. Iran was able to achieve its objective in this legitimate manner which is based on a rule of jurisprudence which states that one must harm the enemy any way one can, small or big."[15]

The Egyptian fundamentalists are, ironically, unaware that the funds were frozen only after the hostages were taken. But it is important to remember that serious misconceptions about the United States are common among the fundamentalists. Moreover, various international events may be interpreted quite differently by observers. Western – or even Egyptian – politicians or generals may conclude that another war with Israel would be disastrous for Egypt, that Iran's Islamic republic is a failed experiment or that an alliance with the United States benefits Egypt. Islamic fundamentalists do not have to agree.

Positive Attitudes toward the United States

Despite this theoretical attitude of hostility, the Brotherhood's more moderate line, its interest in avoiding clashes with the Egyptian government, and its exaggerated fear of U.S. power, lead occasionally to some surprisingly positive statements about the United States. Al-Tilimsani, for example, stated that President Carter asked him to mediate with Tehran to help free the American diplomats held hostage there. Al-Tilimsani tried, with permission from Sadat, but the Iranians told him that anyone attempting to liberate the hostages was a U.S. agent. He returned to Cairo empty-handed but claimed he informed Khumayni of his view that taking diplomats as hostages was sinful.[16]

Al-Tilimsani also had nice things to say about Americans. They are "people of the book," the Islamic term for Jews and Christians who – as monotheists – are considered closer to Islam than are pagans. Given this status, al-Tilimsani added, "We would be with you unconditionally" in the event of a war between the United States and those who were not peoples' of the book. This statement could only be a veiled way of saying that the Brotherhood preferred the United States to a Soviet Union ruled by atheistic Communism. Revolutionary and radical fundamentalists would view such a statement as quite heretical, another proof of the Brotherhood's deviation from proper Islam. But it is also an example of the contradiction between the Brotherhood's more militant theory and more moderate practice over foreign policy issues.[17]

Al-Tilimsani's successor as leader of the Brotherhood, Shaykh Muhammad Hamid Abu al-Nasr, has also evinced some softness toward the United States. Asked if he supported Egypt's special relations with America, al-Nasr replied, "We welcome any relations with any country that does not interfere in our faith and our policy."[18]

It is important to note that the Brotherhood has made many anti-American statements as well over the years. But that group faces a paradox parallel to that of other Middle East forces – including the leaders of Libya, Syria, and the PLO – who have argued that the United States is the world's most powerful force for evil. If, in fact, America is so strong and omnipresent in the domestic politics of one's country, anybody who would hold power must reconcile Washington to that idea. Since the Brotherhood has followed a non-revolutionary path, it has to deal with its perception that the United States has veto power over Egypt's future leadership and policy. Having tried to convince Mubarak that it is an acceptable political factor, the Brotherhood also feels some need to convince the United States as well. But any initiatives in that direction are constrained by the group's Islamic fundamentalist ideology and the fear of criticism from more radical sectors that the Brotherhood, too, has become a U.S. puppet.

THE USSR

Al-Tilimsani's mild remarks about the United States do reveal an important point. While the Brotherhood is not pro-Western, if it had to choose between the two superpowers it might prove even more hostile toward the USSR. Sadat's original support from the Brotherhood was based partly on his break with Moscow. The USSR was the main target of fundamentalist criticism when it was deemed to have the upper hand in Egypt during the 1960s and early 1970s. If the fundamentalists talk less about the Soviets today, it is largely because their influence in Egypt, and in the region generally, seems much reduced.

Qutb, writing at a time when the Soviet factor still loomed large in Egypt, spent more time attacking Communism. Since his writings are the most important single source for the jama'at and jam'iyat, these warnings undoubtedly continue to affect their thinking. Qutb considered Communism the inevitable enemy of Islam. He portrays Communism as the secret ally of Zionism. This approach ignores the USSR's pro-Arab policy but also rests on the basis that Moscow – in contrast to the fundamentalists – has not favored Israel's destruction. In fact, the Soviets urged Egypt to avoid another war with Israel throughout the 1970s.[19]

Qutb also sees strong parallels between Communism and the Western system. His interpretation of the idea of convergence is that Western "democracy has reached what is close to bankruptcy [and] is now borrowing and assimilating features from the Eastern bloc, especially in the economic order under the name of socialism. Similar to the Eastern bloc, all policies have failed, and they now must import even their own food." He thus identified Marxism–Leninism with the Christian West as well as equating Communism and Zionism. Siding with one against the other thus becomes senseless since they are all part of the four-headed threat to Islam. "America and Russia are the same," Qutb wrote, "they both base themselves on materialistic thinking. The real struggle is between Islam on the one hand and Russia and America on the other."[20]

Another, far less well-known, Islamicist tried to persuade the

Soviets that they are wrong about Islam. While praising Lenin for having a "high regard . . . for anti-imperialist Islamic movements," his successors are criticized for their "recurring characterization of Islam . . . as the worship of traditions." He argues that Islam has a progressive social content (allegedly including the idea of class struggle) and is anti-clerical. American imperialism is the main enemy of Islam, he claims.[21]

This kind of leftist interpretation of Islam had some real intellectual impact in Iran, where it produced the Mujahaddin-i-Khalq group and influenced the thinking of many fundamentalists who later became leaders in the Islamic Republic. But it is rare in Egypt, where it has found no major individual or groups as advocates. Part of the reason for this difference is that the secularist left in Iran was almost non-existent whereas in Egypt it has long been a real rival to the fundamentalists. Thus, the Egyptian fundamentalists tend to have a lively antagonism to Marxist thinking. Although they sometimes borrow some leftist ideas in attacking the United States, it can equally be argued that they borrow Western views in criticizing Communism. Egyptian fundamentalists prefer a non-alignment equidistant from East and West and as far removed from them both as possible. But if they had to choose between them, the moderates' preference would more likely be with the West.

ISRAEL

The fundamentalists see the Arab–Israeli confict as a Jewish–Muslim conflict in which Israel is only the most visible symptom. The Muslim Brotherhood's literature blames the Jews as a major force behind both Western imperialism and international Communism. Egyptian fundamentalists tend to believe in a doctrine of anti-Semitism which would be quite familiar to the ideologists of the Tsarist pogroms or the Nazi party. The Jews are the central challenge and foremost danger for the Islamic world. The roots of this struggle lie so deep as to make it totally unresolvable save by the total victory of one side over the other. "Their aim is clearly shown by the Protocols [of the Elders of Zion]. The Jews are behind materialism, animal sensuality, the destruction of the family and the dissolution of society. Principal among them are Marx, Freud, Durkheim, and the Jew [sic] Jean-Paul Sartre."[22]

Brotherhood leader Muhammad Hamid Abu al-Nasr sees the

struggle as one between two civilizations rather than a theological dispute. "We do not fight the Jews because of their religion, but rather because they confiscated land that does not belong to them and because they desecrated Jerusalem."

In this context, then, the Camp David agreements are completely unacceptable. In their magazine, *al-Da'wah*, the Brotherhood called the Camp David agreement "the Stable of David Accords" and declared that Sadat's visit was a "murder of a people of the faith and will not be forgiven."[23] They are a betrayal of Islam which carries with it the subordination of Egypt to anti-Muslim forces. While a radical nationalist would decry the accords for allegedly ignoring Palestinian national rights, an Egyptian fundamentalist views them as, almost literally, a bargain with the devil. The fact that Sadat made the agreement was a major aspect of the fundamentalists' quarrel with him. While Mubarak's willingness to maintain the treaties is also rejected by the fundamentalists, they find it harder to mobilize their own passions or mass support against a *fait accompli*.

Furthermore, as long as the PLO remained intransigent, it was easy for the fundamentalists to claim that their maximalist objectives were in line with the Palestinians' goals. With the more moderate, diplomatically-oriented line of the PLO following the 1988 Palestine National Council, however, the situation became more confused. And the central role played by Egypt in pushing Yasir Arafat to be more flexible – along with Cairo's recognition of the Palestinian state – undercuts the fundamentalists' ability to use the issue for their own political advantage.

One of the few fundamentalist comments which saw any resolution short of war comes from al-Tilimsani, though it is not clear whether this was due to his status as most moderate of Brotherhood theoreticians or is a foretaste of how that organization might deal with an era in which the PLO seeks negotiations. "I am not one of those who speaks of driving Israel into the sea or claiming that we will declare victory in Tel Aviv," al-Tilimsani commented, "for all these gleaming slogans are without balance." Instead, he suggests a different approach. The United Nations and other organizations should declare that the Palestinian Arabs were illegally expelled from their homeland and this decision should somehow be implemented. "For restoring the right to its owners, by any means, however long they take. Events have taught us that right must eventually triumph, no matter how long the time; no matter how long conflicts endure there can be no end until Allah settles the matter effectively. The day that the rulers of the Islamic countries are of one view, of one line, we could then begin effectively to find the right path to solve this problem." All existing treaties are void because they accept "all Israel has done and is doing as an aggressor state, not only in Palestine, but in all the . . . area."[24]

While this legalistic approach is rare, it does express some common premises of the fundamentalists: the Palestine issue should be the focus of all Arab efforts, nothing can be accomplished until the Muslim countries are united, and the Arab cause will inevitably win. Saying that victory is certain sometimes serves as a rationale for doing so little in practice; pointing to Arab and Islamic disunity can be used to suggest – as Nasir did – that the time is not yet ripe for a holy war against Israel.

At their trials, revolutionary fundamentalists proclaimed that the Jews were the enemies of Allah and so Palestine must be conquered. Historical and Qur'anic arguments were often used to prove such ideas. One activist claimed, the Jews "had joined the prophet Mohammed's pagan enemies, stabbing the Prophet in the back after he had made peace with them." Negotiations were impossible partly because the Jews were so cunning that they would turn any such arrangement to their own advantage.[25]

While pan-Arab nationalists blamed Israel for the failure of the Arabs to unite, fundamentalists found the same scapegoat for the inability of their brand of Islam to achieve power. In a 1951 essay, Qutb wrote, "With their spite and deceit, the Jews are still misleading this nation, and distracting her away from her Qur'an in order that she may not draw her sharp weapons and her abundant ammunitions from it. They are secure so long as this nation turns away from the access to her real strength and the sources of her pure knowledge. Anyone who makes this nation turn away from her religion and her Qur'an is the agent of the Jews, whether he know it or not, and whether he wishes it or not."[26]

There are several interesting points in this claim. First of all, the demonization of the Jews (and of Israel) indicates the extremist nature of the fundamentalists' analysis, which will yield neither to reason nor compromise. Second, an Islamic revival is necessary to defeat Israel – a success which Arab nationalism cannot achieve. Thus, Egyptians must fight Israel as Muslims rather than as Arabs. Third, anyone opposing fundamentalism is a Zionist agent. It is interesting to note that this passage was written in 1951, two decades before the Egypt–Israel peace accord.

Camp David

During the 1950s and 1960s – and even when *al-Da'wah* began republishing in 1976 – the wild denunciations of Israel were in line with the kinds of statements made by Egyptian leaders and articles published in the government-controlled media. If peace with Israel was treasonous to the fundamentalists, it was also unthinkable for the nationalists. If the Brotherhood called on all Muslims to participate in a jihad against Israel, this did not conflict with the official line. Religious arguments were freely employed by the Egyptian army, for example, during the 1973 war. In 1975 the ulama of al-Azhar issued a fatwah saying that a ruler who concluded peace with Israel was an unbeliever.[27]

All this changed with Sadat's November 1977 trip to Jerusalem and the Camp David accords. The Brotherhood was still committed to Israel's destruction but now the government was committed to peaceful co-existence. Egypt's leaders felt that they had fought enough wars, lost enough territory, wasted enough treasure, and forfeited enough lives in the battle to eliminate Israel. They accepted peace as a necessity. After Sadat's visit to Jerusalem, al-Azhar issued a fatwah legalizing the treaty with Israel. If the Prophet Muhammad could negotiate with the Jews of Medina, said the shaykh al-Azhar 'Ali Jadd al-Haqq, then Arab states should be prepared to negotiate with Israel.[28]

To the fundamentalists, this was all an illusion. If Egypt would only become a truly Islamic society and if the Muslim countries would unite – two things they thought were quite possible – Israel could still be wiped off the map. Said a pro-Iranian Egyptian fundamentalist, the great powers were trying to act as if "a departure from Camp David would be suicide for the Egyptian people." The fundamentalists argued that Egypt could abrogate the treaty without suffering, whereas more realistic minds knew that such a step would lead to a costly, losing war with Israel.[29]

In a special *al-Da'wah* editorial, al-Tilimsani denounced the Camp David accords, stressing that the Brotherhood – unlike nationalist opponents – protested on the grounds that Islamic law made it a sin to leave any Muslim lands in the hands of usurpers. The Brotherhood organ also claimed that the Qur'an forbade peace with Israel. The Brotherhood demanded a halt to Egyptian–Israeli negotiations on Palestinian autonomy, called on members of parliament and the government to resign when Israeli President Yitzhak Navon visited

Egypt in November 1980, and campaigned against the visit of Israeli Prime Minister Menahem Begin in August 1981. But there was no wave of outrage among Egyptians to support these efforts. Instead, Sadat cracked down on the Brotherhood and suspended *al-Da'wah*.[30]

Revenge was taken against Sadat by al-Jihad, whose advisor, 'Abd al-Rahman, complained, "We reject Camp David and we reject the normalization of relations with Israel. We also reject all the commitments that were made by the traitor Sadat, who deviated from Islam." He even accused Sadat of planning to unify Islam, Christianity, and Judaism on the basis that Sadat once held an ecumenical prayer service. "As long as the Camp David Agreement stands, this conflict between us and the government will continue." And al-Jihad's murder of Sadat was part of that war.[31]

After Sadat's death, the Brotherhood campaigned against any normal relations between Egypt and Israel. Al-Tilimsani suggested that if implementation of the Camp David accords was blocked, the evil would be reduced. Thus, the Brotherhood urged a boycott against buying Israeli goods and demanded the expulsion of Israeli diplomats from Cairo. Any contacts or Israeli presence was said to be an "economic and cultural imperialism which threatened the very survival of Muslim Egypt." Yet Tilimsani implicitly seemed to accept a *de facto* "cold peace" with Israel as long as relations were not "normalized." The Egyptian regime's minimalization of relations with Israel was, in part, motivated by a desire to avoid inflaming fundamentalist anger. While this stance made it easier for fundamentalists to attack Israel, it made it harder for them to stir up passion over the issue.[32]

There are thus two key elements in the fundamentalist analysis in regard to Israel. The stakes were so high that the battle must be fought; Islam provides a way in which the battle could be won. The wars had been lost not by Egypt but by the secularist, Arab nationalist regime which lacked the proper spiritual weapons. Yet the mainstream clerics and the Brotherhood are not willing to take dramatic action themselves to bring about this jihad. Their belligerency is more theoretical.

Kishk certainly sees things in this light. His sermons are often laced with the most virulent hatred for Israel and Jews. They are even the cause of secularism in Egypt. Kishk said in one sermon, "Since Israel entered Egypt and set up an embassy in Cairo, I am absolutely certain that there is a suspicious sect that receives its instructions from a hidden hand to spread rumors and doubts about God and

[Muhammad]." Yet on the strategic level he is unsure as to how to proceed. "We cannot achieve victory in confronting Israel on the military level or on the peaceful level or through negotiations." Arab disunity is a reality not easily overcome, "Israel fights us under one slogan and we fight Israel under 1001!" Like Abu al-Nasr, he views the conflict with "Israel as a struggle between civilizations rather than between religions. Israel is the last of the Crusader wars," he says. But he does not see the West as standing behind Israel, rather, it is the other way around: Israel is an integral part of a West inevitably opposed to Islam.[33]

All the anti-Muslim civilizations are seen as being united behind Israel which is, in the words of one Brotherhood article, the result of a "Crusader plot." Even mainstream clerics express such ideas. Al-Azhar's chief, 'Ali Jadd al-Haqq argued, "I believe that colonialism and the countries which occupied the Islamic Arab East are still pulling some strings and international Zionism is still acting as a front for colonialism and working behind it in order to break the Arab and Islamic world into little principalities" to keep the Muslims divided and supine.[34]

How to Resolve the Conflict

The Muslim Brotherhood greeted the uprising in the West Bank and Gaza Strip which began in December 1987 and opposed a proposal by President Mubarak to suspend the intifadah for six months so that Israel–Palestinian negotiations could take place. Abu al-Nasr praised the uprising as an effective movement in contrast to "the false diplomatic methods from which the fraternal Palestinian people reaped nothing but a loss of time and territory." He wished success for any international peace conference but expressed skepticism that such an approach would bring success.[35]

It was easy, of course, for mainstream clerics and Brotherhood leaders to express verbal support for the uprising. Egypt–Israel relations continued and the government maintained – though it downplayed – the peace established by the Camp David accords. While Egypt recognized the Palestine National Council's declaration of a Palestinian state in November 1988, it pushed the PLO toward a more moderate rather than a more militant policy.

But Egyptian fundamentalists were just observers in this development. Al-Tilimsani had implied earlier that the job of waging a jihad belonged to the Palestinian Arabs. "We have fought the Israelis via organizations and commandos," he commented. "Governments decided to fight with armies and failed. Jihad can be in several forms, the most preferable of which is popular resistance."[36]

The Muslim Brotherhood, as do other Egyptian fundamentalist groups, concludes that peaceful co-existence with Israel is impossible. They hold the most caricatured view of that state. The Brotherhood's publications, when they were legal before Sadat's crackdown, carried articles in each issue with titles like "Muslims of the World, Liberate the Captive [al-Aqsa] Mosque," "Economic Cooperation with the Zionist Enemy by Force," "Loss of Palestine is a Warning for Muslims to Go Back to Their Religion," "How to Turn Around the War Between Us and The Trio of Crusade, Zionism, and Marxism," "Zionism in America Controls Writers and Publishers to Smear the Arabs and Islam," "International Zionism Controls Major TV and Radio Networks in the United States," "The Jews are Behind the Usury System in the World," "A Destructive Jewish Cultural Invasion of Muslim Egypt," "The Normalization Process Destroys Egypt's Linkage With Islam," "Hidden Invasion and Not Normalization," and "When Do We Carry the Banner of Jihad on the Promised Land?" *Al-Da'wah* concluded that war was the only way of "liberating Palestine" because all other means had failed and Israel had only increased in strength. As a result, the Arabs had been terrorized, divided, and drained. The West had given the Arabs no assistance.[37]

Yet there was an abstract quality to all of the bloodcurdling, extremist rhetoric. When it came time to propose how Egypt should prepare for this war, *al-Da'wah* said that the country had to strengthen itself by instituting justice and moral improvement at home, form a broad front of Arabs and Muslims, sever all ties with the West, and mobilize all Arab resources. In short, only an Islamic state at home – or perhaps in the whole Arab–Islamic world – could perform these tasks. Thus, the confrontation with Israel had to be postponed until such changes were in place.

The Radicals and Israel

The attitude of revolutionary and radical fundamentalists was even less focused than the Brotherhood on the immediacy of a confrontation with Israel and put a priority on waging the battle at home. This view is expressed over and over again in the revolutionary fundamentalists' literature.

For example, al-Jihad's leader, Faraj, stated, "As for those who call for directing the Islamic energies to liberate the . . . occupied homelands from Zionism and Imperialism, the Jihad group says to them, 'This is not the immediate fight . . . and this is not the true path to liberating these holy sites! For the path to the liberation of Jerusalem runs first through the freeing of our own country from the rule of unbelief, because these rulers are the basis of the presence of imperialism in the land of Islam.' "[38] In other words, there is no sense even trying to "liberate" Palestine when the nature of the Egyptian regime makes it impossible to succeed in this task. It is interesting to compare this view to the Muslim Brotherhood's far vaguer position on the necessary preconditions for a victorious jihad abroad: justice at home, unity with other Arabs and Muslims. These tasks could perhaps be completed without an Islamic revolution in Egypt.

Not only did the current leaders' apostasy make them unfit to carry out the struggle against Israel but also the Arab–Israeli conflict was actually strengthening the regime. The issue promoted a broad and popular nationalism which rallied support for the government and provided a substitute for an Islamic-oriented ideology. As Faraj puts it, "Through the ideas and battles of 'nationalism' these rulers increase their stock of power, and strengthen their grip on the neck of Islam and its people. There is no escaping the need to get rid of them first, then to burst out, under Islamic leadership, to liberate the holy sites!"

Even the destruction of Israel would be counterproductive if achieved under the current leaders. Faraj summarizes his case as follows: "First, that fighting the near enemy comes before fighting the enemy afar." Second, "The question now is, 'Shall this victory benefit the Islamic state, or the existing rule of unbelief?' . . . For though these rulers seize the opportunity offered by the patriotic ideas of these Muslims to realize their un-Islamic objectives . . . struggle must be under the banner of a Muslim leadership . . . It is encumbent upon us to focus on our Islamic issues . . . The enactment of the word of God is the highest obligation. There is no doubt that the first objective of Islam today is the uprooting of these pagan leaderships and their replacement with a completely Islamic regime."[39]

While al-Jihad was fighting against Muslims in Egypt, an interviewer asked its Spiritual Guide, 'Abd al-Rahman, "Why aren't you fighting against the Jews? We haven't heard about a single battle that you fought against Israel." He responded that this would have to wait until "Egypt can once again become an Islamic national country. Israel is a state, and a state can only be fought by a state." Only when Egypt's "identity and its soul" had been reinstalled could it stand up to Israel. "We believe that a confrontation with those who are dealing with Israel is a prerequisite to a confrontation with Israel itself." Egypt would have to become a secure rear base for jihad and its present leadership could not be depended on for help. The Egyptian government would "turn us over to the Jews."[40]

The leader of al-Takfir, Shukri Mustafa, expressed similar sentiments. Israel had won victories because the Muslims had forgotten God and had not carried out His law. Thus, God punished them by giving power to the Jews. In the spirit of revolutionary defeatism, Mustafa argued during his trial that "if the Jews or anyone else came [to invade Egypt], our movement ought not to fight in the ranks of the Egyptian army, but on the contrary ought to flee to a secure position." This approach was reminiscent of Lenin's call for Russia's defeat as a way of promoting revolution during the First World War, but is scarcely calculated to appeal to most Egyptians. Al-Takfir's members did, in fact, refuse to serve in the army or any part of the state bureaucracy. The external enemy was no worse than the internal one – the "kafir" (unbelieving) government.[41]

While passionately advocating Israel's destruction and the abrogation of any peace with Israel, Egyptian fundamentalists also postpone the day of reckoning until after their proposed revolution comes to power. It is necessary to liberate Egypt from jahiliyyah before liberating Palestine, they say, and only the prior liberation of Egypt can make possible the liberation of Palestine. If additional Arab states and even the PLO recognize or make peace with that country, however, the currently powerful argument against Israel will be reduced in strength. Even more, then, "Zionism" would become a metaphor for the forces reducing Islam's role in Egyptian life – modernism, secularism, Westernism.

IRAN AND THE ARABS

But what of Iran, the one state which can claim to be already liberated in an Islamic sense and to be actively fighting against these threats? Yet it posed a major problem for Egyptian fundamentalists since Iran also came to fight those who were not only fellow Muslims but were, for Egyptians, fellow Arabs as well.

After the victory of his revolution in February 1979, Ayatollah Khumayni established an Islamic republic. This triumph filled Islamic fundamentalists throughout the world with enthusiasm and converted a number of people to the belief that this political ideology was the most effective way of achieving their aims. The Iranian regime claimed to be fulfilling Islamic law and combating the Muslims' enemies. The long confrontation between Tehran and Washington over the holding of American diplomats as hostages could be taken to confirm both Iran's militancy and relative success in expelling U.S. influence.

Shortly after Khumayni's victory, Egyptian jama'at organized demonstrations and rallies in solidarity with it and against giving the Shah asylum in Egypt. These developments coincided with the fundamentalists' growing opposition to Sadat over his new policies. The jama'at tried to argue away the Shi'ite/Sunni differences and were encouraged by the idea that a mass uprising might topple the regime in Egypt as it had the rulers of Iran. During 1979 and 1980, a host of Islamic groups in Egypt began to stage "sit-ins" and street demonstrations trying to imitate Iranian precedents. The Brotherhood's publications also praised Iran's revolution.[42]

Nevertheless, Iran did not become the leader of an Islamic revolutionary bloc the way the USSR (the first "workers' state") came to dominate and direct a world Communist movement after its revolution. Nor did the fundamentalist movement prosper in other countries. Perhaps one should be more patient in assessing these results: after all, the USSR (except in Mongolia) took a quarter of a century to replicate itself when the Red Army advanced into Eastern Europe. Still, at least five factors can be identified which inhibit the spread of the Iranian revolution's techniques and influence.

First, the Iranian regime is a Shi'ite state. Arabs are overwhelmingly – and Egyptian Muslims are entirely – followers of the Sunni brand of Islam. While some Muslims play down the distinction, it is substantial in the eyes of many believers on both sides. The Muslim Brotherhood leader al-Tilimsani said there were clear differences between the two sects. Some of these variations have important political implications. For example, the Shi'ite clergy has substantially more autonomy in theological terms and a great deal more freedom from government controls. Furthermore, the Shi'ite's history, as rebels and outsiders during centuries of Sunni caliphates, give them a stronger potential revolutionary strain to their tradition.[43]

Second, Iran is a Persian state. Again, while fundamentalists may play down national distinctions among fellow Muslims, the Persian/Arab differentiation is of the greatest importance in the minds of many Arabs and particularly Egyptians. While Egyptian fundamentalists explicitly reject Arab nationalism, they are often subject to its premises and their audience is even more influenced by it. Persians are alien and viewed by Egyptians with some suspicion and sense of superiority.

Third, many good Muslims, including clerics, reject the legitimacy of the Iranian revolution because they question its violence, tactics, elevation of the clergy to power, or for other reasons. Those who hold a traditional view of Islam understandably see Khumayni's ideology – as they do that of the Egyptian jama'ats – as a heretical innovation which contradicts Islamic beliefs held for centuries. Individuals may react based on class or interest group as well as out of a sincere belief in the illegitimacy of Khumayni's claims. Minister of Awqaf Dr Muhammad 'Ali al-Mahjub attributed Iran's terrorist acts and killings to the Iranian ruler's aggressiveness and said they had nothing to do with Islam's teachings and rules. In addition, Arab governments have tried to use Islam themselves to underpin their own positions and Egypt's rulers have been relatively successful in doing so.[44]

An Egyptian commentator pointed to certain perceived characteristics of Iran's regime which were unattractive to Egyptian Muslims. Khumayni, he charged, had made the Revolutionary Guard the guardian of the Shari'ah to displace the clergy. "Any Guard can decide that a certain person is an infidel, or that a certain woman has violated the laws of God and so deserves maximum punishment, which is immediately carried out. There is no law governing Iran . . . They are merely ignorant gangs driven by their desires; they interpret the Shari'ah any way they like, and probe into people's minds, something which Islam has totally banned." In contrast, Egyptian revolutionary and radical groups have a strong anti-clerical streak and are not enthusiastic about the clergy's rule in Iran.[45]

Fourth, Iran's own chauvinism in seeking to dominate other Islamic fundamentalist movements also stirred resentment. Leaders of the Brotherhood and groups like al-Jihad believe themselves to be possessors of the truth and the rightful leaders of Egyptian fundamentalism. They are not willing to accept Khumayni as their leader. Even Khumayni's writings have been little read by Egyptian fundamentalists.

Fifth, the Iran–Iraq war brought the Shi'ite/Sunni and Arab/Persian conflicts to the forefront in Egyptians' views of Iran. Tehran's identification with a bloody, inconclusive war between 1980 and 1988 raised additional questions about its methods and aggressive propensities. Iran also threatened the Gulf Arab states, which all supported Iraq. Given Iraq's final emergence as the winner and a consciousness of some of the failures of Iran's revolution, Egyptian Muslims became more skeptical about Tehran.

"Khumayni's failure with Iran is even greater," writes one Egyptian commentator, "We heard about it through news agencies but we said that they were exaggerating and were deliberately destroying Islam's image. However, if we examine closely what happened in [Mecca], what is happening on the borders with Iraq and in Lebanon, and the threats that are being made against Kuwait – all this goes to confirm that Khumayni's internal crisis is worsening and that he is trying to cover up his failure through a foreign peril that would once again rally the Iranian people around him."[46]

Egyptian fundamentalists thus had ample reason for criticizing the Tehran regime and they also knew that support for Khumayni would very much undermine their efforts to win popular support. Any explicit backing for Iran would also virtually guarantee repression by the authorities. "What is happening in Iran is totally rejected in Egypt both by the masses and the government," concludes a pro-government writer with a large degree of accuracy.[47]

When government supporters accused the Brotherhood-dominated Islamic Alliance of being "Khumaynites," the latter became very nervous and eager to refute the charge. A Brotherhood leader denied that "an Islamic state" for them meant a "'Khumaynite' state that will erect gallows for the people." Anyone who thought the Brotherhood was pro-Khumayni was "scandalously ignorant." Contrary to Iran, Egypt follows "true Islam which is Sunni and not Shi'ite: We are people of the Sunnah, and there is not a single Khumayni among us." One of his colleagues added, "You cannot find anything in the Muslim Brotherhood's writings and statements showing that it has ever called for a religious state similar to the one in Iran."[48]

The Iran–Iraq War

Egyptian clerics and fundamentalists were unanimous in proclaiming that the Iran–Iraq war was a waste of effort and damaged the Islamic world. They blamed Iran for the war's continuance. While Iran's agreement to a ceasefire in July 1988 relieved some of this antagonism, pro-Iran sentiment did not seem likely to develop in Egypt.

Shaykh Muhammad Hamid Abu al-Nasr, leader of the Muslim Brotherhood, called the Iraq–Iran conflict "a baseless and senseless war . . . We reject this war because the Iraqi and Iranian people are Muslims." Asked about the fact that Iran was fighting the war in the name of Islam, he replied, "Islam is innocent of this war."[49]

Shaykh 'Ali Jadd al-Haqq, head of al-Azhar, tried to organize a Ramadan ceasefire in 1987 and concluded with frustration that this initiative "like other efforts, have come up against the rigidity of the Iranian position." Tehran was to blame for the continued fighting while Iraq was willing to have a ceasefire and negotiate peace. The "stubborn position" of Iran "is something which is detrimental to all Muslims!"[50]

"This war," Jadd al-Haqq complained, "has undoubtedly created many cracks in the Islamic world. If it continues, it will cause other wars between Muslims to break out. In fact, it may even drag the whole world into a disaster. The Iranians have always said publicly that they want to overthrow the Iraqi regime . . . Such a goal is not legitimate." Islamic law was very simple and straightforward on this matter. God commanded Muslims:

> If two parties of believers take up arms the one against the other, make peace between them . . . The Iranian regime should have yielded to God's judgment and consented to the arbitration effort. If Iraq is found guilty in the arbitration process, the arbitrators will then make the judgment they will see fit . . . Believers are brothers and . . . we should make peace between our brothers. The goal should be peace, not provocation and not prodding our fellow Muslims to fight. Nor should our goal be supporting one of the parties in a fight. Instead, we should try to bring the fighting to an end and to spare Muslims' blood because [Muhammad] said, "Muslims are forbidden from wasting the blood, property and honor of other Muslims."

The war also distracted Muslims from more important issues. "No one mentions Palestine, Jerusalem, and the captive al-Aqsa Mosque which is being attacked every hour at all times. No one mentions Afghanistan. Nor does anyone mention Lebanon . . . The [Iran–Iraq] war, which is being fought between two Muslim, neighboring countries without any rational or legitimate reason is prevailing over all of that."[51]

The Battle of the Hajj

If Egypt's Islamic leaders were disturbed by Iran's refusal to end the war, they were scandalized by the violent demonstrations which erupted during the 1987 pilgrimage to Mecca. Iranian pilgrims had demonstrated during several previous years. The Saudi authorities had issued stern warnings for them to stop and there had been some lull in these activities. During the massive violence of 1987, hundreds of Iranians seeking to demonstrate – and a large number of bystanders – were shot or stabbed by Saudi police. Al-Azhar criticized Iran for assaulting a friendly Arab country while even the Brotherhood, careful to maintain the appearance of neutrality, seemed to view the event as another case of Iranian misbehavior and a sign of their strange interpretation of Islam.[52]

The Brotherhood pronounced itself "utterly saddened by any event that leads to division and conflict among Muslims." The incidents "harmed every Muslim" and Islam itself since "The holy house of God should not have become a stage for political differences, especially in the hajj season during which more than two million Muslims gather to perform the religious duty of the hajj in peace, security, and spiritual happiness . . . The Muslim Brotherhood calls upon all governments and rulers in our Islamic countries to promptly embark on steps to eliminate differences, put an end to the Gulf war, unify views, eliminate the tense atmosphere, and respond to the words of Almighty God."[53]

A pro-government writer was even more critical, "Khumayni's attack on the Ka'bah was his major downfall. His threats to Saudi Arabia mean that he insists on committing crime and aggression against that nation in its capacity as custodian of the two holy places, a role which it is performing as well as possible. Khumayni's order that his picture be carried to the Ka'bah is polytheism and a call to idolatry . . . And so Khumayni deserved the Islamic world's contempt and scorn."[54]

Iranian Subversion

Given this attitude toward Iran, Tehran's efforts to organize pro-Khumayni groups in Egypt met with little success. The most ominous attempt was a plot, directed by the Iranian chargé d'affaires in Cairo, to recruit and pay Iranians, Jordanians, and Palestinians in Egypt for acts of terrorism. This group was to be linked with the officials in charge of exporting the Iranian revolution, Iranian intelligence, the pro-Iran Lebanese Hizbollah, and the pro-Khumayni Iraqi Al-Da'wah Party.[55] Instead, the Egyptian government uncovered these plots, broke relations with Iran, and expelled Iranian diplomats. Yet while detailing the activities of Iran's agents, the authorities also pointed out how hard it had been for them to recruit Egyptians. The main concern was that groups like Hizbollah might be able to carry out terrorist attacks on Egypt's soil against foreigners.

Tehran tried to win sympathy by sponsoring trips for intellectuals and ulama to Iran. Among the more important visitors were Shaykh Muhammad al-Ghazali, who participated in the Fourth Conference on Islamic Thought held in Tehran in February 1986, and member of parliament Shaykh Yusuf al-Badri. There were a few enthusiasts, like the Egyptian judge 'Abd al-Jawwad Yasin, who said he "found much prosperity" in his visit there and praised Iran's "bursting energy of spirit." If this enthusiasm was revived among the Islamic masses, where it remained alive but hidden, they would be able to "start on the path toward the establishment of the religion of God on earth, removing . . . every obstacle, authority and force that resists the light of God."[56]

This was a distinctly minority view. Even though leaders of the jama'at and jam'iyat may have agreed with Yasin's view on the need and results of reviving that Islamic spirit, they certainly did not say that Iran was a model for this process. Thus, it seems that another commentator expresses Egyptian views better when he writes, "There is no fear of Egypt being infiltrated by Khumayni-style terrorism and rebellion because all the signs indicate the . . . total failure of this terrorism after having harmed both itself and Islam . . . Yet caution is necessary because just as terrorism was aimed at [Mecca] it could be aimed at al-Azhar, and just as it exploited myths and legends in mobilizing Iran's children against Iraq, it could likewise fool some of our youths."[57] While Islamic fundamentalism may still shake Egypt, it would do so in spite of, rather than because of, the Iranian example.

THE ARABS AND ARAB NATIONALISM

Egyptian fundamentalists usually criticize Arab nationalism as a competing ideology but frequently show that they share some of its sentiments. Furthermore, they are aware that most of their potential audience would be offended by excessive criticism of pan-Arab or Egyptian nationalist notions. Given the lack of a communal conflict, Egyptian fundamentalists find it easier to co-exist with nationalist feelings than do their counterparts in Syria (where Sunni fundamentalists oppose an Alawite government), Iraq (where Shi'ite fundamentalists oppose a Sunni government), and Lebanon (where Shi'ite fundamentalism is virtually a form of nationalism).

Al-Tilimsani gives the official Islamic line in these words: "Islam does not recognize nationalism . . . which brings about divisions and conflicts between people, who are the fruits of one father and one mother. We know that the world was once a community under the powerful and noble Islamic caliphate, then its people were divided under differing governments." The result was "factions, weakness and disputes, and our condition grew worse and worse. As for the relationship between Arabism and Islam, Islam did not come to the Arabs alone, but all people together, 'Oh people, I am the Messenger of God to all people together' . . . We are Muslims, both Arab and non-Arab, and this is more accurate and more inclusive in strengthening harmony, good relations and progress among the whole."[58]

Arab nationalism is, then, a deviation. The archvillain who brought nationalism to the Muslim Middle East and dismantled the Islamic caliphate was Kemal Ataturk, who is described as a "traitor" and a "Jew" whose doctrine was against Islam.[59] Although the fundamentalists express their criticisms of him in milder terms, Nasir could be subjected to similar accusations for making Arab nationalism hegemonic in Egypt.

Kishk has suggested a synthesis of Islam and Arabism that is reminiscent of the ideas brought forward by Islamic thinkers in the late nineteenth century and during the 1930s and 1940s. Civilization, he argues, is largely a matter of religion. Islam is the faith of the Arabs and only it can revive the Arab nation. Israel is the last of the Crusader offensive wars of the West against Islam and the Arabs. Nationalism was intended to destroy Islamic unity and replace it with division, but Islam cannot be separated from its Arab origins. Thus, Islam and Arabism must together form the identity of Egyptians (and others) and together rebuild the glory that the Islamic Arabs knew in past centuries. He calls for one united Arab nation which will transcend the artificial borders which exist today. Kishk even coupled this call with praise for Mubarak as attempting to restore Egypt to the Arab world.[60]

In practice, though the fundamentalists try to avoid being drawn into commenting on Arab affairs. The mainstream clergy usually follow government policy and so, while reluctant to become involved in inter-Arab affairs, share the regime's definition of friends and enemies. In the case of Libyan leader Mu'ammar al-Qadhafi, and enemy of Egypt who has a very idiosyncratic view of Islamic belief, pro-government ulama can sometimes be quite critical. On the other hand, however, the bonds of Islamic solidarity led Jadd al-Haqq to criticize the U.S. bombing of Libya as an attack on an Arab Muslim people.[61]

Although the Brotherhood does not openly praise Saudi Arabia, it has historic links to the kingdom. Its leaders have taken refuge there and at times Riyadh has provided subsidies. Many of the organization's activists and main contributors have also spent time as merchants in Saudi Arabia or the smaller Gulf Arab states. This special connection thus endures, though its exact significance is unclear at present. The Saudis supply literature and try to gain influence. Egyptian fundamentalists have also become more interested in the anti-Soviet mujah'din in Afghanistan. These fighters, in contrast to the Iranians, have two advantages: they won their war and are also Sunnis.

It might be expected that the Muslim Brotherhood would also have a particular interest in the status of Islamic fundamentalist struggles in Syria and Jordan, where sister groups exist which were influenced by the Egyptian movement in the pre-Nasir period. Nevertheless, the Brotherhood largely avoids these topics. Its official position seems to be that such interventions are divisive while, implicitly, there is also probably some concern about raising the wrath of the Egyptian government over relatively marginal issues. Finally, the disinterest seems to reflect the inward-looking nature of the Brotherhood and of the other Egyptian fundamentalist movements as well.

Thus, the Egyptian Islamic groups have a clear sense of who they see as enemies. Four forces, America/the West, the USSR/Communism, Israel/Jew/Zionism, and secularism, are trying to destroy Islam and to prevent the fundamentalists from coming to power. While the fundamentalists' view is that these evil efforts are consciously designed and carefully planned, another interpretation is possible. Inasmuch as Egyptians adapt foreign and "modern" ideas or habits – through observation, consumerism, and imitation – Islam may well become a less important factor in Egyptian life. The fundamentalists oppose the patterns of modern life which have already eroded religious belief in the West. The Islamic fundamentalist critique of Jews, for example, parallels that of anti-modernist movements in nineteenth and early twentieth century Europe.

These Islamic groups, however, have much less of a sense of who their allies might be. Other than vague calls to their fellow Muslims abroad, the fundamentalists neither have nor are seeking foreign patrons or models. A higher priority for the Islamic forces are domestic questions. They argue over how to implement the Shari'ah, whether Egypt can be made into an Islamic state by reform or revolution, and when – if ever – violence is justified. Beyond this, they see external issues in mainly internal terms. Their concern with the United States, for instance, relates largely to American influence on Egypt's culture and support for the government.

8 Strategy and Doctrine

Each Islamic movement in Egypt has an ideology and strategy to gain power for itself or make Egypt a more Islamic country. This chapter discusses the views of the Muslim Brotherhood, the jama'at, the jam'iyat, charismatic preachers, and mainstream clerics on contemporary Egypt's key domestic issues, the tactics they use to promote their aims, attitude toward reform and revolution, and their vision of a proper Islamic polity.

The Muslim Brotherhood has developed a reformist strategy with three objectives: to gain full legal status, increase its leverage in parliament through its own party or alliance with other forces, and implement the Shari'ah. Mainstream clerics support current government policy. They favour making the Shari'ah the basis for Egypt's laws but urge patience. Radicals ridicule the use of electoral politics and official channels. All sides justify their strategies ideologically by references to the Qur'an, the Prophet Muhammad's teachings, and great Islamic teachers of the past.

The Brotherhood insists that implementation of the Shari'ah will provide a transitional stage on which an Islamic society can be constructed. It opposes violence. The militants, in contrast, find the existing system totally illegitimate. While the radical jam'iyat try to ignore the authorities, the revolutionary jama'at want to fight them. The jam'iyat may sometimes adopt, at least temporarily, the latter tactics.

On the nature of the future Islamic state, all fundamentalists are remarkably vague. They assert that it will solve all problems. Since, by definition, the new system would not have any internal contradictions and the rule of Islam would produce utopia, advocates of an Islamic state feel no need to detail the mechanisms by which it would be governed. Of course, the ideologists of the Russian and Iranian revolutions did not provide exhaustive blueprints in advance either, but the Egyptian fundamentalists are, if anything, even less clear about their plans.

By the same token, these groups do not admit to having an explicit, fully developed worldview of their own. Their theory and practice, they maintain, is Islam as presented in the Qur'an, the sayings of the Prophet Muhammad, and the writings of the leading theologians of the middle ages. What reveals the ideology of contemporary fundamentalists, then, is how they interpret these texts and where they place the emphasis. While the mainstream ulama and, to a lesser extent, the Brotherhood, cite passages stressing tolerance and patience, the revolutionaries use the Islamic tradition of perfectionist purity and extremism to demand struggle and revolution.

MUSLIM BROTHERHOOD: POLITICAL PARTY OR ELECTORAL ALLIANCE?

As parliamentarians, Brotherhood legislators seek public approval by showing themselves to be moderate and incorruptible. They are frustrated by their status as a minority opposition in a system which can, at best, be described as semi-democratic. But while the government always wins parliamentary majorities, the Brotherhood's assembly members claim that they have been effective in order to justify their electoral strategy. For example, Hasan al-Jamal, one of the more successful campaigners, explained that he worked hard to serve his constituency's practical needs. His appeal to implement the Shari'ah was phrased with an ecumenism generally alien to Islamic fundamentalism, "The Shari'ah is for the good of all mankind," giving each individual "rights and duties regardless of his religion . . . Some of those religions do not differ from the Islamic Shari'ah." Aware that only the government majority can legalize the Brotherhood, he tries to convince the rulers that his group is a moderate one. By strengthening it, he argues, the regime would provide an alternative to attract the youth away from the jama'at extremists. His own experience in campaigning for election and seeking to win votes in parliament seems to have moved him toward the political center.[1]

If these statements define the Brotherhood's softer tone, the group is also capable of sharply and bitterly criticizing the regime's behavior. It understands that no matter how well it does in elections, the government will never allow them to gain a majority and take power. Thus, while the Brotherhood has good reason for pursuing a strategy which allows it to survive, prosper, and gain some influence, playing the electoral game can never lead to an Islamic state. The government has resisted even accepting the Shari'ah as the foundation for all Egypt's laws, a step which the Brotherhood claims – rather questionably – would be the first stage in establishing the rule of Islam in the country.

These tensions are well expressed by Professor Ahmad Sayf

al-Islam Hasan al-Banna, son of the Brotherhood's founder and himself one of its leaders and members of parliament. "I would say without the least inaccuracy: There are no freedoms in Egypt, however much the government tries to repeat talk about freedoms and democracy." His main complaint in this regard are the restrictions still put on the Brotherhood. When "we tried to hold a single election [rally] ... all the police stations located in my electoral district refused on the grounds that security arrangements were not available. When the ruling [party] held an election [rally], we said to them that we would hold a conference in the same place. Again they refused, claiming that sufficient forces were not available to guard the election tent. Thus we were deprived of all the means of expression and of contact with the public. The government ... threatened everyone who was cooperating with us. In the elections themselves, there was heavy falsification. Where are the freedoms? Where is democracy?"[2]

But if elections are rigged, then how can the Brotherhood justify placing its faith in them? The answer can only be either that the Brotherhood's main goal is to be a lobbying group – seeking relatively more Islamic observance and giving its leaders some power and prestige – or it hopes to build an organization to take advantage of some future political crisis to seize power.

As has been noted, the Muslim Brotherhood wants to be granted status as a fully legal organization. There is a debate within the organization as to whether it should form its own political party to run in parliamentary elections. It has also sought remedies through the court system, which the jama'at and jam'iyat disdain as collaboration with the rulers.[3]

Within the Brotherhood, some leaders suggest that a political party of its own is needed to increase its effectiveness. Two problems often raised about this idea are that a party might become factionalized and that it could deepen Muslim–Christian antagonism. Salah Shadi, one of the top Brotherhood leaders, responds with the *a priori* logic often used by fundamentalists. There can be no polarization within an Islamic party because Islam rejects factionalism and its message is clear to all believers. This kind of thinking does not explain, however, why factions willing to fight each other developed even in the midst of Islam's "golden age," a few years after the death of the Prophet Muhammad. Nor does it account for the burning antagonism of fundamentalist jama'at and jam'iyat toward Christians which has inspired physical attacks against them. Similarly, Shadi's declaration that Islam does not accept false or extremist ideas is at odds with his own negative view of Khumayni's Iran.[4]

Salah Abu Isma'il, however, opposes the creation of a separate Brotherhood party. As the Brotherhood faction's leader in the Wafd and later the Liberal Party, his career benefited from the policy of joining existing groupings. In order to gain government sanction, he warns, a new party would have to accept the Camp David treaties and declare itself "non-religious." Under these conditions, a Muslim Brotherhood party would be pointless.[5]

One of Isma'il's colleagues in parliament, Dr Muhammad al-Sayyid Habib from Asyut, claims that the Brotherhood's strategy has already effectively affected the regime's policy. As Brotherhood leader in the center of radical fundamentalism, Habib often has to defend its strategy against more extremist critics. In parliament, he points out, the government's National Democratic Party majority controls all legislation. But before the opposition became organized in the mid-1980s, "Laws were issued without surveillance or review." When the Islamic opposition came into the assembly, "legislation began to be reviewed on the basis of an Islamic comprehension of things." In short, the Brotherhood deputies limited the government in certain ways.

Bad legislation might still pass but such an outcome has become less probable. A proposed bill totally at odds with Islamic law, through the Brotherhood's legislative efforts, "might end up 60 percent contrary to Islamic law. Through our criticism of many acts of corruption, we have helped lessen their magnitude." One can almost hear the sneers of radicals at the idea of accepting a law "only" 60 per cent contrary to the Shari'ah. Such a statement illustrates a major ideological divergence among fundamentalists.

Habib also points out that the Brotherhood's presence in parliament allows it to voice its views and mobilize popular support. Participation in parliamentary life has also improved the Brotherhood's image: "Many deputies continue to imagine that the Brothers carry out a dialogue with knives and their teeth are dripping blood. The ministers are still astonished when they hear a 'Brother' talking with intelligence and balance." Indeed, he even proudly claimed that President Mubarak himself was astonished when he heard parliamentarian Ma'mun al-Hudaybi speak in a scholarly manner and made the comment, "So you are talking like us."

The revolutionary or radical would see this pride in the Brotherhood's new respectability **as an unhealthy** aping of unbelievers in order to win their approval. Yet this desire for acceptance may be an inevitable outcome of a reformist strategy. The Brotherhood's members serve on the legislature's committees and learn the art of governing, "We are no longer men who talk about the provisions of Islamic jurisprudence or say 'God' and say 'the Prophet' and leave it at that. Rather, we have gone into the streets with experts. Since we are intending to establish a government, it is necessary to assemble technical expertise in various areas of life ... We are establishing schools, clinics, shops, and economic installations, and we are presenting solutions to current problems and carrying them out in our own institutions." In short, the Brotherhood sees itself as pragmatic, an approach which is the enemy of radical ideology.[6]

The recent history of the Brotherhood's electoral alliances and the emergence of Salah Abu Isma'il as its leader in such matters shows the development of a flexibility – or opportunism – so decried by revolutionary fundamentalists. The relatively secularist Wafd and the Brotherhood formed a partnership due to their shared antipathy for the Nasirist revolution and the incumbent Mubarak government rather than to any common Islamic piety. The Brotherhood's leader, al-Tilimsani, defended the alliance on the basis of mutual patriotism and the need for unity to save Egypt "from devasting dangers." The fragile arrangement ended in 1986, with mutual recriminations, when the Wafd leadership favored one of its own members over Abu Isma'il as leader of the opposition. Still, the Brotherhood had successfully used the Wafd as a way of getting into parliament.[7]

Abu Isma'il gave a candid explanation for the Brotherhood's ensuing alliance with the Liberal Party, of which he became deputy chairman. "We have chosen it not because it is the strongest party but because it is the weakest party. The strongest parties impose their conditions on us, but the Brotherhood was able to dominate the Liberals." The Brotherhood pressured the Liberals into withdrawing recognition of Camp David, eliminating the word socialist from the party's name, and firing the secularist editor of its paper, *al-Ahrar*. The Brotherhood, as an illegal organization, was eager to obtain control of the publication since it could not have its own newspaper. The Liberal Party's chairman went so far as to grow a beard and perform the pilgrimage to Mecca. "Thus," concludes Abu Isma'il, "we feel that we have purged the party and have moved it in the direction of our objective." He appealed to the "faithful masses wishing to apply God's Shari'ah to join the Liberal Party." The politicians leading that group, who had hitherto been little identified with piety and won only half of 1 per cent of the vote in the previous election, were eager to reap the "tens of thousands" of new members promised by Abu Isma'il.[8]

While making significant gains from this alliance of convenience, the Brotherhood wanted even more. It sought to set a new agenda for Egyptian politics, one in which the fundamentalists' most immediate concern must be addressed. Although the government tied up in committee the Liberal Party's new Islamic legislative program, including a bill to abolish interest as usurious, the Brotherhood and its allies asserted themselves as the representatives of Islam, embarrassed other opposition parties into taking a more Islamic tone, intimidated secularist intellectuals, and pressured the government toward compromises.[9]

Obviously, such a situation was not likely to produce either a revolution or an end to the existing regime. Yet the Brotherhood's material accomplishments on behalf of Islam went beyond anything the revolutionaries could show.

CRITICS OF BROTHERHOOD STRATEGY

Naturally, revolutionaries and radicals were skeptical about the Brotherhood's strategy. In their eyes, the Brotherhood had only strengthened the system and weakened the forces of Islam. If Egypt was in a state of jahiliyyah, no compromise or reforms would mend the problem. Some questioned whether the Shari'ah should be submitted to the parliament at all, since God's law was not something which could be voted up or down. Others asked whether adoption of the Shari'ah alone would really change the country in any but the most formal sense since the "impious" regime would still have to implement it.

From a secularist perspective, the Brotherhood and its partners are only hypocritical opportunists. As one writer puts it, "The Wafd is no more faithful nor more Muslim than the other parties, the Wafd's chairman does not wear a turban on his head." And even the Liberal Party leader's beard and pilgrimage did not make him a fundamentalist. But from a fundamentalist standpoint, the Brotherhood was behaving much worse by distorting and betraying Islam. One critic of the Brotherhood's doctrine and strategy was the populist preacher Hafiz Salamah, leader of the Islamic Guidance Society: "By God," he proclaimed, "how can the Nasirists work with Wafdists, and the

Islamicists with the secular Wafdists? Almighty God says [in the Qur'an]: 'You do not find those who believe in God and the hereafter friendly with those who opposed God and his messenger.' If the [ruling party] accepts that the word of God shall be the final word then we will be the first to join it."[10]

THE SHARI'AH AS RATIONALE

The response from the Brotherhood is that the battle to institute the Shari'ah is so important as to justify its entry into politics, alliance with secular parties, and use of all available legal channels. The Brotherhood's ideological perspective is that if it could have the Shari'ah made the basis of all law, this would establish a new stage in which Egypt would become a *de facto* Islamic society. To act otherwise would be sinful. Isma'il stated that the Brotherhood could hardly stand by while "Every party is going after a non-Islamic goal."[11]

This is the answer given by a member of the mainstream ulama who entered parliament on the Wafd ticket in 1984. Dr 'Abd al-Ghaffar Muhammad 'Aziz, a professor and dean of the Islamic Call Department at al-Azhar University, explained his ideology in this way: "I must work for the institution of the Islamic system through the legislative council for I believe that the call to Islam must use all possible, available, and legally permissible means. The best means in this age is to be in a legislative position to bring about change, if not personally, then at least through influence within the assembly via personal contacts and attempts to explain the Islamic system's superiority over other world systems." In short, he argues that refusal to use the system's channels to try to implement Islam in Egypt would be a profoundly immoral and un-Islamic act:[12]

> The Islamicists are not only the Muslim Brotherhood deputies, but can be found in all other parties. A huge number of [the ruling] National Democratic Party's members are also Islamicists who support the Islamic Shari'ah. We have actually succeeded in winning a decision forbidding the enactment of any law by the People's Assembly incompatible with the Islamic Shari'ah provisions. We are watching such laws very closely ... to prove to the assembly that some of them are incompatible so that it may amend them or drop them altogether. If this is the only job of the

Islamicist deputies in the assembly, then it is enough. It is not the number that counts. A very small group that believes in what it is doing can bring about change.[13]

Participation in legal politics offers hope for creating an Islamic society. Yet Dr 'Aziz's optimistic brand of fatalism also suggests that victory is too inevitable to worry about the strategy employed. "Good will triumph in the end. God said: 'The scum disappears like froth cast out while that which is for the good of mankind remains on earth.'" On a more immediate level, he is persuaded that others in parliament, including members of the ruling party, will be persuaded to support the fundamentalists' efforts. Tilimsani, the Brotherhood's leader, expressed similar ideas. A belief that the righteous should advise and convince the rulers toward proper action is a long-accepted doctrine among Sunni Muslims. But it is a view quite different from Qutb's notion that there must be a struggle to the death between those in power who promote jahiliyyah and those in opposition who are the true Muslims.

HOW TO IMPLEMENT THE SHARI'AH

The Brotherhood and the mainstream ulama agree that the Shari'ah should be implemented as the sole foundation of Egyptian law. But must this be done all at once or over a long period of time? And how do pro-government clerics justify the regime's continued refusal to let parliament pass such a law?

Certainly, the fundamentalists have shown a large measure of patience on this issue. Egypt's 1971 constitution mandated that the Shari'ah was to be the country's "principal source of legislation," but this formulation denied it the monopoly demanded by the fundamentalists. In 1978, the People's Assembly formed a committee to study how to make the nation's laws conform to the Shari'ah. Its study was completed in 1982 and the People's Assembly recommended in July of that year that there should be a transitional period to revise the existing legal system where necessary, retrain lawyers and judges, and prepare the public. The People's Assembly set up another special committee to do this job, though clerics and fundamentalists complained that parliament and the government were merely procrastinating.

In 1985, demanding the Shari'ah's rapid implementation became the principal activity of the Brotherhood members of parliament. Abu Isma'il called for the "immediate enforcement of the Shari'ah, without any delay or excuses." Those speaking about "gradual progress," he charged, were "like a sick man who refuses to take medicine, saying: 'I shall take it once I am cured.' The only way to 'prepare the ground' is through Islam." Religious figures argued in all available forums that only full implementation of the Shari'ah would solve Egypt's material and spiritual problems.[14]

The showdown between government and fundamentalists finally came on May 4, 1985, when the People's Assembly discussed the implementation of the Shari'ah. Using parliamentary technicalities, Assembly Speaker Rif'at al-Muhjub cut short the debate. A group of opposition members left the session in protest, whereupon the Assembly voted for a "gradual and scientific" revision of laws that contradicted the Shari'ah rather than imposing it immediately. Bringing Egyptian law theoretically into accordance with the Shari'ah, the government met the demands of the mainstream ulama while denying the fundamentalists a symbolic victory. In addition, the changes would take additional years to be made – if they ever would be – and left the definition of what contradicted the Shari'ah in the government's hands.

What should the fundamentalists do if the parliament did not act properly? Tilimsani attempted to reconcile the seeming contradiction between the categorical imperative to implement the Shari'ah immediately and an attempt to be effective by compromising with those favoring gradual change. "No Muslim who has an ounce of faith can claim that he would pursue a gradual approach to sanction what is permissible or ban what is forbidden. There is absolutely no room for opinions or wavering in this regard," al-Tilimsani wrote. But he also advocated "orderly and gradual application of the Shari'ah." To justify this, he quoted passages from the Qur'an which were not among the kind of verses usually cited by the jama'at: "He that forgives and seeks reconciliation shall be rewarded by Allah [al-Shura: 40]. To endure with fortitude and to forgive is a duty incumbent on all [al-Shura: 43]."[15]

Other fundamentalists were outraged, however, and denounced the government for ignoring the Egyptian people's wishes. On May 24, Shaykh Hafiz Salamah gave a sermon at his al-Nur mosque demanding that the government implement the Shari'ah by June 14 or face a massive march of 50,000 people, praying with Qur'ans in hand, on the presidential palace. The government invoked the emergency law banning marches and threatened to use force to stop the demonstration. Salamah appealed in court and, when it was clear there would be no decision by his deadline, announced he would defy the ban. The Brotherhood did not support him. Between 4000 and 7000 people gathered at the mosque to pray on June 14 and were surrounded by 1000 to 2500 riot police armed with batons, shields and tear gas. Salamah agreed to postpone the march, "until the court ruled in their favor; then the march [would] be from one end of the country to the other." The court, however, turned down Salamah's request the next day.[16] While the pro-government clerics could claim some progress, both the Brotherhood's parliamentary strategy and the jam'iyat's protest tactics had been soundly defeated.

Handling the Defeat on Shari'ah

The importance of these turbulent events cannot be overestimated. The government had rejected the fundamentalists' most important immediate demand, the implementation of the Shari'ah as the basis of Egyptian law. The mainstream clergy, the Brotherhood, and literally millions of Egyptians agreed that application of the Shari'ah was absolutely just and totally essential. The jam'iyat also wanted this step to be taken, though many of them questioned parliament's right to vote on the matter. Nevertheless, the issue was once again postponed after seven years of debate and procrastination. And in the following years, the regime did no more to address the fundamentalists' demands on this issue.

Despite this supreme provocation, nothing happened. The ulama continued to support the government, the Brotherhood still worked within the system, the jam'iyat did not launch a wave of violence, and membership in the jama'at did not grow. While the Shari'ah issue will certainly continue to be important – and may return to haunt Egypt's rulers – this outcome illustrates the strength of the government and the constraints operating on the fundamentalists.

The Brotherhood's response was to increase its electoral activities. In the 1987 parliamentary elections, it conducted a highly organized, well-publicized campaign whose slogan was "Islam is the solution." In frequent meetings and press conferences, its leaders expressed continued determination to convince the People's Assembly to adopt the Shari'ah. Yet given the fact that the campaigns and elections were managed to ensure government majorities, the prospects for such a victory were questionable, if not impossible.[17]

Muhammad Abu al-Nasr, al-Tilimsani's successor as head of the Brotherhood, adjusted to this situation by asking only for a gradual implementation of Shari'ah, "We demand well-considered and balanced steps," he declared, which would allow "sufficient time to shape public opinion." After all, he noted, Muhammad had prohibited wine only over a number of years and in three stages. "Hence the people must be moved gradually toward being convinced because for many years they have not experienced this way of life." In short, the Brotherhood sought no confrontation with the regime.[18]

Some fundamentalists, while maintaining that the Shari'ah was of the highest priority, turned their attention to other issues and argued more explicitly for gradual implementation. They accepted a mildly reformist approach, confessing the government's greater strength and their own limited support. One of them commented it would "take time to develop an Islamic course in [the] social, economic, and political fields." Another maintained, "The most important thing is to create the appropriate psychological atmosphere and reassure the people . . . Is there any harm in reducing the volume of wine sales [or] in lessening the obscenities in TV serials and songs and night clubs?"[19]

While intimidating fundamentalists, the government's tough stand on the Shari'ah issue also emboldened secularists who portrayed the question in political and practical rather than religious terms. They pointed to the unrest which implementing the Shari'ah had provoked in neighboring Sudan ("To what physical and psychological pain is an innocent person subjected when his hand is cut off?") and warned that the Shari'ah issue was a stalking horse for those whose real goal was to seize power. The politicization of religion, they suggested, undermined Islam and Egyptian sovereignty. In one writer's words, "The canonical law of Islam was not revealed so that we could organize a demonstration." Those who protest or resort to violence were misled by foreign powers or political parties who sought to create civil strife. They "demand the application of Islamic law without thinking about applying [it] to themselves . . . Any change that would be brought about will be merely superficial . . . It will be just like what Numayri did in Sudan: he cut the hands of thieves who stole 10 pounds, but spared and pardoned those who stole millions!"

Unattractive foreign examples were invoked, as was the lack of consensus over the exact meaning of applying Islamic law. "Khumayni says that the canonical law of Islam is being applied in Iran.

Mu'ammar al-Qadhafi says that it is being applied in Libya, and Ziya [al-Haqq] says that it is being applied in Pakistan. Which one of these methods of applications do the demonstrators want? In Saudi Arabia prescribed legal punishments are actually enforced. The hands of thieves are cut off, and fornicators are stoned. And yet [an armed] gang carried machine guns and went to the Ka'bah claiming that they wanted the canonical law of Islam to be applied." Instead, people must start by reforming themselves and change should come gradually. Egypt's new mufti, Dr Muhammad Sayyid Tantawi, sounded quite similar: hope in the good faith of the parliament, a preference for gradual imposition of the Shari'ah.[20]

Such counter-arguments put the fundamentalists in a bind. To win mass support, some of them suggested that invoking the Shari'ah would not, in the words of Islamic thinker Khalid Muhammad Khalid, "mean a feared and dreaded change in our lives ... Nine-tenths of [existing law] is consistent with Islamic jurisprudence. The penal code needs only the legal punishments which, if we know the philosophy of Islam ... will not kindle ... the least amount of fear and dread. The civil and commercial laws will only need an additional provision excluding usury. I do not think this is difficult since Pakistan has eliminated all forms of usurious transactions and has transformed all the banking institutions, including the foreign ones, into Islamic transactions ... The step-by-step approach is the ideal way to uplift society and refine its behavior." But such claims open themselves to another criticism: if so little will be changed then how can the Shari'ah dramatically improve Egyptian society and make it so much more pious? [21]

In a more wordly sense, major contributors to the Muslim Brotherhood were wealthy businessmen who run Islamic investment companies. Many of them would benefit materially from making the Shari'ah the basis of Egypt's laws. These enterprises offered high rates of return without actually paying interest. If the Shari'ah were to be invoked, their competitors would be placed at a real disadvantage, at least for a while, and these "Islamic" funds would boom. By the late 1980s, however, rampant corruption and the strain of paying such large dividends drove the largest such companies to the verge of insolvency and may have promoted second thoughts about the efficacy of "Islamic transactions."

The fundamentalists, of course, argue that the Shari'ah's provisions are of value simply because they implement God's word. As Shaykh Salamah declared, "Islamic legislation had descended upon us from the Omniscient, through its application we are bound to solve all our problems."[22]

Fundamentalists are going to have to decide what to do if the government, as seems likely, continues its refusal to implement the Shari'ah fully. They can call for gradualism and express faith in the legal channels, they can protest, or they can seek a revolution. Yet the government has been largely succesful in coopting reformers, suppressing protesters, and repressing violent revolutionaries.

REFORM OR REVOLUTION?

The pro-regime clerics advocate reform and this is, less explicitly, the strategy followed by the Muslim Brotherhood as well. Tilimsani said that "the Muslim Brothers don't aim to rush into government, but they desire that there be a philosophy of government which derives its most fundamental principles from the book of Allah and the Sunnah."[23] They are willing to settle for an Islamic society in which Muslim norms are obeyed and even sanctioned by law. Underground groups like al-Jihad want a total change in Egypt, demanding an Islamic state in which the fundamentalists are in power, while the jam'iyat have diverse, and usually less articulated, views on the matter.

One reason for the Brotherhood's endorsement of reform is that it doubts the likelihood of revolution. It argues that the revolutionaries have little support and obstruct practical improvements. The Brotherhood's leader in Asyut characterizes revolutionary fundamentalism as "a hollow drum," loud but impotent. "They have no base among the people . . . [Their] credibility with the masses is zero, and public opinion is always on the side of moderation and mediation." If not for the ineptness of the authorities, he states, the revolutionaries would be even weaker. The Brotherhood has no interest – particularly after its experiences in the 1950s, 1960s, and 1970s – in sacrificing itself for such a futile cause.[24]

The revolutionaries and radicals accuse the Brothers of having sold out to the government. In Asyut, they distributed leaflets calling on people to boycott elections for the "apostate" parliament. Most of them do not vote.[25] Those who believe that Egypt is in a state of jahiliyyah cannot accept reform when the very foundation of society is rotten. Further, the extremists argue that the Brotherhood's strategy makes a revolution even less likely. Mubarak's system allows the opposition to operate, have access to the press, and express itself as long as it does not directly attack the president or military. The same opportunities are accepted by some charismatic preachers and jam'iyat. By the late 1980s, even Kishk moderated his rhetoric and was allowed to appear on the state-owned television. As we have seen, when Salamah refused to back down, the government took over his mosque.

Some of the other key radicals have also criticized the use of violence. Muhammad al-Maraghi, leader of Alexandria's Islamic Dawn Association, said, "Our rejection of violence is proved by the fact we did not use it against the hundreds of thousands of tourists who violate Islamic traditions on Alexandria beaches. The Islamic community calls for rejecting evil-doing and preaches about what is right and what is wrong with forgiveness and gentleness. Those who want to remain misguided will bear the brunt of their action before God." These protestations of peaceful intent are not always kept by jam'iyat on communities or campuses but do limit their violent activities.[26]

Despite the Brotherhood's sometimes heated rhetoric, even the skeptical *Ruz al-Yusuf* concludes that it rejects violence and follows a parliamentary strategy. At one time, in al-Tilimsani's words, it concluded that an alliance with Sadat was the "shortest road to achieve this dream." It fell out with Sadat but did not return to terrorism. As to tactics, al-Tilimsani said that while the Brotherhood opposes the government, it is also against "the burning of means of transport, the looting of shops, and the pillaging of public establishments," which is a corrupt practice. "What is pillaged is the property not of the head of state or the government but of the people." Coups are made by those "who seek power for its own sake." "Force and violence . . . is a futile use of the people's strength which benefits no one but the enemies of this country." After Sadat's death, al-Tilimsani repeated his request that the opposition be given a real place in Egypt ("as in all advanced countries") and could even help the ruling party overcome Egypt's crises. He praised Mubarak: "The people are enjoying freedom, and security . . . We are not enemies of the ruler himself, but rather watch actions alone, and for what is good in them we praise God, and for what is otherwise, we admonish, advise and investigate." Al-Tilimsani's successor, Abu al-Nasr, denied that the movement was appeasing the government but claimed that its deputies were successful and, "In the end only what is right prevails."[27]

The Extremists and Violence

The militants argue that not only is the existing society unacceptable, but also that the authorities will not agree to make the needed changes and will corrupt or repress opponents. Speaking against reform and parliamentarianism, one revolutionary argues, "Al-jahiliyyah does not permit its enemies to . . . destroy it . . . How can the Islamic movement use the methods of al-jahiliyyah to destroy al-jahiliyyah? . . . These institutions are secular jahiliyyah institutions arising from secular concepts found in a secular constitution, which must be erased from the face of the earth so that the structure of Islam may be built on it once again."[28]

In rejecting the jahiliyyah concept – and thus much of the rationale for using violence against fellow Egyptians – a Brotherhood writer notes, "Egyptian society has a deep-rooted belief in a single God and, in the view of the fair-minded, is one of the best of Islamic societies – we would not say the best of all of them." Contrasting traditional Islam with the radical fundamentalists, the writer says that the extremist groups are "not satisfied that the five pillars of Islam be present in order for a person to be a Moslem, rather, the . . . avoidance of sins is incumbent upon him, lest the person be considered an infidel. They thereby pursue a course which is the opposite of that the public pursues and consider that a person who commits a major sin is not refractory but rather is an infidel."[29]

This is a very accurate analysis. The revolutionaries go beyond what most Egyptians consider proper Islamic practice and are too rigid in their demand for individual perfection. The leader of al-Jihad, Faraj, had written, "Rulers . . . establish their governments by power," and citizens cannot get rid of them except "by violence and the establishment of the Islamic state." These rulers "do not have the right to force Muslims to obey them [but] will disappear only at sword-point." Consequently, Islamic jihad is incumbent on every Muslim. Jihad is such a high priority, he adds with a bow toward the strong ties of Egypt's traditionalist (and anti-revolutionary) family structure, that individuals do not need their parents' permission to wage it. The Qur'an, too, can be a barrier to the revolutionaries' ideology because it has about 124 passages which speak of "forgiveness," "modesty," "clemency," "avoidance," and "patience." Faraj must argue that they are all overruled by the verse in which God tells the Muslims to "besiege and seize and disable and kill the idolators, wherever you find them" (al-Turbah, verse 50).[30]

While the revolutionaries glory in talk about violence, the jam'iyat are more circumspect. Dr Badr al-din Ghazi, a Cairo University teacher and jam'iyat leader comments, "The markets are full of books which repeatedly speak of torture carried out against Muslim brothers and Islamic groups in detention centers and prisons. The state's iron-fist policy is not reform. They should conduct dialogue with us and if that fails they should seek other means." Another jam'iyat leader, Dr 'Ala Muhyi al-Din, says his group has been involved in only "a few incidents" and blames this violence on government security agents. He adds, that "associations, unions, and other bodies" are important places for "rectifying wrongdoing, [though] we strongly warn against using the People's Assembly."[32]

A non-fundamentalist advocate of reform argues that such mechanisms are in place and are actually being used by the Islamic groups. "Any child in politics would see that there is absolutely no justification for the use of violence ... For the first time, this [fundamentalist] current has clear and practical legal channels for expressing its ideas. There are about 35 deputies who have entered parliament and are exercising the right of public oversight ... They also have many newspapers that express even their most extreme viewpoints. They carry on their missionary activities either in writing or in sermons in mosques." They hold public prayers for the 'Idd al-Fitr holidays, demonstrate in public squares, and campaign for implementation of the Shari'ah. The government also has altered television programs to meet their objections, despite complaints from more secular quarters. Of course, there are many restrictions on these groups, but the operating room they do have is sufficient to constrain the great majority of them from seeking violence and revolution.[31]

To all this, the true revolutionary answers with intransigence. Qutb made this position clear: "We cannot just accept that such weakness, complacency and failure are part of human nature without doing anything about it. We still have to motivate that nature to seek the sublime and to reach for the highest standard." To do this the Muslim must always be ready to wage jihad. "Allah knows that those who hold the reins of power in their hands are hostile to Islam and that they will always try to resist it."

Confrontation "between armed evil and armed goodness" is inevitable to counter "the well-equipped forces of falsehood ... Otherwise, it would be a case of suicide." A willingness to sacrifice possessions and lives is something "Allah has required the believers to do, purchasing all these from them in return for admitting them into heaven. He either gives them victory or martyrdom ... All people die when the time comes, but only those who fight for Allah's cause can be martyrs."[33]

Al-Jihad's 'Abd al-Rahman concurs, "Muslims thus have a right to rebel against every unjust and despotic ruler. We are convinced to the point of certainty that those despotic rulers will never step down or change their despotic ways because they were advised to do so or because they were invited to attend international conferences ... That is why Muslims must rebel against them ... We are not being fooled by the democracy whose praises are being sung. Democracy is a false and misleading phenomenon. God commands us to rebel against those oppressors. He says, 'Fight against them until idolatry is no more and Allah's religion reigns supreme.'"[34]

Faraj criticizes everyone who does not take the revolutionary path. He writes that participation in political life – which is what the Brotherhood has done – only strengthens the system. He ridicules the idea that the rise of true Muslims to professional and political positions of power – the jam'iyat strategy – as "pure fantasy." He labeled a dependence on preaching – the Brotherhood and Kishk – or building a mass-based movement – the Brotherhood and jam'iyats – as "a diversion from jihad." He made fun of those who would withdraw from society – al-Takfir – as "an evasion that forsakes the sole authentic and legitimate means of building the Muslim state." Faraj is right in saying that preoccupation with other strategies forestalls a turn to armed struggle, but he is wrong because the battle he advocated against the state was quite unwinnable. Most Egyptians – even most fundamentalists – make sounder evaluations about the balance of forces. The number of those who will seek martyrdom, as Qutb advocated and put into action, are limited.[35]

For 'Abd al-Rahman, the matter is clear and simple. A ruler who commits an act that deviates from Islam is disobeying God and it is the duty of believers to overthrow him. He cites a Qur'anic passage as justification: "Unbelievers ... transgressors ... [and] evil-doers are those that do not base their judgments on Allah's revelations" (al-Ma'idah: 44, 45, 47). The same applies to those who speak piously but do not so act. "You shall find no believers in Allah ... on friendly terms with those who oppose Allah and His apostle, even though they be their fathers, their sons, their brothers or their nearest kindred" (al-Mujadilah: 22). According to the Qur'an, he concludes, "there are two parties: the party of God and the party of the devil."

Those who apply the Qur'an and Shari'ah "make up the party of God, and those who apply other laws make up the party of the devil. You may apply this rule to the many parties that can be found in Egypt now, and you will have the answer."[36]

Some observers make the mistake of equating such statements with the beliefs of all fundamentalists or even of all Muslims. Since Qutb and 'Abd al-Rahman so glibly quote the Qur'an as endorsing their position, it is possible to see their viewpoints as embodying the only Islamic interpretation of that tradition. Yet the majority of believing Muslims in Egypt do not accept these claims. The clergy generally denounce them and the Brotherhood calls them "the trap of haste and rashness."[37]

Nevertheless, the revolutionaries will persevere in trying to force unrest and instability in Egypt. To achieve this end – admitting the perilous odds but with faith in their inevitable victory – they have enunciated several strategies whose contents and fates were discussed above in Chapter 4. The Islamic Liberation Organization thought that a spectacular act of terrorism would stir a spontaneous revolt. Al-Takfir advocated withdrawal from the existing society and the creation of a parallel Islamic one, but became caught up in a suicidal wave of violence after its members were arrested. Al-Jihad advocated a protracted underground struggle to build a mass base which would lead a popular uprising. But it sacrificed much of its organization to the assassination of Sadat and a limited revolt in Asyut. Kepel reminds us that even the assassination of Sadat was not so impressive in revolutionary terms. The Jihad group consisted of two branches which collaborated only loosely with each other; the killing was an adventurous act which al-Islambuli, seeking personal revenge, pushed through by the force of his personality. Since it was so disconnected from any broader plan, the murder led only to the destruction of al-Jihad and the weakening of the fundamentalist forces.[38] An opponent of Faraj within al-Jihad, a Jordanian national named Muhammad Salim Rahal, called for a revolt within the armed forces. Yet none of these paths to power have been followed with much cohesiveness or continuity. If forces are going to arise capable of waging a serious revolutionary struggle or creating an Islamic state, they are not yet apparent in Egyptian politics.

The Nature of the Islamic State

Islamic fundamentalists are characteristically vague about the shape of the state which they wish to create. Iranian ideologists produced little in the way of guidelines before their revolution; their Egyptian counterparts, if anything, have provided even less in the way of hints. In part, this follows a long history of revolutionary thinking. Marx provided few specifics for his Communist state other than generalized utopian promises. This failure, however, did not prevent real Communist regimes from coming to power. They looked far different from what Marx or his comrades would have expected. The same could be said for the Iranian experience.

There are also more immediate reasons for this paltry forecasting by Islamic movements. By definition, the Islamic state is the fulfillment of the Qur'an and Shari'ah, a resurrection of the era of the Prophet Muhammad and the first four caliphs. Consequently, a revolutionary fundamentalist believes that the state's nature is quite clear without further commentary. All problems will be resolved once these laws are put into effect by virtuous men. Just as Marx thought the workers would wield power in a socialist state without much difficulty, the fundamentalists consider the details as unimportant and the process as an automatic one. On a more practical level, any debate over the state's functioning can only be divisive since ideologists might have different interpretations of Islamic law or varying preferences. Thus, the discussion usually falls back on generalities and a few much-repeated catchwords – no alcohol, no usury, no pornography, proper modesty by women, and so on.

At the same time, it is possible to predict some characteristics of an Islamic state in Egypt. The revolutionaries clearly want a contemporary state in terms of modern technology. Decades ago, traditionalist Muslims debated over the Islamic propriety of radio or television, for example, but contemporary fundamentalists have no such qualms. They seek to purge – not eliminate – the educational system, culture, the media, and science to adapt them for Islamic purposes. Many of the fundamentalist leaders have university educations and even a background in technology.

An historical indication of the state's program might be the Muslim Brotherhood's 1939 platform. It called for a constitution based on the Qur'an, making the Shari'ah the basis for all law, an anti-corruption campaign, reinstituting jihad, and subsuming nationalism by the total identification of Islam with the state. On the economic front, usury and stock exchanges were to be prohibited; there would be an agrarian reform, the nationalization of natural resources, and replacement of income tax by the Islamic tax (zakat). Since the Nasir revolution instituted a wide range of land reform and nationalization, such "socialist" demands are not heard from revolutionary fundamentalists today though an Islamic state could institute them to centralize power in its own hands.[39]

The Islamic state would be a dictatorship. The Qur'an accepts the idea of a "shura" (consultative council) and this fact makes it possible to justify parliamentary institutions as Islamic. But the revolutionaries' determination to impose their values and interpretations on society requires a concentration of power beyond what a genuine representative system is likely to supply. Moreover, the fundamentalists believe that God has specified right and wrong; the people have no right to do what they wish. Revolutionary Egyptian fundamentalism is essentially anti-pluralist. Iran, of course, has maintained a parliamentary institution which sometimes acts independently of the executive and even, at times, has permitted different parties (which must be approved by the government). But Iran also had Ayatollah Khumayni as its velayat i-faqih (supreme jurisprudent) to make the ultimate decisions. This concept is totally alien to Egypt.

Indeed, absent from the program of both the Brotherhood and the revolutionary groups today is any central role for the clergy. No one in Egypt has called for direct rule by the ulama, whom fundamentalists look down on both as supporters of the status quo and as being corrupted by the system.

Any Islamic regime in Egypt would also have to come to terms with the country's Arab identity. The lack of any strong concept of Iranian nationalism made it easier for fundamentalism to triumph there. A fundamentalist regime in Cairo might develop its thinking along the lines of combining Islam and Arabism suggested by Kishk and discussed above.

Women and non-Muslims would lose rights they currently enjoy. A large number of women might nonetheless support an Islamic regime, though it seems reasonable to say that the modernization process has gone further among women in Egypt and thus there might be more feminist resistance than in Iran. The Coptic Christian minority – which can be estimated at about 10 per cent of the population – would also be likely to oppose an Islamic regime in a more cohesive way than did minorities in Iran.

A fundamentalist regime in Egypt would advocate more self-reliance, austerity, and hard work. Despite their assertions to the contrary, the fundamentalists have no magic solution to Egypt's economic woes. Egypt must find a major supplier of aid and the only two apparent possibilities are the United States or the Gulf Arab states. The USSR, a financial source in the past, seems too overextended and sunk in its own problems to provide the needed money. Yet a fundamentalist regime would find it difficult to ask or obtain a continued high level of U.S. aid, while the Gulf Arab states have less revenue to spare than they did when they bankrolled Egypt in the past. Saudi Arabia and Kuwait might be unwilling to help a radical fundamentalist Egypt, though they could welcome a moderate Islamic regime.

Finally, a fundamentalist regime would not necessarily seek foreign conflicts since it would first want to concentrate on consolidating control and promoting development at home. Yet, as in Iran's case, its extremist rhetoric and frightening presence could well make it blunder into a war with a neighbor, most likely Israel.

One might expect that an Islamic revolution would bring purges and repression; banning of political parties, closing of newspapers and theatres, burning of books, barring Western-style entertainment, the end of tourism, and major changes in the school system.[40] But the Muslim Brotherhood is at pains to disavow such intentions. "Some propaganda claims that if we get to power we will apply the divine stature immediately and cut off the hands of thieves and kill this one and do this and that," said Abu al-Nasr, but these claims should not be believed. The Brotherhood also allegedly wants to co-exist peacefully with the Copts. Al-Tilimsani noted that during Islam's early years, "Byzantine employees filled the offices of the Islamic government and, during the era of the Abbasids, Christians participated in government and, during the era of the Fatimids, Copts served in the ministries." But the Coptic Christians are a particular target for the revolutionaries, especially those in the Christian centers of Minya and Asyut. The Copts are accused of provocations and attacks on Muslims.

Abu al-Nasr went so far as to promise a moderate foreign policy. "Even those countries that espouse religions and philosophies other than Islam must receive our cooperation . . . so long as they do not interfere with our belief or our country's internal policy. This is one of the fundamentals of our faith."[41] Furthermore, the new Brotherhood explicitly pledges to install democracy since that system "opens the door for all thoughts and minds, as opposed to dictatorship, in which no ideas are permitted except those of the ruler." Democracy is "able to uncover every mistake, and no one is above criticism, while in a dictatorship the decisions are all orders from the ruler, and everyone must obey without discussion or criticism." Whether or not this intention is true, however, is another matter.[42]

In contrast, 'Abd al-Rahman explicitly rules out any pluralism in a state ruled by al-Jihad: "In Islam there are no multiple parties . . . There are only . . . the party of God and that of the devil. The party that believes in the Book of God and asks that judgments be made according to it is the party of God. If it asks for anything else it is the party of the devil. This is not a distinction that we made up; this is a distinction that comes from God." Obviously, any opposition would be deemed to be in the satanic category. The community, say the revolutionaries, can select the ruler, who must be a pious male. He will follow the Shari'ah and consult fellow Muslims when Islamic law is not clear but his duty is to follow the word of God as he sees it and not the dictates or the interests of the people.[43]

The Brotherhood's leader, Abu al-Nasr, puts the same basic thesis in a more palatable form. An Islamic system is similar to that in other countries, he explained, except that in most states "power stems from the people [who] can apply laws which may violate God's laws if that is what they want. Islam maintains that the difference between right and wrong is quite clear, that everyone must obey the rules of Islam and God's law, not man's choice.[44]

Qutb thought that one way to achieve this totalistic society would be through a large measure of decentralization, an approach that Libyan dictator Mu'ammar Qadhafi has advocated more recently. The Brotherhood's founder, al-Banna, suggested that a mass Islamic party might play the role of a consultative council.[45] Some of these ideas have been tried in Iran, with local committees and other institutions. At the same time, Tehran also established an elected parliament and a series of high-level committees with largely clerical membership to determine what legislation is properly Islamic. The Islamic Republican Party, however, was dissolved precisely because it became the forum for conflicting factions. In short, whatever mechanisms are created, the system must be a dictatorship of the pious. And like the "dictatorship of the proletariat," it will usually finish by being a dictatorship by a dictator.

Can economics be so easily defined in Islamic and satanic categories as is moral behavior? Radical fundamentalists dismiss both capitalism and Communism as inhuman and ungodly but have no coherent idea of an Islamic economic system. They merely refer to an idealized version of past Muslim society, decrying excesses of wealth and poverty while advocating fair wages, hard work, honesty, and payment of the Islamic alms tax. They denounce extravagance, hoarding, and interest. There is talk about benefiting "the poor," "the wretched," and the "weak on earth." Marxism is said to be successful inasmuch as it emulated Islam. Sometimes, they point to Islamic strictures against private monopolies in public utilities, though they support private property, profit, and inheritance. In short, this is a prescription for a mixed economy, one which might be slightly more or less socialist than is Egypt's current statist system. One writer likens this approach to the stance of the British Labour Party.[40]

Although the Brotherhood has consistently denounced corruption and conspicuous consumption, it argues that the Shari'ah fully supports private enterprise. In the 1930s and 1940s, the Brotherhood's members were largely peasants and urban shopkeepers who liked its attack on monopolists and big capitalists "for reducing small property owners to bankruptcy," and its advocacy of "an economic system similar to that which existed in Nazi Germany and Fascist Italy." Social justice would be the main criterion for the economy, private property should be limited, and the wealthy would be taxed to benefit the poor. Many of the worst abuses, however, were curbed in the Nasir era. The Brotherhood itself now has some wealthy supporters and after decades of Arab socialism it is harder to suggest that populist programs will resolve all economic problems.[47]

In general, the answers given by Islamic groups about their goals are clever obfuscations. A good example is a statement by Dr 'Asim Fahim, a Cairo University teacher and jam'iyat leader:

> The Islamic program is clearer than anything else. We propose general guidelines and when we have the power of implementation then you can judge us . . . Islam can resolve all current problems because it is not a theoretical religion. For example, if we look carefully into the Egyptian economic system we will find it combines socialist and capitalist systems. This system could lead to the total collapse of the society's main infrastructure. Then there is the issue of prosperity. The problem arose when people were paid when they did not work for it or received payment illegally.[48]

For fundamentalists, belief in Islam's ability to achieve success in all fields is tautological. Either one has faith or one does not. If the

Shari'ah is God's direct word and command, then implementing it cannot help but produce material and spiritual prosperity. Of course, the assumption is that an Islamic state would fully carry out Islamic norms and that the majority of its citizens would act properly. The utopian nature of these expectations are apparent. True believers will not be swayed by facts about events in Iran or probing questions about their blueprints. By the same token, however, fewer people will become true believers.

An example of this highly idealistic and theoretical approach is couched in the following terms:

> In an Islamic system the book of God would not be a book . . . that people merely read. Instead every verse must be applied and every expression in the Qur'an and the Sunnah must be carried out. All of life must proceed according to Islam since . . . everything is included in the universal Islamic system. What we want is for people's lives to be regulated by Islam. We do not want Islamic law to be one of the sources of legislation. Instead, [it] must be the only source of legislation.[49]

Even a domestic utopia, however, was too limited for Faraj's ambition. He saw an Islamic state in Egypt as a stage toward recreating the Islamic caliphate and reuniting all Muslims. "The serious effort to bring back the caliphate . . . is encumbent upon every Muslim," who must swear allegiance to it. He quoted Muhammad as saying, "God shrank the earth so that I could see its east and west, and that my nation's domain shall reach all that had been shrunk for me to see." Faraj adds, "This has not happened yet, because there are still countries which the Muslims have not conquered in any of the ages past. But, God willing, it shall come to pass." Faraj tried to take the first step in that direction by assassinating Sadat.[50]

The wide gap between this maximalist position of the revolutionary fundamentalists and the Brotherhood's view is illustrated by al-Tilimsani's response to that deed: "I oppose violence in any form . . . This is not only a political position, but also a personal position bound in my own character . . . Even if I am oppressed, I shall never turn to violence . . . Never in all my days has it come into my mind to take part in an assassination . . . or a conspiracy against any person . . . regardless of who that person was . . . Despite the fact that Sadat was most evil to me . . . I felt sad."[51]

While fundamentalists suggest that only Islamic government can restrain the ruler from being tyrannical, it is appropriate to recall

Marx's dictum that even the educator must be educated. In short, the true interpretation of God's law may seem obvious to each fundamentalist but they cannot even agree among themselves on which is correct. Thus, the ruler in an Islamic state can be arbitrary and fundamentalist groups within Egypt can be so divided because they have a diversity of views on how to apply Islam. The fundamentalists would probably not be united in seeking Islamic revolution; only force could settle their differences over how to govern an Islamic state.

In these battles, the mainstream clergy are more likely to appeal to Egypt's Muslims than are revolutionary fundamentalists who question the people's piety and demand that they embrace new, radical doctrines. Three leading clerics – Shaykh Muhammad Mutawalli al-Sha'rawi, Shakyh Muhammad al-Tayyib al-Najjar, and Shaykh Muhammad al-Ghazali – ridiculed the radicals at a conference in al-Azhar. How can they claim that Egypt is full of infidels, al-Sha'rawi asked, while there are thousands of mosques and millions of believers? Islam, the trio insisted, is based on education and knowledge, not on "victory through oppression" or "shouting and clamor."[52]

In the 1950s, the Brotherhood had two leading figures. Qutb considered Egyptian society as based on "opposition to God's rule over the earth . . . by allowing man to unduly arrogate to himself the right to establish values, to legislate . . . and to take positions, all without regard to divine ethnics . . . For Islam, there are only two kinds of society: Muslim and jahiliyyah." In contrast, Hudaybi argued that Egypt is a Muslim society but that it was necessary to preach within the existing regime to overcome ignorance and advance toward an Islamic society.[53]

This debate still characterizes the arguments among fundamentalists in contemporary Egypt. The revolutionary fundamentalists and some jam'iyats insist that violent revolution is necessary to create an Islamic state. More numerous groups – the mainstream clergy, the Brotherhood, and other jam'iyats – call for energetic, militant organization to seek reforms which can create an Islamic society. Qutb argued that only a vanguard could rebuild Islam, while more moderate fundamentalists favor education and mass organization. The struggle within fundamentalism is as important as that between the Islamicists and the regime. Egyptians will have to decide whether to see their own Muslim identity in traditional terms – asserting authenticity by reviving their own historic practices – or to redefine it radically by accepting the revolutionaries' view of their religion.

9 Assessments and Conclusions

Islamic fundamentalism became an increasingly important political factor in Egypt in the late 1970s and the 1980s. Several developments indicated the growth of radical Islam in Egypt:

- Believers in its cause assassinated President Sadat in 1981.
- Students and young people have become drawn to Islamic groups in their search for spiritual meaning and a moral ideology to guide the adaptation of Egyptian society of modern life.
- Muslim Brotherhood activists following an electoral strategy made their organization the leading opposition movement in the late 1980s.
- Secular and leftist Egyptians, shocked at the rise of fundamentalism, rushed to accommodate it, further reinforcing the influence of the new current.

While the importance of Egyptian fundamentalism should not be ignored, the barriers to its seizure of political power should equally not be neglected.

The burden of history weighs heavily on Islamic fundamentalist organizations. They were subjected to tremendous repression in the Nasir and Sadat years, a lesson which still intimidates many older activists and makes them doubt that the regime can be overturned. On the one hand, the successes of the nationalist revolution undermined the attractiveness of fundamentalism and created an appealing alternative ideology. On the other hand, disappointment with decades of "revolution" has made many Egyptians more cynical about creating a new one.

Due to its past defeats at the hands of the government, the sufferings of its leaders, and the opportunities permitted under Mubarak, the Muslim Brotherhood has significantly changed its strategy and tactics. The Brotherhood has not been involved in any violence since Sadat permitted its reactivation. While the group's rhetoric is often fiercely radical, its actions have been far more moderate. It professes itself to be a reformist organization, combating extremism by its own example, and committed to working within the system. This approach might be altered if new leadership takes over the group or in the event of a national crisis which discredited the current political leadership.

The revolutionary fundamentalist groups – the jama'at – have remained small, divided, and generally unsuccessful. The three best known organizations each failed to survive the aftermath of a spectacular terrorist action. There are few signs of broad popular support for revolutionary fundamentalist groups which advocate violent revolution to establish an Islamic state. It is particularly important to note that the ideology of each group differs in significant ways from traditional Islam as practiced in Egypt. This factor alienates many Muslims from these groups.

A still developing phenomenon is that of the jam'iyat. These campus Islamic groups remain strong and often attract the most energetic and able students. Their ideology is diverse, ranging from pro-jama'at to pro-Brotherhood. One should be careful of judging the success of all jam'iyat by the standard of Asyut, which is their stronghold. Even more interesting has been the development of community jam'iyat groups which, in some cases, have resorted to low-level violence. These organizations may fuel future crises by engaging in economic or anti-Christian rioting.

While the Egyptian government may be unable to solve many of the country's most pressing problems, it has learned how to adopt flexible tactics to cope with the fundamentalists. The Mubarak regime has had a good deal of success in suppressing extremists and coopting moderates. One of the regime's main assets in handling the revolutionary fundamentalist threat has been the support it has enjoyed from most Islamic clerics. The regime's control of al-Azhar, the awqaf (religious trusts), the Muslim school system, the appointment of preachers, religious programming on television and radio, and most of Egypt's mosques is a powerful instrument. As a consequence, almost all fundamentalist groups are led by lay people and there is a strong element of anti-clericalism in Egyptian fundamentalism.

A sharp distinction should be drawn between the appeal of traditionalism and Islam as a psychological/cultural force shaping people's behavior and the appeal of radical fundamentalism as a political movement capable of seizing power in Egypt. In other words, a return to Islamic norms is more supportive of the orthodox ulama and a relatively non-political Islam than it is of revolutionary fundamentalism. Despite its name, radical "fundamentalism" is a movement of innovation, challenging the way in which Islam has actually been practiced in Egypt over generations. This makes it harder for the extremists to recruit large numbers of Egyptians than an outside observer might expect.

Egyptian fundamentalists are inward-looking and foreign policy issues have relatively low priority for them. They believe, however, that the West, the Communists, and the Jews are waging a battle against Islam and seek to control – or are already controlling – Egypt. Any increase in American cultural influence, political leverage, or presence is extremely worrisome for them. Fundamentalists have the capability to become a major force for anti-Americanism in Egypt and a source for anti-U.S. terrorism. The Brotherhood tends to see the villains in their country as external forces, making it possible for the Muslim Brotherhood to cooperate with the government. The revolutionaries see the government as the puppet of the foreigners. Both fundamentalist streams resent any close Egyptian relations with Washington or Moscow, and prefer a policy of neutrality in the superpower conflict, though the Brotherhood may prefer the United States as a somewhat lesser evil to the USSR if forced to choose between them.

Egyptian fundamentalist groups do not have foreign sponsors nor do they seek foreign models. They are not particularly friendly toward Iran, whose regime they have criticized. Their contacts with fundamentalist groups in other countries are relatively limited.

Though the fundamentalists are opposed to foreign influence, reject any peace with Israel, and usually oppose close relations with the United States, they also argue that there is nothing they can do about these things until they are in power. Thus, they tend to postpone actual actions against foreign interests. Even when they resort to terrorist actions, they usually attack Egyptian targets.

Moderate and radical groups have demanded the immediate implementation of the Shari'ah (Islamic Law). The government has refused, while promising a gradual implementation in the future. In the short run, the fundamentalists – who enjoy a great deal of popular support on the Shari'ah issue – have been quiescent. But frustration could lead to intensified activism on this question.

A central question among fundamentalists is whether or not it is appropriate to use violence against fellow Muslims. It is difficult for the revolutionaries to justify killing or other terrorism against Egyptians and such actions lead to an erosion of support for them. The mainstream ulama and the Brotherhood argue for non-violent means of activity; jam'iyats usually eschew violence – except in limited cases of attacks on men talking to women students or against stores selling videos or alcohol – in order to continue operating above ground.

Similarly, the ulama and the Brotherhood argue that education, persuasion, and reform can make Egypt a more Islamic society. Revolutionaries respond that the current system is too corrupt and anti-Islamic. An Islamic state must be created to impose the Shari'ah. Fundamentalists provide an unclear picture of what an Islamic policy would look like. They favor a private enterprise or mixed economy along with an authoritarian political structure.

It seems reasonable to suggest that fundamentalism has peaked in Egypt for at least the time being. In the case of a systemic crisis – most likely brought about by a breakdown in Egypt's already weak economic order and infrastructure – revolutionary Islamic fundamentalism could become a popular movement. Such an outcome, however, is by no means inevitable. Fundamentalists would have to overcome their deep divisions in doctrine and leadership. The forces opposing the idea that revolutionary Islam is the answer for Egypt's woes are stronger than expected. But a moderate brand of Islam, combined with nationalism, might be an instrument for a military or successor national leadership to govern in a crisis.

There are sharp distinctions between the different kinds of fundamentalist groups. Each has its own ideology, strategy, and constituency which is not easily transferable to the other types of organizations. These divisions – and the lack of charismatic leaders who bridge them – weaken the overall Islamic movement and make it particularly hard for the revolutionaries to recruit followers.

The Muslim Brotherhood has adopted a reformist strategy. The government does not grant it fully legal status but allows it to engage in propaganda and electoral activity through other groups. This relative freedom contrasts in the leaders' eyes with their long imprisonment in past decades. The Brotherhood has wealthy supporters who have much to lose in the event of a thorough-going repression or social instability. Thus, the Brotherhood has become a status quo organization, even opposing street demonstrations.

The Brotherhood's strategy is to conduct educational activities; increase its role in parliament; convert non-fundamentalist politicians; and build support among campus, professional, and neighborhood groups. The immediate objective is to win the implementation of the Shari'ah as the basis for Egypt's law. This step, the group's ideologists argue, would begin the transformation of Egypt into an

Islamic society. The Brotherhood often expresses sharp criticism about social and economic conditions in Egypt, corruption, and foreign influence in the country. Still, it also sometimes complimented President Mubarak and praised his semi-pluralist system. Moreover, it attacked revolutionaries as being immature and deviationist. The government's obduracy created these movements, it charges, but the revolutionaries were incapable of overthrowing the regime and were counterproductive in terms of Islam.

The jama'at disdain the Brotherhood as reformist. They recruit mostly among students, though sometimes from poorer immigrants to the cities. In contrast to the bureaucratic Brotherhood structure, the jama'at are semi-underground cults centered around a charismatic leader. These groups – deeply divided among themselves – generally adopted the concept of jahiliyyah, branding Egypt as a profoundly pagan society. The parliament has no right to decide about the Shari'ah, the jama'at argue, and even if it is "implemented," the government is too corrupt to do so properly. Jama'at strategy is armed revolution but these groups have been repeatedly drawn into small-scale terrorist activity and crushed by the government. Yet their goal remains the creation of an Islamic state.

The jam'iyat stand as intermediate between the Brotherhood and the jama'at, with some supporting each side and serving as a pool of recruits for them. These groups produce less theoretical writing than do the Brotherhood and revolutionaries because they are more action-oriented. The student organizations complain about the problems faced by those attending universities and take some steps to improve the situation. The community groups try to become a type of local council which opposes crime, Western films, and alcohol. Many jam'iyat have been involved in small-scale intimidation and violence but have not used arms. Doctors, lawyers, and other professional groups have been formed which are close to, though not necessarily controlled by, the Brotherhood. Some jam'iyat are built around independent mosques led by charismatic preachers.

The jam'iyat's strategy is to organize growing sections of Egyptian society to create islands of Islamic practice. Rather than seek to overthrow the government or to gain power through legal channels, the jam'iyat try to ignore the government and create their own alternative institutions. They are less concerned about parliament invoking the Shari'ah, instead they try to live within their own interpretation of Islamic law. The jama'at remain the most inchoate and flexible type of group which bear close watching in the future.

The mainstream clergy are generally pro-government. The regime uses its control over al-Azhar, the awqaf, the religious school system, the media, and other institutions to ensure that prominent ulama support its policies. While the clergy receive material benefits from the government, they are also genuinely horrified by the jama'ats' interpretation of Islam. They worry that radical activity will bring instability, which they sometimes see as the product of foreign conspiracies. They favor the invocation of the Shari'ah and hope the government will do so. They stress the need to educate the people and for individuals to begin implementing Islam in their own lives.

Each of these groups, then, has a clear doctrine, strategy, and goal. The key question is how the masses of Egyptians seeking a more Islamic identity will relate to these options. It seems likely that most of them will find the Islam of the clerics to be most congenial and familiar, even when they criticize the ulama for ineffectiveness or hypocrisy. It is important to remember that the ulama represent traditional Islam while the revolutionaries have sought to institute a revolution in Muslim doctrine as well as a political revolution.

10 The Islamist Revolt

During the 1990s, Egyptian Islamists—especially the older al-Jihad and the Islamic Group (IG) which emerged from the jam'iyat movement—staged a revolutionary war against the regime which peaked during the decade's first half and declined thereafter. They were defeated for a variety of reasons including the government's clever, multilayered strategy; the strength of the regime's institutions and the security agencies' loyalty; the lack of popular support for the radicals; and divisions among the insurgent groups.

Mubarak constantly portrayed Egyptian Islamism as the product of outside forces, especially hinting at Iranian involvement, while minimizing the domestic problem and claiming that the insurgents were being defeated. Even in 1992, when it was clearly untrue, he insisted that "The terrorist organization has effectively been destroyed."[1] He maintained the same line continuously throughout the decade.[2]

The government, however, did not underestimate its opposition and developed a multilevel strategy for victory. Repression was the foundation stone, with an energetic policy of raids, arrests, trials, torture, intimidation, and executions. But at the same time, large amounts of money were offered to those helping the police, while repentant extremists ready to denounce their former groups were rewarded and freed from prison. Several thousand defectors accepted this deal.[3]

The regime worked hard to discredit the revolutionaries as improper Muslims and to deny them popular support. In addition, it tightened control over all institutions, including schools, professional associations, village governments, and religious institutions to deny control of them to the Islamists and punish supporters of the revolutionaries. It also pursued domestic cultural and foreign policies designed to appease the largest elements of its own public and especially the Muslim sectors. Al-Azhar was strengthened and put under moderate leadership to combat the extremists, but this step thus gave it as well as the non-radical ulama more influence in Egyptian society.[4] This was the area where the government could be said to practice the most appeasement of its critics. Finally, the government argued that economic development would undercut the radical cause. The one thing the regime did not do—and which was beyond its power to do—was to solve Egypt's deep-seated social and economic problems that had partly led to the profound discontent.

PROBLEMS WITHIN THE REVOLUTIONARY MOVEMENT

Among the radicals' own weaknesses were their many splits. A cleric involved in al-Jihad remarked that the real reason there were "thousands" of groups and factions was that "everybody wishes to be a leader."[5] Some jam'iyat groups and activists remained faithful to their earlier non-violent strategy; others, swept along by revolutionary enthusiasm and the urgings of some extremist clerics, took up arms. Yet jam'iyat insurgents were also the first to abandon the armed struggle when they concluded it was not working. Defeat also split al-Jihad among those who wanted to give up violence, those who wished to continue the battle against the Egyptian government, and those who switched to American targets in alliance with Usama bin Ladin.

Another shortcoming of the movement was that many of the enthusiasts for armed struggle took their ideas from foreign rather than Egyptian realities. An estimated 300 to 700 al-Jihad members had fought with the mujahidin in Afghanistan against the Soviets, which gave them military experience but also a basis for misestimating the problems of staging an uprising at home.[6]

Moreover, as the original Islamist activists from the 1970s and 1980s were killed, imprisoned, or lost interest in revolutionary action, those staging the revolt became younger and less educated. According to an Egyptian study, only 33 percent of the militants of the 1970s had been under 25 years of age, while this was true of 71 percent in the 1990s. While in the 1970s, 79 percent of the activists had some higher education, by the 1990s this number had fallen to 20 percent. And while as little as 8 percent of the militants in the 1970s had come from rural areas, in the 1990s 54 percent were from villages and shantytowns. The revolutionaries' profile had moved closer to that of the typical Egyptian, but the quality of leadership was falling and the movement became more tied to Upper Egypt, where organizing was easier but seizing state power harder.[7]

There were also particular problems with the revolutionaries' selection of violent tactics. These included the assassination of officials, attacks on security forces, attacks on Coptic Christians, and assaults on tourists. All of these types of actions raised problems for the radicals. Killing Arabs and Muslims challenged both nationalist and traditional Islamic thinking and was unpopular: Copts were at least fellow Egyptians, and striking them seemed to undermine national unity. Murdering tourists—though they be foreigners and non-Muslims—damaged the livelihood of many Egyptians. Thus, the armed struggle failed largely due to two fundamental problems: the government overpowered the rebels militarily and the masses did not rally to the rebels' side.

In carrying out assassinations, the radical Islamists tried to repeat what they considered their greatest accomplishment, the killing of Anwar Sadat. On October 12, 1990, members of al-Jihad assassinated parliament speaker Rifa't Mahgub and his bodyguards in Cairo.[8] In 1993, Islamist radicals attacked the information minister in April, the interior minister in August, and the prime minister in November, wounding the first two and injuring numerous bystanders.[9]

At the insurgency's peak, several attempts were made to assassinate Mubarak.[10] This goal was almost realized on June 26, 1995, in Addis Ababa, Ethiopia, as Mubarak was arriving to attend the Organization of African Unity summit. A group fired at the president's car killing two Ethiopian bodyguards. Later that year, an Egyptian diplomat was murdered in Switzerland and, in November, Egyptian Islamists bombed Egypt's embassy in Pakistan, killing 15 and wounding about 70 people. The Islamic Group declared that killing Mubarak remained its "sacred duty."[11] But the attempt to win a quick, decisive victory by decapitating Egypt's government or intimidating the rulers clearly failed.

Most Islamist attacks were against security forces. While there were sporadic clashes in Cairo, especially in poor neighborhoods where radical Islamists had gained a foothold, most violence took place in the south. Each attack was followed by police raids, which sometimes led to additional shoot-outs and mass arrests. Clash followed clash and shoot-out followed shoot-out, year after year. The government's goal, said Asyut security chief, Major General Mahmud al-Fakhrani in 1990, was "The total elimination of radical strongholds everywhere." By July 1990, 1,225 al-Jihad members were jailed and the number of prisoners would increase sharply in the next few years.[12]

Nevertheless, violence increased in 1992, Egypt's bloodiest year since Sadat's assassination in 1981, with constant attacks on police in Upper Egypt and Cairo along with the beginning of the anti-tourist campaign. The government tried new strategies against the insurgents. A revised anti-terrorism law increased sentences for aiding, encouraging, or even expressing sympathy for terrorists. Trials were held by military courts. And large-scale military operations were staged to sweep areas with large concentrations of rebels. Among them was the week-long December 1992 campaign in Cairo's Imbaba district involving 14,000 soldiers and resulting in 700 arrests along with the seizure of weapons.[13] Afterward, Mubarak said, "Perhaps as many as 90 percent of the extremists and terrorists have been captured and . . . the terrorist organization has been destroyed, crushed."[14]

But in March 1993, 21 people were killed and hundreds more arrested in nine raids in Cairo and Aswan.[15] And in December an attack on an island in the Nile near Asyut resulted in the arrest of scores of suspected IG members who, the government declared, were planning to assassinate officials and bomb government offices. Between the end of 1992 and the end of 1994 Egyptian military courts sentenced 58 Islamists to death (20 of them in 1994), of whom 41 were executed (13 in 1994).[16] Still, for a time, the level of insurgency continued to grow. At least 70 people were killed during 1992 in terrorist attacks and in subsequent clashes with police, with twice as many injured.[17] But in 1993 more than 300 people were killed, about the same number in 1994, and around 400 in 1995.[18]

For a while, Islamist revolutionaries were able to stage more sophisticated attacks, using small squads to shoot up police cars and stations as well as assassinating high-ranking officers. In Asyut alone, 54 people were killed between January and March 1994, including 30 policemen, 11 militants, and 13 civilians, showing that the rebels were winning. In addition, 67 people were injured there.[19] On January 2, 1995 alone, the Islamic Group claimed responsibility for killing 11 people and wounding 6 in 4 separate attacks.[20] By 1995, however, most of the casualties occurred in Upper Egypt and fewer in Cairo.[21] "They suffered backbreaking blows that eradicated their infrastructure and smashed their criminal acts," Mubarak claimed in May 1995.[22] Between 1992 and 1995 the war had caused the death of around 1,000 people, including Islamists, police, and civilians. As Mubarak suggested, the pace of violence slowed in late 1995 and fell off further in 1996 to less than 200 dead (some figures put it far lower) and 78 wounded.[23] Meanwhile, the police kept up the pressure, arresting 3,630 alleged extremists in 1995 and 3,933 in 1996.[24] A number of Islamic Group leaders were killed or captured. During 1996, al-Jihad was so hard hit that it did not claim any attacks in Egypt.

Yet even in 1996, only about 20 percent of those killed were extremists. The Islamic Group continued hit-and-run attacks in Upper Egypt against police and began robbing jewelry stores to finance its operations.[25] In a fitting symbol of the continuing insurgency, on April 18, 1996, one day after the Egyptian cabinet congratulated Interior Minister Hasan al-Alfi on his "victory in the war against terrorism," Islamic Group gunmen killed 18 Greek tourists and wounded 14 outside a Cairo hotel.[26] More government offensives followed, further depleting the radical forces and reducing, but not altogether eliminating, the insurgency. In 1997, the government introduced new identity cards and passed a law requiring a license to preach in mosques. It was designed to control the huge numbers of private mosques often used by the radicals. This regulation was endorsed by the state-backed clerics of al-Azhar.[27] In Upper

Egypt there continued to be attacks on policemen by the Islamic Group, despite the efforts of some of its leaders to declare a ceasefire. Fatalities rose in 1997 but by 1998 it was clear that the government had broken the insurgency.[28] There were constant splits from al-Jihad and the Islamic Group which tried to restart the battle with little success. The government stepped up its long-standing efforts to get militants extradited from Europe and Pakistan and to cut off the flow of funds to them from the Gulf Arab states, with some success,[29] and kept the Muslim Brotherhood on the defensive through frequent arrests.

Thus, the government did defeat the insurgency, although it could not eliminate the radical Islamists altogether.[30] In 1998, the number of deaths from terrorist-related incidents was 47, less than one-third of the previous year and the lowest since 1992.[31] It was at this moment that the radical Islamists split, sensing the need for an entirely new strategy. One group, mainly from al-Jihad but including some Islamic Group members, joined forces with Usama bin Ladin and redirected their target from Egypt's government to the United States.[32] Another faction, mostly from the Islamic Group, called for a ceasefire with the government, seeking to return to their earlier strategy as a militant version of the Brotherhood.[33] As a result, the level of violence fell even further in 1999.[34] The government, despite its refusal to negotiate, released more than 2,000 Islamic Group prisoners during the year.[35] The regime continued, however, to arrest, kill, and try insurgents still active, including Farid Kidwani, the Islamic Group's operational leader in Egypt,[36] killed in a shoot-out.

Despite the massive amount of suffering, casualties, and wasted resources they had inflicted on Egypt, the Islamists had come nowhere near to staging a revolution. They had assumed that God was on their side, that their ideology properly mirrored divine intentions, and that the masses would inevitably follow them. All their strategic and tactical ideas were proven wrong. Some were willing at least to reconsider their tactics, while others persisted in the belief that victory was inevitable.

While far higher levels of support for the Islamists in Upper Egypt were reactions to the government's neglect of that region and perhaps the area's more traditionalist tone, a key element in the movement's limited success was interreligious hatred. Although the Islamists' official line was that they would protect the rights of Coptic Christians if that group accepted subordinate status, anti-Christian violence was one of the Islamists' main themes. For example, one Brotherhood leader praised his movement's good relations with Copts but also said they should pay the special jizya tax as non-Muslims and claimed they would betray Egypt if a Christian nation attacked it.[37]

There were constant attacks on Coptic Christians, mainly in southern Egypt. In March 1990, for example, Islamists set fire to two Christian churches, a Christian hospital, and other property in the Minya province after being stirred up at a Friday prayer service by groundless rumors that a Christian boy had seduced a Muslim girl. Islamist leaflets had urged Muslims to "Wipe Out the Disgrace," calling Christians "Crusaders." About 100 demonstrators were arrested.[38] In April, after a false rumor that a five-year-old Muslim girl had been raped by a Copt, Muslims attacked a church in the Fayyum province, killing a guard and wounding 12 others.[39] There were many such riots in Upper Egypt, resulting in numerous deaths. In virtually every case, Muslims attacked Christians, setting fire to houses, shops, and churches, killing people merely because of their religion. The same pattern happened in the Inbaba district of Cairo, an Islamist stronghold where Copts were harassed.[40]

THE ANTI-TOURIST CAMPAIGN

Another main feature of the Islamists' revolutionary campaign in the 1990s was the anti-tourist campaign. This tactic could be attributed to several motives: to mobilize Egypt against wealthier, unpopular, non-Muslim foreigners; to gain international publicity; to strike at the West; to cleanse Egypt of alien cultural influences; and to weaken the regime by destroying one of the country's main sources of income. After all, tourism is Egypt's largest single source of foreign income bringing in $4 billion a year.[41]

Perhaps this tactic began spontaneously. As early as July 13, 1990, an employee of a hotel on the Red Sea threw a Molotov cocktail into the restaurant. A German and a French woman died and three other tourists were severely burned. The terrorist complained that the tourists were "offending Islam" by their behavior.[42]

By 1992, the Islamic Group had launched a systematic, high-priority effort to murder and maim visitors to Egypt. In June and July, homemade bombs were thrown at tourists in Luxor, one of Egypt's greatest tourist attractions.[43] As the main tourist season began later in the year, there were shootings at Nile ships carrying tourists, bombs on trains, and assaults on buses. "Tourism must be hit because it is corrupt," said one of the Islamic Group's leaders, and it "brings alien customs and morals which offend Islam, especially the attire of some women."[44]

Moderate clerics rejected this view. Shaykh Muhammad al-Ghazali remarked, "Whoever attacks a tourist is a traitor against Islam. It is a duty of Muslims to let others acquaint themselves with us. Should we let them know us as murderers?"[45] Officials played down attacks as rare acts by "a perverted minority of outlaws." Egypt, Minister of Tourism Fu'ad Sultan insisted, was still "the safest place in the world for tourists."[46]

Nevertheless, the attacks by the Islamic Group continued. In February 1993, a Molotov cocktail was thrown at a group of South Koreans outside a Cairo hotel. There were many such operations throughout 1994. In February 1994, after it warned foreign tourists and investors to leave Egypt,[47] the Islamic Group made three armed attacks on tourist buses and one on a Nile cruise ship.[48] A German tourist was killed in March. In August, it murdered a Spanish boy and wounded three others in an attack on a bus. In September, three more tourists were killed in a shooting.[49] The Islamic Group also threatened participants in the UN International Conference on Population and Development that took place in Cairo. Though no incidents occurred, many Islamists opposed the meeting as a forum supporting birth control.[50] In September, a German tourist was killed in the south and in October, another German tourist was killed there. Others, both Europeans and Egyptians, were wounded in the attacks.[51]

There were also more attacks in 1995 and 1996, most notably the killing of 18 Greek tourists in Cairo in April 1996 and the November 1997 massacre of 58 tourists and 4 Egyptians in Luxor, one of the most popular destinations for visitors. The Luxor attack was a short-run disaster for Egypt's tourist industry, but it also increased the unpopularity of the radical Islamist forces. The murders were denounced by the leader of al-Azhar, Muhammad Sayyid Tantawi—who came to the town to condemn those responsible as "traitors and cowards who sold their souls to the devil"—and by Brotherhood leaders.[52]

Thereafter, though, there were relatively few attacks, most notably one in September 1997 outside the National Museum in Cairo where 10 were killed. The campaign against tourists had cost Egypt hundreds of millions of dollars but had not destroyed either the government or the tourist industry itself. The radicals "lost public opinion," an Egyptian researcher observed, "especially because of the attacks on tourists. Rank-and-file support has also eroded, with the most capable members in jail or dead."[53]

THE MUSLIM BROTHERHOOD

As with the Luxor attack, the Muslim Brotherhood tried hard to distance itself from the violent revolutionaries and to insist that its own goals and methods were moderate. Spokesman Ma'mun al-Hudaybi claimed the organization did not seek an Islamist regime dominated by clerics, even promised to accept Christians into the government it hoped to form. The radical groups, he said, "have lost hope and despaired of the possibility of a peaceful evolution, hence they resort to violence ... [while] the Brothers believe in quiet change and hold that violence and hatred are un-Islamic. We are trying to educate the public by disseminating the right values and their true meanings."[54]

This stance made the Brotherhood seem an attractive partner for the regime, providing an alternative, non-violent path for Islamist feelings. In effect, the government could wager that the Brotherhood would remain a reformist group which posed no short-term threat and could be ultimately coopted; or at least would make no meaningful progress toward challenging the existing order in Egypt.

At the same time, the government knew that the Brotherhood had a tremendous potential appeal for Egyptians, given both the piety of large elements of the masses and the persuasiveness of the message. Egyptian officials could also observe how the mainstream equivalent of the Brotherhood in Algeria, the Islamic Salvation Front, spearheaded a bloody revolt against the regime there that denied it an election victory. Indeed, while the Brotherhood may have toned down its ambitions of gaining power in Egypt, it made no secret of them. Hudaybi explained that the group opposed the regime but was "in no hurry to attain power."[55] The government was certainly not ready for a fair electoral test. The Brotherhood also blamed terrorism on the government rather than on the insurgents' goals or ideology. In Hudaybi's words, "Terrorism occurs when the government uses violence, pressures the people and rigs elections. The regime is not prepared to remain democratic. Consequently, it rejects the idea of a strong and influential opposition."[56]

Nevertheless, within the Brotherhood there had always been more militant factions which sympathized with the revolutionaries and perhaps even imitated them. Periodically, individuals and groups had left the organization to join or establish radical splinter groups. Moreover, by spreading Islamist ideas and taking over major institutions—including mosques and professional groupings—the Brotherhood was extending its influence throughout society and providing a potential support base for the militants' violence. For example, while Hudaybi condemned Fuda's murder, he blamed the killing on Fuda himself because of his writings "and the provocative manner in which he attacked Islam.[57]

Three specific examples from 1992 illustrate both the Brotherhood's potential power and the reason why the government decided to intimidate it during the 1990s. First, in 1992 the Brotherhood had taken over the lawyers' association for the first time, winning 15 of 25 seats on its board, partly due to a low voter turnout and the group's disciplined membership. This meant that the Brotherhood controlled the organizations of physicians, engineers, dentists, pharmacists, and merchants. Only the journalists' association eluded its control.[58] The government moved to disrupt this situation by passing new regulations and harassing Brotherhood members who were officers in these associations.

Second, when Egypt suffered a major earthquake in October 1992, the Brotherhood proved more effective than the government in providing relief, while distributing propaganda at the same time to those it helped. This humanitarian effort increased the group's popularity. The government then barred such efforts. "If anyone wants to do anything, they should do it through the government," stated Interior Minister Abd al-Halim Musa, who asked, "what is this becoming, a state within a state?"[59]

Finally, three owners of the Salsabil computer company, all Brotherhood activists, were arrested and found to possess data they had gathered on secret military projects and public opinion. It was seen as a Brotherhood intelligence organization and they were charged with, among other things, using computer devices to manipulate professional association elections."[60]

Also as part of this campaign against the Brotherhood, the government—through the court system—repeatedly rejected its requests to be made a legal organization.[61] Since it functioned on the border of the law, it was easy to find pretexts for arresting Brotherhood officials and activists. For example, in June 1992, 50 members were arrested in Zaqaziq for allegedly "planning to topple the government."[62] The government's rhetoric was even harsher than it's actions. Muhammad Sa'id al-Ashmawi, chief justice of the High Court of Appeals and the High Court for State Security, warned, "The Muslim Brothers and the terrorist groups are two sides of the same coin. . . . Experience has shown that they are not a moderate lot."[63]

The Brotherhood continued to condemn terrorism, proclaim its respect for the law, and oppose the anti-tourist campaign. But the regime continued to disbelieve these assertions. It is hard to know to what extent the government had reliable intelligence that some members or even leaders of the Brotherhood did have covert ties with the insurgents, justifying the statements being made by Ashmawi and others, or to what extent it just saw the group as a potential threat.

In May 1994, after an Islamist lawyer, Abd al-Harith al-Madani, died in police custody, the Brotherhood-controlled Bar Association charged he had been tortured to death. It organized large rallies and a one-day strike demanding an investigation and the release of all imprisoned lawyers. Another 37 lawyers were arrested during this conflict.[64]

The more effective and popular the Brotherhood seemed, the more the government was motivated to move against it. Mubarak responded by calling the Brotherhood "an illegal organization that is behind most of the activities of the religious troublemakers." The popular Brotherhood preacher Muhammad al-Ghazali was prevented from giving an Id al-Adha sermon to tens of thousands of worshippers in Cairo. The Brotherhood's leader, 81-year-old Shaykh Hamid Abu al-Nasr, was questioned by police about illegal publications bearing his signature. Dozens of other members were arrested.[65] Hudaybi again denied any connection between the Brotherhood and the militants and said there was no proof his organization had ever been involved in "supporting, inciting or participating in actions violating the law."[66]

But the Brotherhood-backed *al-Sha'b* made the sort of threat that inspired the government's crackdown by warning that the regime would soon be toppled. It could only delay "the date of the funeral, but the funeral [was] inevitable."[67]

At one point, Hudaybi asked whether the anti-Brotherhood campaign was taking place "because the government wants to remind us that it is still there?"[68] Yes, that was precisely the regime's point, not to crush the organization but to contain and intimidate it.

In 1995, the level of anti-Brotherhood activity was even higher. Mubarak again insisted, "The Muslim Brothers, al-Jihad, the Islamic groups, and the rest of them, are all the same."[69] During that year, the government cracked down on the Brotherhood-dominated professional associations and the group's attempts to run parliamentary candidates. New laws let courts supervise association elections and remove serving officers, a power used to take the engineers and lawyers groups away from the Brotherhood. Dozens of association and Brotherhood leaders and parliamentary candidates were arrested, many of them then tried before military courts. In January 1995, 27 activists, including the deputy leader of the doctors' association, were taken into custody and charged with seeking to topple the regime.[70]

As the elections approached, repression increased. Among the Brotherhood candidates arrested in September and October was Sayf al-Islam al-Bana, son of the organization's founder and a prominent leader.[71] In November, a week before the balloting, the court sentenced 54 Brothers to prison terms of 3 to 5 years and ordered closed the organization's headquarters.[72] Finally, according to the Brotherhood, two days before the elections over 1,000 of its members were detained, including 300 who were to be involved in overseeing the polls.[73]

In the end, Mubarak's ruling party and its supporters won more than 400 of 444 parliamentary seats. The Brotherhood won one seat on the Socialist

Labor party ticket.[74] Yet there was also no let-up in 1996. In January, the Brotherhood's 83-year-old leader Hamid Abu al-Nasr died and was replaced by the 74-year-old Mustafa Mashhur, who asked sarcastically how the government could allow drugs and alcohol while waging a repressive war against Islam.[75] Retention of control by the older generation alienated many younger members. So did the leaders' support for a new land law which hurt small farmers.[76] One reaction was the formation of the Wasat party. While the Wasat party apparently was an enterprise by younger dissident Brotherhood members opposed by the leadership, the government saw it as a front for that organization and was determined not to grant it a license.[77] Ironically, in June 1996, 13 leading figures of the Brotherhood were put on trial for allegedly creating the party as part of a revolutionary plot.[78]

As the April 1997 local elections drew closer, there were new rounds of arrests. The Brotherhood decided to boycott the elections due to this harassment, which included accusations of revolutionary conspiracy on the part of their sole parliamentary member, but was ready to let supporters run as independents. These candidates, however, were intimidated in an attempt to make them withdraw while other activists were arrested. Again, the ruling party won a huge victory with 93 percent of the local posts. The opposition was almost totally excluded.

The litany of arrests and trials continued: 34 activists arrested in Alexandria in August, charged with secretly training for revolution and possessing insurrectionary literature; 70 students jailed in September; the dissolution of a Physicians' Union branch in Alexandria; and a criminal investigation which led to the government's taking over the finances of the Bar Association.[79] In November 1997, Minister of Education Husayn Baha al-Oin banned over 1,600 teachers associated with the Brotherhood from teaching in public schools, ordering them transferred to clerical work.[80] "It is inconceivable," he explained, "that Egypt turn into a second Algeria and serve as a hothouse for terror."[81]

If official harassment of the Brotherhood tapered off after 1997, it was largely because the group had been taught its lesson and the insurgency itself had been defeated.

Indeed, some of the revolutionaries were also reaching this conclusion. In July 1997, a military trial began of 97 militants accused of planning to place bombs at Cairo banks and tourist offices. To everyone's surprise, one defendant read a statement by six Islamic Group leaders jailed for life in connection with Sadat's assassination, calling for an unconditional truce with the government. One of them, Abbud al-Zumur, had been an al-Jihad leader who had joined the Islamic Group in jail.[82] Several imprisoned al-Jihad leaders and Umar Abd al-Rahman, from his New York prison, endorsed the proposal.[83]

One of the radicals' main theorists was Umar Abd al-Rahman. Acquitted of involvement in the assassination of Sadat and again of subversion charges in 1990, he moved to New York, which distance removed him from direct involvement in Egypt's politics but it also protected him from punishment by the authorities there. He sent fiery messages on audio cassettes calling for "a merciless war, a no-holds'-barred battle against the pharaohs and atheists of Egypt." He told followers:

> Before the flames go out in Asyut, light more in Cairo. Before they bring Qina under control, set the towns and villages of the Nile Delta aflame. Disperse them before they disperse you. Fear not their threats. They are a motley of cowards. They are in their death throes and will be crushed under your feet like dirty insects.[84]

Yet Abd al-Rahman did not just advocate Islamist revolution in Egypt. On February 26, 1993, those he influenced or directed bombed the New York World Trade Center, killing six people and injuring over 1,000. Abd al-Rahman and 11 of his followers were charged not only for this attack but also with conspiring to wage a "war of urban terrorism" that included plans to blow up the United Nations building, the Lincoln and Holland Tunnels and the FBI headquarters in the city, among other things.[85] More than two years later, he was found guilty and sentenced to life imprisonment.[86]

If a militant like Abd al-Rahman could endorse a truce, the idea certainly had appeal for the most unbending militants. Nevertheless, leaders of both groups outside Egypt, mainly in Europe and Afghanistan, criticized the plan, claiming it as a regime plot to divide the opposition and end the insurgency. Some observers considered the November 1997 massacre of tourists at Luxor as a sign intended to show a rejection of the truce and continuation of the struggle. Abd al-Rahman also withdrew his approval for the peace initiative.[87]

But the government was equally opposed to the initiative, branding it propaganda to prevent the rebels' impending defeat. Deals, it said, could be concluded between sovereign states, not between a government and a "criminal" organization.[88] In November, the jailed leaders renewed their call for abandoning terror and shifting to non-violent action. This time, however, they conditioned any ceasefire on an end to the government's campaign against Islamic groups and its agreement to break relations with Israel. Again, the move was angrily rejected by Egyptian Islamists abroad who termed it "defeatist and submissive" and a "betrayal of the memory of our martyrs."[89]

Nevertheless, the Islamic Group's leaders in March 1999 adopted a decision to stop violence inside and outside Egypt. The long insurgency, or at least the main battle, was over.

While the revolutionary Islamist groups had used violence during the 1990s, other radical or activist Islamists were working through peaceful means with more success to recruit supporters and to control Egypt's social and intellectual life. This cultural struggle involved a wide range of tactics, from the revolutionaries' use of assassination to legal actions, preaching, teaching, non-governmental organizations meeting citizens' needs, and lobbying activities.

There were three important sectors involved in this struggle: militant independent clerics or activists, senior clerics belonging to ostensibly pro-government institutions, and the Brotherhood. On one hand, since these forces did not support or aid the violence—in fact, they usually explicitly condemned it—and gave young people alternatives to picking up guns, the government could decide to treat them as allies. On the other hand, though, inasmuch as such sectors—especially the Brotherhood—were themselves pushing for an Islamist regime through peaceful means and recruiting those who often became revolutionaries later, the government could see them as enemies and as targets for repression.

The most extreme acts in the cultural struggle were the 1992 murder of writer Faraj Fuda, a critic of the Islamists by al-Jihad,[90] and the 1994 attempted assassination of the Nobel prize-winning novelist Najib Mahfuz. But there were many more incidents and battles. Some of these were won by the Islamists, all of them made for an atmosphere of intimidation, conformity, eagerness to appease Islamist demands, and limiting the size of secularist or modernizing Islamist forces.

Among these included the conviction of Ala Ahmad and his publisher for producing an allegedly heretical book. There was a long court battle over a 1994 film by Yusuf Shahin, "The Emigrant," which portrayed the prophet Joseph, called for normalizing relations with Israel, and depicted a Muslim hero as a eunuch. An Islamist lawyer sued Shahin and won initially, although the case was eventually reversed because the plaintiff did not have sufficient standing. Some clerics harassed a liberal Islamic philosophy lecturer, Dr. Hasan Hanafi, of Cairo University in 1997, accusing him of atheism. Other books were attacked by Islamists and banned by the government for alleged sacrilege.

The case that drew the widest international attention was that of Professor Nasir Hamid Abu Zayd of Cairo University. One of his colleagues accused him of blasphemy for a 1992 book that used critical scholarly methods to analyze phrases in the Qur'an. After a series of conflicting decisions in lower courts, a Cairo court ruled that Zayid was an apostate from Islam and that he and his wife should be legally separated against their will. The professor was accused of being an atheist who was targeting Islam; some clerics called on the government to execute him. The couple fled to Europe.[91] "This is just the beginning," Abd al-Sabur Shahin announced in a Cairo mosque, "we will do this to everyone who thinks they are bigger than Islam."[92] In 1995–96 alone, there were 18 legal suits brought by Islamists against intellectuals for blasphemy. Seven books and one movie were also banned on these grounds.[93]

GOVERNMENT-APPOINTED LEADERS

The two most important clerics in Egypt were both appointed by the government. When al-Azhar's leader Jadd al-Haqq died in 1996, he was replaced by Grand Mufti Muhammad Sayyid Tantawi, a relative liberal who had sanctioned banking interest and family planning while opposing female circumcision. Islamists opposed the minister of health's ban on female circumcision, asserting that Islam obligated female circumcision. A lower court ruled that the state had no jurisdiction on the issue but the High Administrative Court, in December 1997, decided that Islam did not mandate this practice and thus it could be prohibited by the state.

The new grand mufti was Nasir Farid al-Wasil. Wasil was a traditionalist but a flexible one. His first major ruling was that the face veil was not a Muslim custom, although a head cover (hijab) was mandatory for all Muslim women. Tantawi agreed.[94] But there were also conflicts between them. Wasil opposed selecting women for senior government positions while Tantawi supported it. On organ transplants, Tantawi saw such donations as praiseworthy Islamic acts to save lives, while Wasil and other ulama opposed them as contrary to Islam."[95]

There were also some radicals, however, who knew that the war was being lost but also rejected making a truce and accepting the reformist path of the Brotherhood and the state-backed clerics. Their idea was to shift the focus of attack from Egypt's rulers, who were after all Muslims, to foreigners who could more easily—and popularly—be hated and attacked.

One critic of the ceasefire was a former al-Jihad (and now al-Qa'ida) leader Ayman al-Zawahiri, whose life embodied the Egyptian movement's history and the ideological crossroads at which it had arrived in the 1990s. An excerpt from Zawahiri's book, *Knights Under the Prophet's Banner* is included as an appendix. Zawahiri joined the first al-Jihad cell in Cairo in 1966 when he was only 16 years old. He came from a very wealthy and influential Egyptian family and studied medicine.[96]

Zawahiri was much influenced by the ideas on jihad of Muhammad Abd-al-Salam Faraj. He was working at a Muslim Brotherhood sponsored medical clinic in 1980 when its director asked him to go to Afghanistan to provide medical assistance for those fighting the Soviets. He returned after four months but was imprisoned for three years following Sadat's assassination. He was released in 1984 and returned to Afghanistan in 1986. There he played a leading role in the development of Usama bin Ladin's al-Qa'ida group. In February 1998, he signed the statement of the Global Front for Fighting Jews and Crusaders. He played a leading role in the August 1998 bombings of the U.S. embassies in Kenya and Tanzania.

Responding to these deeds, Western governments rounded up al-Jihad leaders in exile and put them in prison or extradited them to Egypt, including Zawahiri's own brother, Muhammad. At the subsequent trial, one prominent al-Jihad figure, Ahmad Salamah Mabruk, Zawahiri's right-hand man who had earlier been sentenced to death, testified against his colleagues. As a result of this case, Zawahiri himself was sentenced to death in absentia in April 1999 and became a fugitive after the U.S. offensive in Afghanistan and the Taliban's fall in November 2001.

Despite his criticisms of colleagues and other Islamist groups, Zawahiri depicts the Islamist revolution in Egypt as a succession of heroic battles by courageous warriors whom the masses will soon join. In fact, though, his account chronicles a series of total defeats and almost total failures punctuated by factional splits and quarrels. His description of the movement's greatest moment and crushed uprising—after its assassination of Sadat in 1981—is typical in this regard. About all Zawahiri could do to illustrate his claims for the movement's popularity is to cite one of the lawyers voicing support for Sadat's killing.

The suppression of the movement by Egypt's government in the 1990s, the failure of the masses to respond, and the decision of some of his colleagues to accept a ceasefire, all pushed Zawahiri to shift his own focus to the Islamist internationalism of al-Qai'da and to focusing on fighting America rather than the Egyptian regime. Moreover, it is clear that his confidence that the movement will triumph is based on his ideological view that it represents God's will and not on material evidence. At times, he suggests that victory could take many decades or even a century or two.

Zawahiri makes two main arguments in his book. First, he critiques both the strategy of the Muslim Brotherhood: not being revolutionary and using violence; and some of his own former colleagues for giving up armed struggle. Second, he urges that the main struggle should be waged against America and Israel, or Christians and Jews, rather than in an effort to overthrow Egypt's government directly. He argues, so to speak, that the road to Cairo runs through Washington and Tel Aviv. Of course, despite his claim that the movement was now united on ideology, Zawahiri's own actions show this not to be the case, and in fact brought about a split in al-Jihad. In addition, the strategy he advocated led the al-Qa'ida organization and its Taliban allies to a defeat. While Zawahiri claims that the record of Egypt's Islamist movement was one of glorious advances, his own account shows that it was one of defeat after defeat. The revolutionary movements remained small and marginal. They had many martyrs but few victories.

Thus, the decision of a minority of Egyptian Islamists to refocus their battle onto America rather than Mubarak was dictated by their failure at home more than by some ideological or religious revelation.

Zawahiri makes this choice sound almost like the result of market research. The masses were dubious about the Islamic propriety of killing other Muslims or rebelling against a government constituted by Muslims, Zawahiri admits, and might like a movement based on anti-Americanism better. The distinction and debate over priorities between the "near" and "far" enemies has always been an important feature of Arab politics, especially in revolutionary ideology. The "near" enemy means the government of the country which the movement wants to overthrow because it is deemed corrupt, wrong-minded, and at the service of the "far" enemies, the West and Israel.

The failure to defeat one has periodically led to a shift in emphasis to the other, since the loss is said to prove that the other enemy is preventing success. In light of the defeat by Israel in 1948, for example, Gamal Abdel Nasser and his colleagues decided the real enemy, responsible for this failure, was the Egyptian monarchy. The Arab states' defeat by Israel in 1967 and the PLO's defeat by Jordan in 1970 led to an emphasis on international terrorism in the 1970s. If the nationalist regimes' coups had failed to bring victory and Israel's own army had defeated them, perhaps a focus on anti-Western struggle would fare better.

Iran's revolution began a new wave of "domestic" revolutionary efforts by Islamist groups in the 1980s. But the overall failure of the Islamist movements to seize power, clear by the mid-1990s, led to the rise of Usama bin Ladin and a renewed emphasis on battling the West. This tendency was reinforced by the fact that the most successful Islamist movements in gaining wide support—though not seizing power—were

Hamas and Hizballah which fought Israel and, in Hizballah's case, also hit Western targets.

This is precisely the pattern arising from the defeat of the revolutionary Islamist movement in Egypt. It at first turned to targeting foreigners and tourists and then, when even this tactic brought only increased repression without an increase in popular support, the movement split. Some favored a ceasefire; others, like Zawahiri, turned to strategies that were even more targeted against foreign enemies. In both cases, pressure on the regime eased.

In a remarkable passage in his book, Zawahiri shows clearly why he and others wanted to refocus the Islamist movement against the United States and Israel rather than their own regimes: "The Muslim nation will not participate [in an Islamist revolution] unless the slogans of the mujahidin are understood by the masses of the Muslim nation," he said, and then explained the only tactic he thought could work:

> The one slogan that has been well understood by the nation and to which it has been responding for the past 50 years is the call for the jihad against Israel [and] against the U.S. presence. It has responded favorably to the call for the jihad against the Americans. A single look at the history of the mujahidin in Afghanistan, Palestine, and Chechnya will show that the jihad movement has moved to the center of the leadership of the nation when it adopted the slogan of liberating the nation from its external enemies and when it portrayed it as a battle of Islam against infidelity and infidels.[97]

In general, Zawahiri added, the Islamists had left the Arab-Israeli conflict in the hands of the secularists, who had lost the wars and were committing treason in seeking to make peace. Ironically, the Islamists "who are the most capable of leading the nation in its jihad against Israel are the least active in championing the issue of Palestine and raising its slogans among the masses."[98]

Even the Brotherhood gave at least lip service to this newly fashionable analysis and strategy. In March 2002 it presented a new martyrdom branch, eight of whose members declared themselves ready to be "suicide bombers" in attacking Israel. One of them explained that the Brotherhood had no intention of becoming involved with any revolution in Egypt: "Our preparations are directed only against the Israeli enemy. . . . We do not permit the blood of Muslims [to be shed], and therefore we will not carry out domestic violence."[99]

This statement implied a critique of the radical movements which had shed much Muslim blood during the 1990s. It is consistent with the Brotherhood's attempt to use the strategy in appealing for legitimacy. On one hand, the Brotherhood tells the regime that it has no intention of waging armed struggle within the country and is, in fact, an ally in the struggle against Israel. On the other hand, it appeals for popular support asking, in effect, how the government could ban and repress a group that is waging a struggle in which all Arabs and Muslims believe. In effect, this is what the Brotherhood had successfully done back in the 1940s and early 1950s—the time of its greatest size and success—portraying itself as an anti-Israel (and anti-British) patriotic group. The government, however, ignores this effort and continues to keep the Brotherhood both illegal and in check.

Al-Jihad was split over Zawahiri's "international" orientation, but some members agreed with him, vowing to "send U.S. soldiers back to their country in coffins just as was the case in Somalia, Riyadh, and Dhahran."[100] Yet, of course, what Zawahiri neglected to point out that applies to the Brotherhood also applies to him. Revolutionary Islamists who devote themselves to anti-Israel and anti-American actions are little threat to the regime which is not targeted by their violence and whose state-controlled media can mobilize even more support for the rulers by echoing criticism of America.

Throughout 2001, Egyptian Islamists threatened additional terrorist attacks against American targets, which were often linked with a demand for Abd al-Rahman's release. The appeal of the anti-American orientation is based on the failure of alternative, anti-regime strategies. In the end, the September 11, 2001 attacks on New York and Washington were a realization of Zawahiri's new approach. Many key participants in that operation and earlier al-Qa'ida attacks were veterans of the Egyptian movement. Indeed, it is probable that Egyptian Islamists were the largest group of Arab al-Qa'ida members.[101]

Yet there was no reason to believe that the killings of more that 3,000 Americans in one day—many times more than the death toll in Egypt's decade-long insurgency—would revitalize the movement in Egypt. The conditions that gave rise to Islamist movements there continued, but so did the factors preventing them from winning mass support or seizing power in that country.

Indeed, in June 2002, the Egyptian government sponsored a convention in an isolated prison. The 500 attendees, all members of the Islamic group serving sentences for past armed attacks, discussed ending their involvement in violence. A key element here was a revision in their ideology to argue that Islamic law forbade attacks on civilians. Those deciding to follow a reformist rather than revolutionary path could be released from prison, as had already been done with 1,500 members of the organization.

Appendix

Editor's Note: Ayman al-Zawahiri, a leader of al-Qa'ida and former leader of the Jihad group, wrote *Knights Under the Prophet's Banner* about his views and experiences. The following extracts are based on the text published in *al-Sharq al-Awsat* newspaper, December 2–12, 2001 and are translated by the U.S. Department of Commerce, Foreign Broadcast Information Service (FBIS), December 2–12, 2001 (FBIS-NES-2001–1202–12).

My connection with Afghanistan began in the summer of 1980 by a twist of fate, when I was temporarily filling in for one of my colleagues at al-Sayyida Zaynab Clinic, which was administered by the Muslim Brotherhood's Islamic Medical Society. One night the clinic director, a Muslim Brother, asked me if I would like to travel to Pakistan to contribute, through my work as a surgeon, to the medical relief effort among the Afghan refugees. I immediately agreed because I saw this as an opportunity to get to know one of the arenas of jihad that might be a . . . base for jihad in Egypt and the Arab region. . . .

The problem of finding a secure base for jihad activity in Egypt used to occupy me a lot, in view of the pursuits to which we were subjected by the security forces and because of Egypt's flat terrain which made government control easy, for the River Nile runs in its narrow valley between two deserts that have no vegetation or water. Such a terrain made guerrilla warfare in Egypt impossible. . . .

During my contacts and dealings with [Afghanistan, in 1980–81 and again after 1986], several vitally important facts became clear to me. . . .

1. A jihadist movement needs an arena that would act like an incubator where its seeds would grow and where it can acquire practical experience in combat, politics, and organizational matters. . . .
2. The Muslim youths in Afghanistan waged the war to liberate Muslim land under purely Islamic slogans, a very vital matter, for many of the liberation battles in our Muslim world had used composite slogans, that mixed nationalism with Islam and, indeed, sometimes caused Islam to intermingle with leftist, communist slogans. . . .

The Muslim youths began to have doubts about who was the enemy. Was it the foreign enemy that occupied Muslim territory, or was it the domestic enemy that prohibited government by Islamic shari'a, repressed the Muslims, and disseminated immorality under the slogans of progressiveness, liberty, nationalism, and liberation. This situation led the homeland to the brink of the abyss of domestic ruin and surrender to the foreign enemy, exactly like the current situation of the majority of our [Arab] countries under the aegis of the new world order. . . .

In Afghanistan the picture was perfectly clear: A Muslim nation carrying out jihad under the banner of Islam, versus a foreign enemy that was an infidel aggressor backed by a corrupt, apostatic regime at home. . . .

3. Furthermore, the Afghan arena, especially after the Russians withdrew, became a practical example of jihad against the renegade rulers who allied themselves with the foreign enemies of Islam. [Communist President] Najibullah in Afghanistan was an example that we had seen before. He prayed, fasted, and performed pilgrimage. At the same time he prohibited government by Islam and allied himself with the enemies of Islam, allowed them to enter his country, and brutally oppressed the Muslims and the mujahidin.

4. A further significant point was that the jihad battles in Afghanistan destroyed . . . the USSR, a superpower with the largest land army in the world. . . .

That jihad was a training course of the utmost importance to prepare Muslim mujahidin to wage their awaited battle against the superpower that now has sole dominance over the globe, namely, the United States.

It also gave young Muslim mujahidin-Arabs, Pakistanis, Turks, and Muslims from Central and East Asia-a great opportunity to get acquainted with each other on the land of Afghan jihad through their comradeship-at-arms against the enemies of Islam. . . .

[Zawahiri then explains why the Egyptian movement opposes the government:]

The issues that were triggered by the killing of Sadat and the events that followed became basic issues in the minds of the Muslim youth. Thus the issues of the supremacy of the shari'a, the apostasy of the regime from Islam, and the regime's collaboration with America and Israel, became givens. . . . Khalid al-Islambuli said when he was asked why he killed Sadat: "because he did not rule in accordance with the shari'a, because he concluded [peace with Israel], and because he insulted the scholars of Islam." . . .

Military secularism always claimed that it respected Islam. But this respect had only one meaning for it, namely, employing religious scholars to pour praise on it to justify its acts. Indeed, the military court based its judgment on a fatwa by Shaykh Jad-al-Haq, the mufti of Egypt and later on the shaykh of Al-Azhar. It used his fatwa to massacre young fundamentalists. . . .

[Zawahiri's discussion of the de facto war between the fundamentalists and the regime only alludes to its brutality:]

[On] Friday August 12, 1988 . . . the government carried out an aggression against the Ayn Shams neighborhood in Cairo. After the sunset prayers, police troops stormed Adam Mosque, where the Islamic Group held its weekly seminar. . . . The raid started with breaking the mosque's windows and firing tear gas and throwing incendiary bombs inside the mosque to force the people to leave. When the worshippers started to leave, the police forces stormed the mosque and opened fire indiscriminately. . . .

The police raided Adam Mosque before the dawn prayers [again on December 7, 1988] and arrested those inside the mosque. It conducted a large-scale arrest campaign against all members of the Islamic group [in several neighborhoods]. More than 180 persons were arrested. . . .

The fundamentalist movement decided to respond to the Ayn Shams incidents. The answer was to ambush Interior Minister Zaki Badr's motorcade using a booby-trapped car in December 1989. However, the ambush failed when the explosives in the car malfunctioned and its driver was arrested.

The Interior Ministry responded to us by killing Dr. Ala Muhiy-al-Din in broad daylight in the street on September 2, 1990. [He] . . . was one of the leaders of the Islamic Group who advocated the dialogue with the government. . . . The Islamic Group responded to the killing of Ala Muhiy-al-Din by ambushing Interior Minister Abd-al-Halim Musa, but God willed that People's Assembly Speaker Rif'at al-Mahjub's motorcade happened to pass by the ambush and he was killed.

Thus, the Islamic Group shifted its policy from long-term [propaganda and organizing] to violence by fighting and resisting the government's aggression. . . .

In the early 1990s . . . a large number of our brothers in the al-Jihad Group were arrested. More than 800 of them were put on trial in what came to be known as the Tala'i Al-Fath cases. The court sentenced to death four of the defendants. . . .

Our response was to attack the convoy of Interior Minister Hasan al-Alfi with a booby-trapped motorcycle. The minister escaped death, but his arm was broken. A pile of files that he kept next to him saved his life from the shrapnel. This was followed by an attack carried out by the Islamic Group against Information Minister Safwat al-Sharif, who survived the ambush.

This coincided with the Islamic Group's attack on the commander of the Central Military Zone in his capacity as the commander who sanctioned all the verdicts issued by military courts [against Islamist radicals]. The attack failed because his car was bulletproof.

Our brothers in the Al-Jihad Group carried out the attack on the motorcade of Prime Minister Atif Sidqi using a booby-trapped car, but the prime minister survived the attack. His car escaped the full power of the explosion by a split second, although some shrapnel hit it.

As a result of the attack, a child named Shayma was killed. She was a student in a nearby school who was standing near the site of the incident. . . . Our brothers who carried out the attack had surveyed the area and noticed that there was a school under construction. They thought the school had no students in it. It transpired later that only the external part of the school was being renovated but the rest of the school was operating normally.

The unintended death of this innocent child pained us all, but we were helpless and we had to fight the government, which was against God's Shari'a and supported God's enemies.

We had warned the people several times before that, particularly following the attack on Interior Minister Hasan al-Alfi, to stay away from the pillars of the regime, their homes, and the routes they used. In their homes, offices, and motorcades, these officials are mixed with the public and they take cover behind them. So we have no choice but to hit them while cautioning the general public.

Our colleague Al-Sayyid Salah summed this up by saying, when asked by investigators about the death of Shayma, that he regretted the killing of this child, but the jihad must not stop. . . .

Our colleagues in the Al-Jihad Group set up an ambush for Husni Mubarak's motorcade along the Salah Salim road, but he did not use that road on his way to perform the Id prayers, so we failed. There was another attempt to assassinate Husni Mubarak at Sidi Barrani Airport by members of the Islamic Group, but the attempt was discovered before implementation.

[The Islamic Group killed Major General Ra'uf Khayrat on April 9, 1994.]

Ra'uf Khayrat was one of the most dangerous officers in the State Security Intelligence Department who fought the fundamentalists. . . . As he was emerging from his home and about to get into his car, one of the brother mujahidin approached him and threw a bomb inside his car, and he was killed instantly.

The Islamic Group escalated the campaign and attacked the convoy of Husni Mubarak in Addis Ababa in the summer of 1995. The attack failed and Mubarak survived because one of the two cars that participated in the attack broke down.

Our colleagues in the al-Jihad group planned two operations at almost the same time. The first was the bombing of the Egyptian embassy in Islamabad in the autumn of 1995. . . . The other was at home against Israeli tourists. It was known as the Khan al-Kkhalili case.

In July 1997 the Islamic Group inside prison announced its initiative to suspend violence unilaterally. However, following this initiative a team from the Islamic Group carried out the Luxor operation against Western tourists. . . .

The Muslim youths demonstrated that undermining the government and its henchmen was not difficult.

The fruits of the jihad resistance go beyond inspiring hope in the hearts of the Muslim youths. The resistance is a weapon directed against the regime's henchmen, who are demoralized as they see their colleagues falling around them. Furthermore, stepping up the jihad action to harm the U.S. and Jewish interests creates a sense of resistance among the people, who consider the Jews and Americans a horrible symbol of arrogance and tyranny. . . .

Egypt is struggling between two powers: An official power and a popular power that has its roots deeply established in the ground, which is the Islamic movement in general and the solid jihad nucleus in particular.

The first power is supported by the United States, the West, Israel, and most of the Arab rulers. The second power depends on God alone then on its wide popularity and alliance with other jihad movements throughout the Islamic nation, from Chechnya in the north to Somalia in the south and from Eastern Turkestan in the east to Morocco in the west. . . .

It is a battle of ideologies, a struggle for survival, and a war with no truce. . . .

[Given the existential struggle, Zawahiri provides an analysis and accounting of the history of the Egyptian Islamist movement, writing:]

1. . . . There is no doubt that the struggling Islamic movement has gained much ground during that period, particularly among the

youths, and that it continues to grow and spread.
2. ... The Islamic movement has been on the offensive against the enemies of Islam.... Major events beginning with the incident at the Technical Military College in 1974 up to the Luxor incident in 1997 provide the best proof of this.
3. ... The Islamic movement has offered tens of thousands of detainees and wounded and tortured people and thousands dead in its continuing struggle....
4. ... The regime had no choice but to turn the battle against the mujahid Islamic movement into an international battle, particularly when the United States became convinced that the regime could not survive alone in the face of this fundamentalist campaign. It was also convinced that this spirit of jihad would most likely turn things upside down in the region and force the United States out of it. This would be followed by the earth-shattering event, which the West trembles at the mere thought of it, which is the establishment of an Islamic caliphate in Egypt. If God wills it, such a state in Egypt, with all its weight in the heart of the Islamic world, could lead the Islamic world in a jihad against the West.

It could also rally the world Muslims around it. Then history would make a new turn, God willing, in the opposite direction against the empire of the United States and the world's Jewish government.
5. ... The regime and its media try in vain to convince the people at home and abroad that the battle is over, despite the continuation of the emergency law and the costly security budgets. All these signs indicate that the regime is still in a state of panic, anticipation, and extreme caution because of the continuing battle and that the situation could explode at any minute....
6. ... The Islamic movement has largely succeeded in clarifying the main elements of its ideology, relying on strong evidence from the Koran, the prophet's tradition, and the respected scholars....
7. [There has been, however, a] weakness of planning and preparations for the jihad actions....
8. [There has also been a] weakness of the message to the people: The fundamentalist movement's message continues to be mostly geared toward the elite and the specialists. The public and the masses do not understand this message....
9. Failure of some leaders to continue the confrontation: The best proof of this is the initiative made by the Islamic Group leaders in the Turah Prison to suspend military action....

10. Conclusion: Has the jihad movement failed or succeeded in the past 36 years?. . . .

A. We must admit that the fundamentalist movement's goal of establishing an Islamic government in Egypt is yet to be achieved.

B. The jihad Islamic movement, however, has not set a specific date for achieving this goal. More importantly, this is a goal that could take several generations to achieve. The Crusaders in Palestine and Syria left after two centuries of continued jihad. . . . The British occupied Egypt for 70 years. The French occupied Algeria for 120 years.

C. What I see clearly is that the jihad Islamic movement has gone a long way on the road to victory.

1. It possesses a clear-cut ideology based on firm Shari'a foundations and tangible and realistic facts.
2. It has succeeded in outlining to the youths issues that were absent from the minds of the Muslim masses, such as the supremacy of the Shari'a, the apostasy of the rulers who do not rule according to God's words, and the necessity of going against rulers who are affiliated with the enemies of Islam.
3. The jihad movement has exposed the close links between the international regime and the Egyptian regime.
4. The jihad movement has not confined itself to a theoretical debate of these issues. It has put them to practice with an offensive that has shaken the pillars of the regime several times. It also succeeded in assassinating the former president.
5. Based on the above, the jihad movement has strongly influenced the Muslim youth in theory and practice. This has led to the spread of the fundamentalist spirit among large segments of the Egyptian youths. In addition, the fundamentalist movement has influenced broad sectors of the Egyptian people.

. . .

8. Thus, we could affirm that the jihad movement is growing and making progress in general. It may retreat or relax for a while, but this happens because of the campaigns of brutality or during the periods of siege.

Therefore, the jihad Islamic movement must not stop the resistance and must get the entire nation to participate with it in its battle. . . .

The persistence of the resistance will keep the volcano in a state of continual eruption and ready to blow up at the least provocation. The persistence of the resistance will transfer the popular wrath from one generation to another and keep the desire for revenge alive in the people's souls. In contrast, the spread of the concepts of conciliation, acquiescence, and acceptance of the facts will make our generation leave a legacy of despair and a willingness to surrender to the next generation. . . .

If I fall as a martyr in the defense of Islam, my son Muhammad will avenge me, but if I am finished politically and I spend my time arguing with governments about some partial solutions, what will motivate my son to take up my weapons after I have sold these weapons in the . . . market? More important than all the foregoing is the fact that resistance is a duty imposed by shari'a. . . .

[Zawahiri quotes a saying by Sayyid Qutb], the most prominent theoretician of the fundamentalist movements, who said: "Brother, push ahead, for your path is soaked in blood. Do not turn your head right or left but look only up to heaven."

[Zawahiri was very critical of those members of the fundamentalist movement who advocated and adopted an unilateral cease-fire, rejecting violence in the fight against the government. He criticizes especially the Islamic Group for not getting anything in return for its cease-fire and weakening its moral standing, asking:]

In exchange for what has it done so? What is the alternative? Does the alternative consist of repeated requests to the government, made by the people who presented the initiative, to show responsiveness to their initiative? Does the alternative consist of asking the leaders of the political parties to intercede with the government to make it respond to their initiative?

Is this the Islamic Group's alternative method to jihad and incitement to jihad? Does the work of the jihadist groups—that is governed by shari'a, an understanding of the jurisprudence of the historical imams, the nation's ulama, and proof of adherence to shari'a—consist nowadays of repeatedly soliciting the secular governments to give us permission to establish an Islamic state? . . .

The Muslim Brotherhood has [also] reneged on its history of struggle . . . [and] on its principles and creed . . . creating a new generation who only cares about worldly things now and in the future. . . .

[Zawahiri discusses the jihad movement's future and strategy:]

A. . . . The Western forces that are hostile to Islam have clearly identified their enemy . . . as Islamic fundamentalism. They are joined in this by their old enemy, Russia. They have adopted a number of tools to fight Islam, including: the UN; friendly rulers of the Muslim peoples; multinational corporations; the international communications and data exchange systems; the international news agencies and satellite media channels; [and] the international relief agencies, which are being used as a cover for espionage, proselytizing, coup planning, and the transfer of weapons.

In the face of this alliance, a fundamentalist coalition is taking shape. It is made up of the jihad movements in the various lands of Islam as well as the two countries that have been liberated in the name of jihad for the sake of God (Afghanistan and Chechnya). . . .

B. . . . There is no solution without jihad. The spread of this awareness has been augmented by the failure of all other methods that tried to evade assuming the burdens of jihad. The Algerian experience has provided a harsh lesson in this regard. It proved to Muslims that the West is not only an infidel but also a hypocrite and a liar. The principles that it brags about [such as democracy] are exclusive to and the personal property of its people alone. They are not to be shared by the peoples of Islam, at least nothing more that what a master leaves his slave in terms of food crumbs.

The Islamic Salvation Front in Algeria . . . rushed to the ballot boxes in a bid to reach the presidential palaces and the ministries, only to find at the gates tanks loaded with French ammunition, with their barrels pointing at the chests of those who forgot the rules of confrontation between justice and falsehood. The guns of the Francophile officers brought them down to the land of reality from the skies of illusions. . . .

Someone may ask: Don't you think that you are contradicting yourself? A short while ago you talked about the spread of despair in the hearts of some leaders of the jihad movement and now you are talking about a widespread jihad awakening?

The answer is simple. All movements go through a cycle of erosion and renewal, but it is the ultimate result that determines the fate of a movement: Either extinction or growth. . . .

In waging the battle the jihad movement . . . must be extremely careful not to get isolated from its nation or engage the government in the battle of the elite against the authority.

We must not blame the nation for not responding or not living up to the task. Instead, we must blame ourselves for failing to deliver the message, show compassion, and sacrifice. . . . The Muslim nation will not participate with it unless the slogans of the mujahidin are understood by the masses of the Muslim nation.

The one slogan that has been well understood by the nation and to which it has been responding for the past 50 years is the call for the jihad against Israel. In addition to this slogan, the nation in this decade is geared against the U.S. presence. It has responded favorably to the call for the jihad against the Americans.

A single look at the history of the mujahidin in Afghanistan, Palestine, and Chechnya will show that the jihad movement has moved to the center of the leadership of the nation when it adopted the slogan of liberating the nation from its external enemies and when it portrayed it as a battle of Islam against infidelity and infidels.

The strange thing is that secularists, who brought disasters to the Muslim nation, particularly on the arena of the Arab-Israeli conflict; and who started the march of treason by recognizing Israel beginning with the Armistice Agreement of 1949, as we explained earlier, are the ones who talk the most about the issue of Palestine.

Stranger still is the fact that the Muslims, who have sacrificed the most for Jerusalem, whose doctrine and Shari'a prevent them from abandoning any part of Palestine or recognizing Israel . . . and who are the most capable of leading the nation in its jihad against Israel, are the least active in championing the issue of Palestine and raising its slogans among the masses. . . .

Through this jihad the stances of the rulers, their henchmen [pro-government clerics], writers, and judges, and the security agencies will be exposed. . . . They have allied themselves with the enemies of God against His supporters. . . .

Tracking down the Americans and the Jews is not impossible. Killing them with a single bullet, a stab, or a device made up of a popular mix of explosives or hitting them with an iron rod is not impossible. Burning down their property with Molotov Cocktails is not difficult. With the available means, small groups could prove to be a frightening horror for the Americans and the Jews.

. . .

D. . . . The jihad movement must adopt its plan on the basis of controlling a piece of land in the heart of the Islamic world on which it could establish and protect the state of Islam and launch its battle to restore the . . . caliphate based on the traditions of the prophet. . . .

E. . . . We must respond in the arena that we choose; namely, to strike at the Americans and the Jews in our countries. By this, we win three times:

First, by dealing the blow to the great master, which is hiding from our strikes behind its agent.
Second, by winning over the nation when we choose a target that it favors, one that it sympathizes with those who hit it.

Third, by exposing the regime before the Muslim people when this regime attacks us to defend its U.S. and Jewish masters....

F. ... Our path, as the Koran and our history have shown us, is a long road of jihad and sacrifices, we must not despair of repeated strikes and recurring calamities. We must never lay down our arms, regardless of the casualties or sacrifices.

We must realize that countries do not fall all of a sudden. They fall by pushing and overcoming.

G. The Islamic movement and its jihad vanguards, and actually the entire Islamic nation, must involve the major criminals—the United States, Russia, and Israel—in the battle and do not let them run the battle between the jihad movement and our governments in safety. They must pay the price, and pay dearly for that matter.

The masters in Washington and Tel Aviv are using the regimes to protect their interests and to fight the battle against the Muslims on their behalf. If the shrapnel from the battle reach their homes and bodies, they will trade accusations with their agents about who is responsible for this. In that case, they will face one of two bitter choices: Either personally wage the battle against the Muslims, which means that the battle will turn into clear-cut jihad against infidels, or they reconsider their plans after avknowledging the failure of the brute and violent confrontation against Muslims.

Therefore, we must move the battle to the enemy's grounds to burn the hands of those who ignite fire in our countries.

H. The struggle for the establishment of the Muslim state cannot be launched as a regional struggle.... The Jewish-Crusader alliance, led by the United States, will not allow any Muslim force to reach power in any of the Islamic countries. It will mobilize all its power to hit it and remove it from power. Toward that end, it will open a battlefront against it that includes the entire world. It will impose sanctions on whoever helps it, if it does not declare war against them altogether....

I. The struggle against the external enemy cannot be postponed.... The Jewish-Crusader alliance will not give us time to defeat the domestic enemy then declare war against it thereafter....

J. ... The jihad movement must realize that half the road to victory is attained through its unity, rise above trivial matters, gratitude, and glorification of the interests of Islam above personal whims....

K. Rallying around and supporting the struggling countries: Backing and supporting Afghanistan and Chechnya and defending them with the heart, the hand, and the word represent a current duty . . . We must seek to move the battlefront to the heart of the Islamic world, which represents the true arena of the battle and the theatre of the major battles in defense of Islam. . . .

L. . . . We concentrate on the following:

1. The need to inflict the maximum casualties against the opponent, for this is the language understood by the West, no matter how much time and effort such operations take.
2. The need to concentrate on . . . martyrdom operations as the most successful way of inflicting damage against the opponent and the least costly to the mujahidin in terms of casualties.
3. The targets as well as the type and method of weapons used must be chosen to have an impact on the structure of the enemy and deter it enough to stop its brutality, arrogance, and disregard for all taboos and customs. . . .
4. . . . Focusing on the domestic enemy alone will not be feasible at this stage. . . .

What will we tell the future generations about our achievements? Are we going to tell them that we carried arms against our enemies then dropped them and asked them to accept our surrender? . . .

This goal must remain the basic objective of the Islamic jihad movement, regardless of the sacrifices and the time involved.

Notes and References

1 Introduction

1. Sa'ad Eddin Ibrahim, *Misr Turaji'u Nafsaha* (Cairo: Dar al-Mustaqbal al-'Arabi, 1983) pp. 5–7.
2. *Al-Majallah*, "*Al Majallah* Uncovers the Plans for the Secret Religious Societies to Seize Power in Egypt" (October 14, 1981); Abdelwahab el-Affendi, "The Islamic World in Review," *Arabia*, (November 1985).
3. Fouad Ajami, *The Arab Predicament* (Cambridge: Cambridge University Press, 1981) p. 117.
4. Salib Zaytun, "Application of Islamic Sharia in Egypt Inevitable," *Al-Ahd* (June 4, 1985), translation in *Joint Publications Research Service, Near East and South Asia Report (JPRS)* (July 25, 1985).
5. Cited in Emanuel Sivan, *Radical Islam* (New Haven: Yale University Press, 1985) p. 14.

2 Contemporary History of Fundamentalism in Egypt

1. The best history of the Muslim Brothers during this period remains Richard Mitchell, *The Society of the Muslim Brothers* (London: Oxford University Press, 1968). On the group's involvement in the Palestine question, see Barry Rubin, *The Arab States and the Palestine Conflict* (Syracuse: Syracuse University Press, 1982).
2. Ahmad Hamrush, "Issue is not Shari'ah But Government," *Ruz al-Yusuf*, (August 12, 1985), translation in *Joint Publications Research Service (JPRS)* (October 8, 1985) p. 18. According to one anecdote, "Mustafa al-Nahhas [leader of the Wafd party and Egypt's most popular politician] summoned Hasan al-Banna to meet him at Mena House where al-Nahhas lived ... and told the shaykh with his well-known frankness: 'Listen, Shaykh Hasan: Religion yes, politics no.'", Hamrush, p. 17.
3. Sayyid Qutb, *Ma'alim fi al-tariq* (Cairo, 1964) quoted in Elie Kedourie, "Anti-Marxism in Egypt," in Michael Confino and Shimon Shamir (eds), *The USSR and the Middle East* (Jerusalem, 1973). See also John Waterbury, *Egypt, Burdens of the Past, Options for the Future* (Bloomington: Indiana University Press, 1978).
4. *Ruz al-Yusuf*, "The Islamic Societies" (September 28, 1981). The best account of the loss of credibility by the Nasir regime and its counterparts is Fouad Ajami, *The Arab Predicament* (Cambridge: Cambridge University Press, 1981).
5. *Al-Ahram* (October 21, 1971).
6. Sadat expresses his self-image in the autobiography, Anwar al-Sadat,

In Search of Identity (New York: Macmillan, 1978). On his attitude toward the Muslim Brothers, see p. 147.
7. Su'ad Aly, 'Abd al-Monein and Manfred W. Wenner, "Modern Islamic Reform Movements: The Muslim Brotherhood in Contemporary Egypt," *The Middle East Journal* (Summer 1982).
8. *The Economist*, "Cairo's Caliph" (July 16, 1977); see also M. C. Aulus, "Sadat's Egypt," *New Left Review*, 98 (July 1976) p. 348.
9. Text of the Egyptian Constitution of 1971 in *The Middle East Journal* (Winter 1972) p. 349.
10. *New York Times* (April 27, 1974).
11. Colin Legum, Haim Shaked and Daniel Dishon (eds), *Middle East Contemporary Survey, 1981–1982* (*MECS*), vol. 6 (New York, 1984–5) p. 447; Robert Satloff, "Army and Politics in Mubarak's Egypt," The Washington Institute for Near East Policy, *Policy Papers No. 10* (Washington D.C., 1988) pp. 29–32; Adil Hammudah, "The Story of Religious Extremism," *Ruz al-Yusuf*, 3034 (August 4, 1986) pp. 28–32.
12. *The APS Diplomat*, "Re-drawing the Islamic map," 5 (5) (May 25, 1983).
13. *Al-Da'wah* (February 1977), translation in Foreign Broadcast Information Service, Middle East and Africa Reports (FBIS) (January 21, 1977) p. 139; Saad Eddin Ibrahim, "An Islamic Alternative in Egypt: The Muslim Brotherhood and Sadat," *Arab Studies Quarterly*, 4 (1–2) p. 81.
14. *The APS Diplomat*, "Re-drawing the Islamic maps."
15. *MECS*, vol. 4 (New York, 1981) p. 350; *The Economist* (March 8, 1986) p. 49; Satloff, "Army and Politics," pp. 29–32.
16. *Al-Ahram* (June 14, 1979).
17. Hassan Hanafi, "The Relevance of the Islamic Alternative in Egypt," *Arab Studies Quarterly*, 4 (1–2) p. 65.
18. Emanuel Sivan, "Intellectual Blues," *Jerusalem Quarterly*, 20 (Summer 1981) p. 126.
19. *Arabia*, "Ikhwan in parliament: Aiming to set an example" (August 1984) p. 34.
20. Interview with Mustafa Mashhur, Muslim Brotherhood leader, *Al-Mujtama'* (April 7, 1987).
21. Colin Legum, Haim Shaked and Daniel Dishon (eds), *MECS*, vol. 4 (New York, 1982); *MECS*, vol. 5 (New York, 1980–1) p. 427; *Al-Da'wah* (July and August 1981). See also Muhammed 'Abd al-Qudus, "Uniting of Two Elements of Nation Will Thwart Conspiracy," *Al-Sha'b* (March 10, 1987).
22. *Al-Ahram* (September 3, 6 and 27, 1981).
23. *International Herald Tribune* (September 12–13 and 19–20, 1981); *Al-Jumhuriyyah* (September 25, 1981); *MECS*, vol. IV (1980–1), pp. 428–32.
24. *Al-Ahram* (October 23 and 24, 1981); *Akhbar al-Yawm* (October 24, 1981); *MECS* vol. V (1980–1) pp. 417–39.
25. Mohamed Sid-Ahmed, "Egypt: the Islamic Issue," *Foreign Policy '88* (Winter 1987).
26. Satloff, "Army and Politics," pp. 29–32.

27. See Ami Ayalon, "Terrorism in Egypt," in Barry Rubin, *The Political Uses of Terrorism* (Johns Hopkins University Press, 1989).
28. Jamal Isma'il, "Shari'ah Laws for Those Who Hurry and for Those Who Procrastinate," *Al-Dustur*, 15 (376) (May 20, 1985) pp 13–14.
29. *Guardian* (July 10, 1985); *Al-Siyasi* (July 14, 1985); *Al-Jumhuriyyah* (July 4, 1985); *New York Times* (July 7, 1985); *Newsweek* (August 5, 1985); Arnold Hottinger, "The Problem of the Shariah in Egypt," *Swiss Report of World Affairs*, 35 (4) (July 1985) pp. 30–1.
30. Ibrahim Abu Dah, "How is the Awqaf Ministry Preparing To Bring 1000 Mosques a Year Under Its Supervision?," *Al-Siyasah* (July 14, 1985) p. 8.
31. *Al-Hawadith*, "We Do Not Believe in Sectarianism" (April 10, 1987).
32. *MECS* vol. 7, (New York: 1986) pp. 353–62; Sid-Ahmed, "Egypt," p. 33.
33. Hamrush, "Issue is not Shari'ah," p. 19.
34. *Ruz al-Yusuf*, "Playing with Fire: The Danger Threatening the Government and Opposition" (August 25, 1986).
35. Interview with 'Abd al-Hawi in *Al-Mujtama'* (June 30, 1987).
36. Sid-Ahmed, "Egypt," p. 31.

3 The Muslim Brotherhood: Ideology and Program

1. Usamah 'Ajjaj, "Reports on Islamic Groups. Where do Political Parties Stand?," *Akhir Sa'ah* (June 11, 1986). See also "Muslim Brotherhood Figure Discusses Groups Role in Society," *Al-Mujtama'* (May 3, 1988) pp. 20–1.
2. *Al-Yamamah*, "Will the Muslim Brotherhood Seize Power?," (July 10, 1985), in *JPRS* (August 14, 1985); Adil Hummudah, "Are the Brothers Abandoning Violence?," *Ruz al-Yusuf*, 3032 (July 21, 1986) pp. 30–4.
3. *Ruz al-Yusuf*, "The Muslim Brotherhood and Sadat Face to Face" (June 28, 1986).
4. Saad Eddin Ibrahim, "Egypt's Islamic Activism in the 1980's," *Third World Quarterly* (April 1988) p. 641.
5. Saad Eddin Ibrahim, "An Islamic Alternative in Egypt: The Muslim Brotherhood and Sadat," *Arab Studies Quarterly*, 4 (1–2) p. 81.
6. Karim Alrawi, "End of an Era," *Inquiry*, 3 (7) (July 1986) pp. 16–17.
7. *Al-Majallah*, "Interview with Tilimsani," 2 (101) (January 16, 1982).
8. *Arabia*, "Tilimsani on Ikhwan Policy" (November 1981) p. 11.
9. *Arabia*, "Tilimsani."
10. *Arabia*, "Tilimsani."
11. *Akhbar al-Yom*, "Your Answer, A Response from 'Umar al-Tilimsani," in *JPRS* (July 17, 1984) p. 16.
12. *Al-Majallah*, "Al-Majallah Uncovers the Plans of the Secret Religion Societies to Seize Power in Egypt" (October 14, 1981).
13. 'Umar 'Abd al-Sami, "I want a Party, The Brotherhood Did Not

Leave the Wafd and Did Not Join the Liberal Party," *Al-Musawwar* (May 2, 1986) pp. 16–19.

14. *Al-Yamamah*, "Will the Muslim Brotherhood Seize Power?," pp. 32–4.
15. See, for example, *Al-Hawadith*, "Independent Party for Muslim Brotherhood" (February 14, 1986) p. 9.
16. 'Abd al-Sami, "I Want a Party," pp. 5–6.
17. 'Abd al-Sami, "I Want a Party," pp. 16–19.
18. For the views of Liberal Party President Mustafa Kamil Murad, see Usamah 'Ajjaj, "Reports on Islamic Groups." On the changing party press see, for example, *Al-Ahram* (November 24, 1986).
19. *Al-Hawadith* (London), "We Do Not Believe in Sectarianism" (April 20, 1987) p. 30. The specific cause behind the break was that, after the May 1984 election, the Brotherhood proposed Shaykh Salah Abu Isma'il as head of the opposition while the Wafd had its own candidate. Jamal Isma'il, "The Split between the Wafd and the Muslim Brotherhood," *Ruz al-Yusuf*, 2924 (June 25, 1984) pp. 10–12.
20. "1. In the 1984 elections the Wafd party was allied with the Muslim Brotherhood and won 778,131 votes. In the 1987 elections the Wafd's share dropped to 746,024 votes.
    2. In the 1984 elections the Labor and Liberal parties won 452,863 votes: while in the latest elections in which the Muslim Brotherhood, Labor, and Liberal parties were allied, the alliance won 1,163,525.
    3. This means if we assume the increase in votes won by the new alliance was from the votes for the Muslim Brotherhood and their supporters for the alliance is 542,863 votes, approximately 8 per cent of the total valid votes.
    4. While the number of votes won by the alliance has increased by that amount, the number of votes won by the NDP in the latest elections increased by 1 million votes; that is, twice as many votes won by the Muslim Brotherhood. (The NDP won 3.7 million votes in the 1984 elections and 4.7 million votes in the 1987 elections.)" Salah Muntasir, "The Strength of the Muslim Brotherhood," *Al-Ahram* (April 12, 1987).
21. Mary Curtius, *The Christian Science Monitor* (July 13, 1987); *Arabia*, "Tilimsani on Ikhwan Policy" (November 1981) p. 11.
22. *Al-Mujtama'*, "Interview with Mr. Mustafa Mashur" (May 3, 1988).
23. Interview in *Al-Sharq al-Awsat* (London) (January 11, 1988) p. 10. See also Alexandre Buccionti, "Le Parti aux Pouvoir et Les Islamists . . . ," *Le Monde* (August 24, 1987).
24. 'Abd al-Sami, "I Want a Party," p. 1.
25. *Al-Majallah* (January 16, 1982) pp 1–5.
26. *Al-Yamamah*, "Will the Muslim Brotherhood Seize Power?" For a similar type of analysis, see 'Abd al-Sami, "I Want a Party," pp 16–19.
27. Olivier Carré, "Le Combat-pour-Dieu et L'État Islamique, chez Sayyid Qutb, l'inspirateur du radicalism islamique actuel," *Revue de Science Politique Française*, 33 (4) (August 1983) p. 683.

28. *Al-Musawwar*, "Brotherhood Supreme Guide Candidate: There are Several Opportunities for Meeting Current Regime in Climate of Freedom and Purity," (May 16, 1986). Interview in *Al-Sharq al-Awsat* (January 11, 1988) p. 14.
29. *Middle East Times*, "Muslim Brotherhood as Moderate" (July 6, 1985) pp. 1–20.
30. Salah 'Abd al-Maqsud, "Interview with Muhammad Abu al-Nasir," *Al-I'tisam* (October–November 1986) in *JPRS* (February 19, 1987).
31. Salah 'Abd al-Maqsud, *Al-I'tisam* (October–November 1986).
32. *Akhir Sa'ah*, "Muslim Brotherhood, Jihad Confrontation in Asyut" (April 6, 1988) pp. 21–3.
33. Salah 'Abd al-Maqsud, *Al-Musawwar* (May 2, 1986). Jamal Isma'il, "Will 'the Society' Become a Political Party?," *Al-Dustur*, 16 (434) (June 23, 1986) pp. 18–20.
34. Salah Abu Rafia, Member of Muslim Brotherhood Guidance Council, "We Reject Violence," *Al-Musawwar* (May 9, 1986). 'Abd al-Sami, "I Want a Party;" see also 'Abd al-Latif al-Minawi, "After the death of 'Umar al-Tilimsani: The Muslim Brotherhood; Middle Selection of Extremism?," *Al-Majallah* (May 28–June 3, 1986).
35. Mustafa Bakr, "The Controversy with the Muslim Brotherhood about the New Guide," *Al-Musawwar*, 3215 (May 23, 1986) pp. 10–11; "Inside the Brotherhood, the Struggle Between the Followers of Money and the Followers of Islamic Scholars," *Ruz al-Yusuf* (June 16, 1986).
36. *Al-Majallah* (January 16, 1982) pp. 1–5.
37. *Al-Sharq al-Awsat* (January 11, 1988).

4 The Jama'at

1. Saad Eddin Ibrahim, "Anatomy of Egypt's Militant Islamic groups; Methodological Note and Preliminary Findings," *International Journal of Middle East Studies*, 12 (1980) p. 429.
2. Ibrahim, "Anatomy," p. 431.
3. *Al-Watan al-Arabi*, "Cairo: Strange Encounters with Extremist Ideas" (September 1, 1982).
4. *Al-Majallah*, "Al-Majallah Enters the Private World of Khalid Islambouli" (January 1, 1982).
5. Muhammad 'Abd al-Salam Faraj, *Al-Rafidah al Gha'ibah* and Muhammad 'Immarah, *Al-Faridah al-Gha'ibah 'Ard Wa-Hiwar wa-Taqyim* (Beirut, 1983).
6. Faraj, *Al-Faridah al-Gha'ibah* p. 30. A more literal translation of the title of Faraj's book would be *The Absent Pillar*. Jihad is one of the five pillars of Islam – the major duties of the faith – which include the belief in Allah and the status of Muhammad as his prophet, prayer, the Ramadan fast, the pilgrimage to Mecca, and jihad. For an assessment of Faraj's importance, see *Al-Akhbar* (September 1, 1987) p. 4.

7. *Al-'Ahd*, "Al-Jihad in Egypt: What is it? How does it think? What does it Want" (January 17, 1987) p. 8, translation in *JPRS* (March 17, 1987) p. 5.
8. On Qutb's life, see Giles Kepel, *Muslim Extremism in Egypt: The Prophet and the Pharaoh* (Berkeley: University of California Press, 1986) Chapter 2. For an Egyptian assessment of his importance, see *Al-Hawadith*, "Will Secret Contacts Between the Nasirists and Islamists Bring Two Opposites Together?" (January 9, 1987) pp. 22–3. Another French scholar calls Qutb, "the inspiration for contemporary Islamic radicalism." See Olivier Carré, "Le Combat-Pour-Dieu et L'État Islamique, chez Sayyid Qutb, l'inspirateur du radicalism islamique actuel," *Revue Française de Science Politique*, 13 (4) (August 1983) pp. 680–703.
9. Kepel, *Muslim Extremism* pp. 38–43. Qutb's father was an official in the National and later the Wafd parties and his house was a meeting place for activists. Graduating from the teacher's college in Cairo in 1925, Qutb then went to Dar al-Ulum College (which Hasan al-Banna had attended), graduating in 1933. In 1945 or 1946, he fell out with the Wafd and began writing social criticism. Many of Qutb's ideas were borrowed from the Pakistani thinker Abu-Allah Mawdoodi. An article in *Ruz al-Yusuf* summarizes Qutb's doctrine as follows: "(1) Man in today's Jahiliyyah society has replaced rule by God with rule by man. (2) Rule by God and rule by man are mutually incompatible. (3) The restoration of the Kingdom of God will only come about by force, not by words. (4) Jihad is necessary to arrive at a true Islamic society. The responsibility for taking the first steps in the Revolution fall to the elite of the faithful." "Sayyid Qutb," *Ruz al-Yusuf* (June 7, 1986) pp. 30–4. See also, Sylvia Haim, "Sayyid Qutb," *Asian and African Studies*, 16 (1) (March 1982) pp. 147–56; Muhammed Tawfiq Barakat, *Sayyid Qutb, Khulasat Hayatihi, Manhajuhu Fi Al-Haraka, Al-Naqd Al-Muwajjah Ilayhi* (Beirut, n.d.) p. 20.
10. Kepel, *Muslim Extremism* p. 155.
11. Kepel, *Muslim Extremism*, pp. 44n.–45.
12. Kepel, *Muslim Extremism*, pp. 61–4; Ibrahim Nafi', "The Personal Theories of a Muslim," *Al-Ahram* (July 5, 12, 1985).
13. Kepel, *Muslim Extremism*.
14. *Al-Akhbar* (September 1, 1987) p. 4.
15. 'Umar 'Abd Al-Sami, "I Want a Party, The Brotherhood Did Not Leave the Wafd and Did Not Join the Liberal Party," *Al-Musawwar* (May 2, 1986) pp. 2–5.
16. Nada al-Qassas, "We approve the Establishment of a Communist Party and One for the Copts," *Al-Dustur* (May 4, 1987) in *JPRS* (June 30, 1987) p. 2.
17. Interview of 'Umar Tilimsani in *Al-Abram* (February 15, 1982); Shaykh Mutwali Shaarawi in *Al-Ahram* (November 8, 1981); Hamied Ansari, "Sectarian Conflict in Egypt and the Political Expediency of Religion," *The Middle East Journal* (Summer 1984) pp. 402, 405. For a Brotherhood polemic against al-Jihad, see the article by Salah Abu Rafiq, member of the Muslim Brotherhood Guidance Council, "We

Reject Violence," *Al-Musawwar* (May 9, 1986). He says al-Jihad is fanatic and "characterized by stupidity and irresponsibility."
18. Saad Eddin Ibrahim, "Egypt's Islamic Activism in the 1980's," *Third World Quarterly* (April 1988).
19. Saad Eddin Ibrahim, "Arab Social Change: Six Profiles," *Jerusalem Quarterly* (Spring 1982) pp. 13–23.
20. Nafi', "The Personal Theories of a Muslim."
21. On Sariyah, see Kepel, Muslim Extremism, pp. 93–4; "The Assassination of Sadat," *Ruz al-Yusuf* (August 4, 1986). On al-Takfir see, for example, "Takfir wal-Hijra Reveals its True Thoughts for the First Time," *Al-Musawwar* (June 18, 1982); "The Assassination of Sadat," *Ruz al-Yuṣuf* (August 4, 1986). In prison, a number of the Islamic Liberation Organization's members, whose leader Salah Sariyah was executed in 1976, joined al-Takfir though there was also some fighting between the prisoners belonging to the two groups. The actual founder of al-Takfir was Ali Abduh Isma'il but al-Hudaybi persuaded him to return to the Brotherhood. The best account of al-Takfir's views is in Kepel, *Muslim Extremism*, Chapter 3.
22. Kepel, *Muslim Extremism*, p. 80. 'Adil Hammudah, "The Leader of the Hippies of Asyut," *Ruz al-Yusuf*, 3035 (August 11, 1986) pp. 28–32; *Ruz al-Yusuf*, "Shukri Mustafa Speaks About Himself" (August 18, 1986).
23. "The Muslim Brothers are with the Wafd while al-Jihad Awaits Trial and al-Takfir wal-Hijra is an unexpected danger," *Al-Majallah* (April 19, 1984). On May 16, 1982, Egypt's interior minister announced the elimination of al-Takfir following the arrest of its fugitive leadership though a few members released from prison tried to form it again.
24. *Al-'Ahd*, "Al-Jihad in Egypt."
25. *Ruz al-Yusuf*, "The al-Jihad Organization Stands Before Justice" (December 13, 1982).
26. *Ruz al-Yusuf*, "Violence Rises to the Top" (September 8, 1986).
27. *Al-Majallah*, "The Mufti of Egypt responds to the Pamphlet: 'The Invisible Religious Duty'" (December 19, 1981).
28. Sawsan al-Jihar, "The Weapons of Those Who Claim to be Prophets," *Ruz al-Yusuf*, 61 (3019) (April 21, 1986) pp. 39–42.
29. For a detailed discussion of Faraj's thought, see 'Immarah, *Al-Faridah al-Gha'ibah*.
30. *Al-Musawwar*, "Inside the Prison with the Islamic Societies" (January 29, 1982); 'Abd al-Basit Hasan, "Al-Jihad and the Brothers: The End of the Honeymoon," *Al-Watan* (May 12, 1988); Kepel, *Muslim Extremism*, pp. 94–5.

5 The Radical Jam'iyat

1. 'Adil Hammudah, "Exit from the Cave: Violence Climbs to the Top," *Ruz al-Yusuf*, 3039 (September 8, 1986) pp. 30–3.

2. Hamid Zaydan, "Hiwar al-Sha'b ma' al-Shabab al-Muslim," *al-Sha'b* (March 22, 1984).
3. *MECS*, vol. 7 (New York, 1984) pp. 398–9.
4. *Al-Majallah*, "Al-Majallah Uncovers the Plans of the Secret Religious Societies to Seize Power in Egypt" (October 14, 1981). On the early history of the student movement, see Giles Kepel, *Muslim Extremism in Egypt: The Prophet and the Pharaoh* (Berkeley: University of California Press, 1986) pp. 129–71.
5. *Al-Mujtama'* (July 29, 1985).
6. *MECS*, vol. 4 (New York, 1981) p. 332.
7. *Washington Post* (April 2, 1986) p. A-15; Karim Jabr, "The Next Step of the Islamic Groups," *Ruz al-Yusuf*, 61 (3021) (May 5, 1986) pp. 12–15.
8. Kepel, *Muslim Extremism* pp. 152–6.
9. Hasan 'Abd al-Basit, "Al-Jihad and the Brothers: The End of the Honeymoon," *Al-Watan* (May 12, 1988).
10. Karim Jabr, "The University of Asyut under the Protection of the Islamic Groups," *Ruz al-Yusuf* (April 28, 1986); Alexandre Buccianti, "Egypt Faced with Rising Tide of Fundamentalist Violence," *Guardian Weekly*, 134 (21) (May 25, 1986) p. 12.
11. *Ruz al-Yusuf*, "Playing with Fire: The Danger Threatening the Government and Opposition" (August 25, 1986).
12. Al-Basit, "Al-Jihad and the Brothers."
13. Salah 'Abd al-Maqsud, "The Islamic Groups Won In Spite of the Comedy of the Student Elections in the Egyptian Universities," *Al-I'tisam* (February 19, 1987).
14. *Al-Jumhuriyyah*, "Ayn Shams University Forbids Wearing of 'Jalabiyahs,' Full Veil" (September 28, 1988) p. 5.
15. *Al-Jumhuriyyah*, "Ayn Shams University."
16. Kepel, *Muslim Extremism*, pp. 148, 152.
17. *Al-Musawwar*, "Interview with the Leader of the Islamic Group in Asyut" (April 11, 1986).
18. Kepel, *Muslim Extremism*, p. 137.
19. *Jordan Times* (September 14, 1987).
20. Mustafa al-Qadi, "Islamic Leader on Islamic Groups, Camp David," *Al-Anba'* (February 23, 1987).
21. *Akhir Sa'ah*, "Muslim Brotherhood, Jihad Confrontation in Asyut" (April 6, 1988).
22. Akhir Sa'ah, "Muslim Brotherhood."
23. Fahmi Huwaydi, "The Real Situation Between Shaykh al-Azhar and Shaykh Kishk," *Al-Arabi*, 279 (February 1982) p. 42.
24. Author's review of tapes of Kishk's sermons and interviews with those attending his Friday services. The best written description of Kishk's methods and presence is in Kepel, *Muslim Extremism*, pp. 172–90.
25. *Al-Majallah*, "The Islamic Societies in Egypt: The Most Prominent Obstacle Facing the New Government" (October 17, 1981).
26. Kepel, *Muslim Extremism*.
27. *Al-Yamamah*, "Will the Muslim Brotherhood Seize Power?" (10 July, 1985), in *JPRS* (August 14, 1985) p. 7.

28. Simon Ingram, "Sheikh Hatea's Challenge," *Middle East International*, 254 (July 12, 1985) p. 9; *Newsweek* (August 5, 1985); *Al-Ahram* and *Al-Akhbar* (July 14, 1985); *New York Times* (July 16, 1985); *MECS*, vol. 6 (1984–5) pp. 352–4; *Africa Research Bulletin*, "Sheikh Freed for Pilgrimage" (September 15, 1985).
29. Muhammad Barakat, "To Me a Death Sentence or a Verdict of Innocence Would be the Same for the Cause of God," *Al-Yamamah* (October 24, 1984) pp. 12–19, translation in *JPRS* (December 28, 1984) pp. 38–40.
30. Hamid Sulayman, "The al-Shaykh Abu Isma'il Phenomenon: Uncovered," *Akhir Sa'ah* (January 21, 1987); Zuhayr Mardini, *Al-Ladudan: Al Wafd wa-al-Ikhwan* (Beirut: Dar Iqra', 1984); Kepel, *Muslim Extremism*, pp. 85, 90.

6 Popular Islam and Official Ulama

1. Saad Eddin Ibrahim, "Egypt's Islamic Activism in the 1980's," *Third World Quarterly* (April 1988) pp. 635–8.
2. Ibrahim, "Egypt's Islamic Activism."
3. "The Real Situation Between Shaykh al-Azhar and Shaykh Kishk," *Al-Arabi* (February 1982).
4. "Prestigious Al-Azhar is Force for Moderation," *Wall Street Journal* (August 10, 1987) p. 22.
5. Fouad Ajami, *The Arab Predicament* (Cambridge: Cambridge University Press, 1981) p. 186; Fahmy Howaydi, *The Qur'an and the Sultan* (Cairo: Dar al-Shuruk, 1982).
6. *Ruz al-Yusuf*, 60 (2969) (May 6, 1985) pp. 30–2.
7. "Muslim Scholars Discuss Islamic Law," *Al-Ahram* (July 5, 1985).
8. Saad Eddin Ibrahim, "Anatomy of Egypt's Militant Islamic Groups," *International Journal of Middle East Studies*, 12 (December 1980).
9. Ibrahim, "Anatomy" p. 434; "Cairo: Strange Encounters with Extremist Ideas," *al-Watan al-Arabi* (September 3, 1982); 'Adil Hammudah, "The Trial," *Ruz al-Yusuf*, 3036, (August 18, 1986) pp. 26–30; Giles Kepel, *Muslim Extremism in Egypt: The Prophet and the Pharaoh* (Berkeley: University of California Press, 1986); 'Isam al-Dallash, "Is this possible? The Holy Quran Has Become a Problem Even at Al-Azhar University," *Al-Nur* (August 10, 1988) p. 4.
10. Muhammed Ma'tuq, "The Mufti of Egypt responds to the Pamphlet: 'The Invisible Religious Duty,'" *Al-Majallah*, 2 (97) (December 19, 1981) p. 14.
11. Mustafa Mahmud, "Against Whom are the Powers of Islamic Law Being Invoked?," *Al-Ahram* (July 9, 1985) p. 7.
12. *MECS*, vol. 6 (New York, 1984) pp. 352–4.
13. 'Abd al-Sattar al-Tawilah, "Terrorism Against the People," *Al-Siyasah* (June 7, 1987).
14. Kepel, *Muslim Extremism*, pp. 98–100.

15. Hasan 'Alam, "Interview with 'Ali Jadd al-Haqq," *Akhir Sa'ah* (April 29, 1987) pp. 12–13.
16. *MECS*, vol. vi, pp. 405ff.
17. Al-Tawilah, "Terrorism."
18. *MECS*, vol. vi, pp. 352–4.
19. A. Chris Eccel, *Egypt, Islam and Social Change: Al-Azhar in Conflict and Accommodation* (Berlin, 1984) p. 512.
20. Ibrahim, "Egypt's Islamic Activism," p. 633.
21. Ibrahim, "Egypt's Islamic Activism," p. 635.
22. *The Economist* (May 21, 1988) p. 46.
23. Eccel, *Egypt*, pp. 370–2, 524.
24. An interesting discussion of Egyptian attitudes in this respect can be found in Rivka Yadlin, "Militant Islam in Egypt: Some Sociocultural Aspects," in Gabriel Warburg and Uri Kupferschmidt, *Islam, Nationalism, and Radicalism in Egypt and the Sudan* (New York: Praeger 1983) pp. 159–82.

7 Attitudes Toward Foreign Policy

1. Muhammad Shams al-Din al-Shinnawi, "The Real Reasons Behind Liquidating the Muslim Brotherhood," *Al-Da'wah* (October 1976); Saad Eddin Ibrahim, "An Islamic Alternative in Egypt: The Muslim Brotherhood and Sadat," *Arab Studies Quarterly*, 4 (1–2) p. 85.
2. Ami Ayalon, "Regime Opposition and Terrorism in Egypt," in Barry Rubin, *The Politics of Terrorism* (Washington: Johns Hopkins University Foreign Policy Institute, 1989).
3. *The Christian Science Monitor* (April 25, 1988).
4. Sylvia Haim, "Sayyid Qutb," *Asian and African Studies*, 16 (1982) pp. 155–6.
5. Haim, "Sayyid Qutb," pp. 154–5.
6. "Religious Strife and Intellectual Figures in Egypt Answer al-Dustur," *Al-Dustur* (April 20, 1987).
7. Haim, "Sayyid Qutb," pp. 154–5.
8. Amr 'Abd al-Sami, "I want a Party, The Brotherhood Did not Leave the Wafd and Did Not Join the Liberal Party," *Al-Musawwar* (May 2, 1986) pp. 16–19. For a Muslim Brotherhood view, see al-Shinnawi, "The Real Reasons."
9. Ibrahim, "An Islamic Alternative," p. 89.
10. Sana Hasan, "Egypt's Angry Islamic Militants," *New York Times Magazine* (November 20, 1983) p. 138.
11. Ibrahim, "An Islamic Alternative."
12. Sawsan Abu-Husayn, "Kuwaiti Paper Interviews Islamic Figures," *Al-Anba'* (March 4, 1987), translation in *JPRS* (April 7, 1987) p. 20.
13. Ibrahim, "An Islamic Alternative," pp. 87–9.
14. "Al-Jihad, What is It? How does it think? What does it Want?" *Al-'Ahd* (January 17, 1987), translation in *JPRS* (March 17, 1987) p. 5.

15. *Al-'Ahd*, "Al-Jihad."
16. "Tilimsani Remembers," *Al-Watan al-Arabi* (July 20, 1984).
17. Interview with al-Tilimsani, *Al-Majallah* (January 18, 1982).
18. Nada al-Qassas, "Interview with Shaykh Muhammad Hamid Abu al-Nasr" (May 4, 1987), translation in *JPRS* (June 30, 1987) p. 51.
19. Haim, "Sayyid Qutb." For Qutb's writings on the subject, see Ron Nettler, *Past Trials and Present Tribulations: A Moslem Fundamentalists' View of Jews* (Oxford: Pergamon Press, 1987).
20. Haim, "Sayyid Qutb."
21. Al-'Aqali, translation in *JPRS* (September 13, 1985) pp, 16, 23.
22. Haim, "Sayyid Qutb."
23. Zuhayr Mardini, *Al-Ladudan: Al-Wafd wa-al-Ikhwan* (Beirut: Dar Iqra', 1984) p. 146; al-Qassas, "Interview with Shaykh Muhammad Hamid Abu al-Nasr."
24. Mardini *Al-Ladudan*, pp. 153–4.
25. Adil Hammudah, "The Trial," *Ruz al-Yusuf*, 3036 (August 18, 1986) pp. 26–30; Hasan, "Egypt's Angry Islamic Militants," p. 138.
26. Haim, "Sayyid Qutb," pp. 155–6.
27. Gabrial Warburg, "Islam and Politics in Egypt: 1952–80," *Middle Eastern Studies* (April 1982) pp. 150–1. "In no single issue of *al-Da'wah* and *al-I'tisam* in the last four years would the reader fail to encounter two or three articles about the Jewish danger or the atrocities of Israel," wrote Ibrahim, "An Islamic Alternative," pp. 87–9. For a contemporary survey of Egyptian attitudes toward Jews and Israel, see Rivka Yadlin, *Anti-Zionism as Anti-Judaism in Egypt*, (Jerusalem: Zalman Shazar Center, 1988).
28. "Grand Imam of al-Azhar Interviewed," *Al-Tadamun* (July 8, 1986).
29. Samir Irshadi, "Islam in Egypt is Shaking the Dust Off Itself and Moving Forward Unrelentlessly," *Kayhan al-'Arabi* (February 21, 1987), translation in *JPRS* (April 10, 1987) pp. 4–6.
30. Warburg, "Islam and Politics," pp. 150–1. "The Muslim Brotherhood and Sadat Face to Face," *Ruz al-Yusuf* (June 28, 1986); *APS Diplomat*, "Redrawing the Islamic Map," 5 (5) (May 25, 1983).
31. "Al-Jihad, What is It?," *Al-'Ahd* (January 17, 1987).
32. Muhammad 'Abd al-Quddus and 'Umar al-Tilimsani, "The Normalization of Relations and the Exchange of Ambassadors," *Al-Da'wah* (January 1980); Said Aly, 'Abd al-Monein, and Manfred W. Wenner, "Modern Islamic Reform Movements: The Muslim Brotherhood in Contemporary Egypt," *The Middle East Journal* (Summer 1982) p. 256; Interview with al-Tilimsani, *Al-Majallah* (January 18, 1982). In a 1985 interview, Tilimsani said he opposed Camp David since full Muslim sovereignty over Sinai had not yet been restored. Even though the land had been returned to Egypt, there were limits on the number of troops it could maintain there. He added that the Jews were welcome to remain in Palestine after it was returned to its rightful owner, the Palestinians. Shirbil Zughayb, "Interview with al-Tilimsani," *Al-Hawadith* (February 22, 1985) pp. 33–5.
33. Daud al-Sharayan, "Jalal Kishk: The Islamic Movement has Gone Beyond Tilimsani," *Al-Yamamah*, 33 (829) (November 21, 1984) pp.

42–6; Kepel, *Muslim Extremism in Egypt: The Prophet and the Pharaoh* (Berkeley: University of California Press, 1986) p. 183.
34. *Ruz al-Yusuf* "Are the Brothers Abandoning Violence?" (July 21, 1986); *al-Dustur* (April 20, 1987).
35. Muhammad 'Abd al-Quddus, "In First Egyptian Reaction, Alliance Leaders Criticize Mubarak Initiative," *al-Sha'b* (January 26, 1988), translation in *FBIS* (February 3, 1988) p. 11.
36. Al Qassas, "Interview with Shaykh Muhammad Hamid Abu al-Nasr."
37. Ibrahim, "An Islamic Alternative," pp. 87–9.
38. Faraj, *Al-Faridah al-Gha'ibah* (Beirut, 1983) p. 25. See also "Violence Rises to the Top," *Ruz al-Yusuf* (September 8, 1986).
39. Faraj, *Al-Faridah al-Gha'ibah*. Additional examples of Faraj's views are offered in Kepel, *Muslim Extremism*, pp. 202–3. "In the Islamic countries, the enemy is at home; indeed, it is he who is in command . . . To launch a struggle against imperialism is therefore useless . . . we must concentrate on . . . the establishment of God's law in our own countries."
40. *Al-'Ahd*, "Al-Jihad, What is It?".
41. *Ruz al-Yusuf*, "Shukri Mustafa speaks about himself" (August 18–19, 1986); Kepel, *Muslim Extremism*, p. 84.
42. Saad Eddin Ibrahim, "Egypt's Islamic Militants," *Merip Reports* (February 1982) p. 13; "Violence Rises to the Top," *Ruz al-Yusuf* (September 8, 1986).
43. Interview in *Al-Majallah* (January 18, 1982); Emmanuel Sivan, "Sunni Radicalism in the Middle East and the Iranian Revolution," *International Journal of Middle East Studies*, 21 (February 1989) pp. 1–30.
44. "Awqaf Minister Criticizes Iranian Practices," *FBIS* (February 8, 1988).
45. Muhammad al-Hayawan, "Word of Love," *al-Jumhuriyah* (August 17, 1987).
46. Al-Hayawan, "Word of Love."
47. Al-Hayawan, "Word of Love."
48. Shaykh 'Abdallah al-Ghawabi, "Our Egypt," *Al-Ahram* (March 30, 1987) p. 2, translation in *JPRS* (April 27, 1987) p. 43; Hasan Amir, interview with Muhammad al-Ma'mun al-Hudaybi, *Al-Jumhuriyyah* (April 23, 1987).
49. Al-Qassas, "Interview with Shaykh Muhammad Hamid Abu al-Nasr."
50. Hasan 'Alam, *Akhir Sa'ah* (April 29, 1987). See also Hibah Abduh, "Interview with Shaykh al-Ghazali," *Al-Ahram al-Iqtisadi*, 839 (February 11, 1985) pp. 50–3.
51. Hasan 'Alam, "An Appeal from Shaykh al-Azhar to the Islamic Summit Conference," *Akhir Sa'ah* (January 28, 1987).
52. The Al-Azhar statement of August 2, 1987 is in *FBIS* (August 3, 1987).
53. Text of statement in *Al-Sha'b* (August 18, 1987).
54. Al-Hayawan, "Word of Love."
55. *Al-Dustur* (November 3, 1986) p. 3. "Egypt breaks all Diplomatic Ties with Iran," *New York Times* (May 15, 1987); "Iranian Backed Terrorist Group Uncovered," *FBIS* (July 13, 1987) p. C-2; "Terrorist Group Admits Planning Operation," *FBIS* (July 16, 1987) p. C-1;

"Prosecutors Investigating pro-Iranian Organization," *Al-Sharq al-Aswat*, translation in *FBIS* (July 23, 1987) p. C-5; "Prosecution Official Says Groups Seek Iranian Ties," *FBIS* (August 31, 1987) p. C-2; "Egypt Says it Arrested Iranian In Terror Plot," *New York Times* (January 10, 1988); "Clandestine Group Uncovered: Defendants Listed," *FBIS* (June 5, 1988) p. 9; "More details on Underground Group Uncovered," *FBIS* (June 16, 1988) p. 6.
56. Irshadi, "Islam in Egypt," pp. 4–6.
57. Al-Hayawan, "Word of Love."
58. Mardini, *Al-Ladudan*, p. 151.
59. "Are the Brothers Abandoning Violence?," *Ruz al-Yusuf* (July 21, 1986).
60. Jalal Kishk, in *al-Sharayan*, "Jalal Kishk."
61. Hasan, "An Appeal;" *FBIS* (April 16, 1986).

8 Strategy and Doctrine

1. "Ikhwan in Parliament: Aiming to Set an Example," *Arabia* (August 1984) p. 34.
2. "Belief, Before Book, Binds Me to My Father," *Al-Mujtama'* (May 5, 1987).
3. "The Muslim Brotherhood is Preparing to Announce its Party," *Al-Sharq al-Aswat* (February 18, 1985).
4. Salah Shadi, "'Umar al-Tilimsani Interview," *Al-Watan al-Arabi* (July 26–August 1, 1985).
5. 'Umar al-Tilimsani, "The Muslim Brotherhood is Preparing to Announce its Party," *Al-Sharq al-Aswat* (February 18, 1985) p. 8.
6. Hasan 'Abd al-Basit, "Al-Jihad and the Brothers: The End of the Honeymoon," *Al-Watan* (May 12, 1988) p. 18.
7. "Wafd and the Brotherhood, Once Again," *Al-Wafd* (October 11, 1984) p. 7; *Al-Hawadith*, "Will Secret Contacts Between the Nasirists and Islamists Bring Two Opposites Together?" (January 9, 1987) p. 9; "Split between the Wafd and the Ikhwan," *Ruz al-Yusuf* (June 25, 1984).
8. Cited in Mahmud 'Awad, "Mahmud 'Awad Answers Salah Abu-Isma'il: Do Not Lie, Shaykh," *Uktubar* (December 28, 1986), (January 11, 1987); *Al-Mujtama'* (February 27, 1987).
9. "Wafd, Muslim Brotherhood Differences Discussed" *Ruz al-Yusuf* (March 17, 1986).
10. Jamal Salim, "Why Does Brotherhood Put its Hands in Wafd's Hand," *Ruz al-Yusuf* (August 12, 1985) p. 14; Mustafi al-Qadi, "Islamic Leader on Islamic Groups, Camp David," *Al-Anba'* (February 23, 1987).
11. "Shaykh Salah Abu Isma'il Relates his experience with the New Wafd party," *Al-Mujtama'* (December 10, 1985); See also *Al-Khalij*, "Muslim Brotherhood Leader Discusses Relations with Wafd," translation in *JPRS* (July 23, 1986).

12. "Design to Exclude al-Azhar 'Ulamas from Political Action," *Al-Mujtama'* (March 18, 1986).
13. "Design to Exclude al-Azhar."
14. *MECS*, vol. 2 (New York, 1974) pp. 335, 344; *Al-Liwa' al-Islami* (May 16, 1985), cited in *MECS*, vol. vi, p. 350; *Al-Dustur*, "Shari'ah Laws for Those Who Hurry and for Those Who Procrastinate" (May 5, 1985).
15. *Al-Hawadith* (April 10, 1987).
16. *MECS*, Vol. iv, pp. 352–3.
17. *The Christian Science Monitor* (June 13, 1987).
18. *Al-Ahram* (May 5, 1985); *Al-Nur* (May 18, 1985).
19. Hasan Abu Husayn, "Kuwaiti Paper Interviews Islamic Figures," *Al-Anba'* (March 4, 1987), translation in *JPRS* (April 7, 1987) pp. 19, 20.
20. Ahmad Hamrush, "Issue is not Shari'ah But Government," *Ruz al-Yusuf* (August 2, 1985) p. 16; Mahmud al-Ahman, "Against Whom Are the Powers of Islamic Law Being Invoked" (July 9, 1985) p. 7, translation in *JPRS* (August 26, 1985). Tantawi said, "I lean towards the point of view which calls for gradual progress in some matters pertaining to the Shari'ah. There is nothing wrong with that," *Uktubar* (January 18, 1987).
21. *Al-Yamamah*, "Will the Muslim Brotherhood Seize Power?" (July 10, 1985).
22. Interview with *al-Shira'* (Beirut) (July 15, 1985) cited in Emanuel Sivan, "Islamic Republic of Egypt," *Orbis* (Spring 1987) pp. 48–9. 'Umar al-Tilimsani, "Wafd and the Brotherhood Once Again," *Al-Wafd* (October 11, 1984).
23. "The Islamic Societies in Egypt: The Most Prominent Obstacle Facing the New Government," *Al-Majallah* (October 17, 1981).
24. Cited in al-Basit, "Al-Jihad and the Brothers."
25. Cited in al-Basit, "Al-Jihad and the Brothers."
26. Mustafa al-Qadi, "Islamic Leader on Islamic Groups, Camp David," *Al-Anba'* (February 23, 1987).
27. *Ruz al-Yusuf*, "Are the Brothers Abandoning Violence?" (July 21, 1986); interview with Tilimsani, *Al-Majallah* (January 16, 1982); Zuhayr Mardini, *Al-Laludan: al-Wafd wa-al-Ikhwan* (Beirut: Dar Iqra', 1984) pp. 153–4. Mahmud Abdallah, Interview with Abu al-Nasr, translation in *FBIS* (August 1, 1988) pp. 13–14. See also *MECS* vol. vi, pp. 349–50; Giles Kepel, *Muslim Extremism: The Prophet and the Pharaoh* (Berkeley: University of California Press, 1986) p. 128.
28. Samir Irshadi, "Islam in Egypt is Shaking the Dust Off Itself and Moving Forward Unrelentlessly," *Kayhan al-'Arabi* (February 21, 1987) translation in *JPRS* (April 10, 1987).
29. Ibrahim Nafi', "The Personal Theories of a Muslim," *Al-Ahram* (July 5, 12, 1985).
30. Faraj, *Al-Faridah al-Gha'ibah* (Beirut, 1983) pp. 3, 20–1, 24, 28, and 33. See Chapter 4 of Muhammad 'Immarah, *Al-Faridah al-Gha'ibah: 'Ard wa-hiwar wa-taqyim* (Beirut: Dar al-Wahdah lil-Nashr, 1983) and Kepel, *Muslim Extremism*, pp. 195–6.
31. Abu Husayn, "Kuwaiti Paper Interviews," pp. 19–20. 'Ala Muhi

al-Din, "Islamic Groups Between Violence and Acceptance of Dialogue," *Al-Sha'b* (January 24, 1989) p. 2.
32. 'Abd al-Sattar al-Tawilah, "Terrorism Against the People," *Al-Siyasah* (June 7, 1987).
33. Sayyid Qutb, "The Philosophy of Jihad," *Arab News* (August 21, 1987).
34. *Al-'Ahd*, "Interview with Dr. 'Umar 'Abd al-Rahman" (January 17, 1987), translation in *JPRS* (March 17, 1987) pp. 9–10.
35. Cited in Kepel, *Muslim Extremism*, pp. 200–1.
36. Muhammad Barakat, "To Me a Death Sentence or a Verdict of Innocence Would Be One and the Same for the Cause of God," *Al-Yamamah* (October 24, 1984), translation in *JPRS* (December 28, 1984).
37. Mahmud Abdallah, Interview with Muslim Brotherhood Supreme Guide Abu al-Nasr, *Al-Majallah* (July 27–August 3, 1988).
38. Kepel, *Muslim Extremism*, p. 204.
39. APS Diplomat, "Re-drawing the Islamic Map," 5 (5) May 25, (1983).
40. Hussein Ahmad Amin, in *Al-Musawwar* (September 26, 1986).
41. Muhammad Abu al-Nasr, in *Al-Hawadith* (April 10, 1987); *Arabia*, "Tilimsani on Ikhwan Policy" (November 1981) p. 11; Kepel, *Muslim Extremism*, pp. 207–10.
42. Said Aly, Abd al-Monein and Manfred W. Wenner, "Modern Islamic Reform Movements: The Muslim Brotherhood in Contemporary Egypt," *The Middle East Journal* (Summer 1982) pp. 352–3.
43. Barakat, "To Me a Death Sentence"; Saad Eddin Ibrahim, "Egypt's Islamic Militants," *Merip Reports* (February 1982) pp. 8–9.
44. Mahmud Sadiq, "Muslim Brotherhood Outlines Aims, Methods," *al-Sharq al-Aswat* (January 11, 1988).
45. Olivier Carré, "Le Combat-Pour-Dieu et L'État Islamique, Schez Sayyid Qutb, inspirateur du radicalism islamique actuel," *Revue de Science Politique Française*, 33 (4) (August 1983).
46. Ibrahim, *Merip Reports*; Aly, al-Monein and Wenner, *Modern Islamic Reform* p. 351; Saad Eddin Ibrahim, "Anatomy of Egypt's Militant Islamic Groups," *International Journal of Middle East Studies*, 12 (December 1980) p. 433.
47. *Ruz al-Yusuf*, "Are the Brothers Abandoning Violence?," APS Diplomat, "Re-drawing the Islamic Map."
48. Abu Husayn, "Kuwaiti Paper Interviews," p. 20.
49. Barakat, "To Me a Death Sentence."
50. Faraj, *Al-Faridah al-Gha'ibah*, pp. 6–7.
51. Mardini, *Al-Ladudan* p. 147.
52. Muhammad 'Arafah *et al.*, "Ulema Meet, Rebut Charge of 'Infidelity,'" *Al-Akhbar* (January 2, 1989).
53. Kepel, *Muslim Extremism*, pp. 45, 48, 63.

10 The Islamic Revolt

1. Mubarak's interview, Cairo TV, December 16, 1992. Translated in U.S. Department of Commerce, *Foreign Broadcast Information Service* (hereafter *FBIS*), December 17, 1992.
2. *New York Times*, August 30, 1995; U.S. Department of State, *Patterns of Global Terrorism, 1995*, http://www.state.gov/www/ global/terrorism/annual_reports.html; Elie Podeh, "Egypt," in Ami Ayalon, ed., *Middle East Contemporary Survey 1993* (hereafter *MECS 1993*), pp. 129–130; Ami Ayalon, "Egypt," in Ami Ayalon, ed., *Middle East Contemporary Survey 1994* (hereafter *MECS 1994*), pp. 120–121.
3. *Agence France Presse*, January 16, 1994, in *FBIS*, January 18, 1994; MENA, March 28, 1994, in *FBIS*, March 29, 1994; *Civil Society*, May 1994, in *FBIS*, September 3, 1994, September 6, 1994.
4. *New York Times*, October 12, 1993.
5. Shaykh 'Abdallah al-Samawi, in *al-Ahrar*, July 28, 1991. Cited in Uri Kupferschmidt, "Egypt," in Ami Ayalon, ed., *Middle East Contemporary Survey 1991* (hereafter *MECS 1991*), p. 354.
6. *Al-Watan al'Arabi*, May 15, 1992; *Ruz al-Yusuf*, May 25, September 14, and November 9, 1992; *al-Ahram*, August 30, 1992; *al-Wafd*, November, 27 1992, cited in Ami Ayalon, "Egypt," in Ami Ayalon, ed., *Middle East Contemporary Survey 1992* (hereafter *MECS 1992*), p. 367.
7. Saad Eddin Ibrahim, "Reform and Frustration in Egypt," *Journal of Democracy*, Vol. 7 No. 4, October 1996, p. 126.
8. Middle East News Agency (hereafter MENA), October 12, 1990, in *FBIS*, October 12, 1990. See also *Al-Ahram*, October 28, October 29, and October 30, 1990; *Al-Jumhuriyya*, October 29, 1990; *al-Ahram* and *al-Wafd*, October 13 and October 14, 1990, respectively, cited in Ami Ayalon, "Egypt," in Ami Ayalon, ed., *Middle East Contemporary Survey 1990* (hereafter *MECS 1990*), p. 322; MENA, April 20, June 8, June 10, and July 7; *Le Monde*, April 25; *Ha'aretz*, May 30; *al-Ahram* Weekly, June 20, July 18, August 8, August 22, and October 17, 1991, cited in *MECS 1991*, p. 354.
9. *Al-Akhbar*, March 18, May 4, and July 17, 1994; *Le Monde*, August 23, 1994, cited in *MECS 1994*, p. 263.
10. MENA, October 17, 1994, in *FBIS*, October 18, 1994.
11. *New York Times*, July 5, 1995; U.S. Department of State, *Patterns of Global Terrorism, 1995* http://www.state.gov/www/global/terrorism/annual_reports.html; *Al'Arabi*, July 29, 1996, in *FBIS*, August 5, 1996, p. 23.
12. *Al-Nur*, April 24; *al-Ahram* Weekly, July 8, 1991, cited in *MECS 1991*, p. 354.
13. *Agence France Presse*, November 19, 1992, in *FBIS*, November 20, 1992.
14. Mubarak Press Conference, Cairo TV, December 16, 1992, in *FBIS*, December 17, 1992.
15. "Tourists Are the Latest Victims of Egypt's Civil Strife," *Africa Report*, Vol. 38, Issue 1, January 1993.
16. *Le Monde*, August 23, 1994.
17. *Middle East International*, December 18, 1992, p. 10.
18. U.S. Department of State, *Patterns of Global Terrorism, 1995*, http://www.state.gov/www/global/terrorism/annual_reports.html.
19. *The Economist, Country Reports for Egypt*, No. 2, 1994, p. 11.

20. *New York Times*, January 3, 1995.
21. U.S. Department of State, *Patterns of Global Terrorism, 1995*, http://www.state.gov/www/global/terrorism/annual_reports.html.
22. Mubarak's May Day speech, Radio Cairo, April 30, 1995, in *FBIS*, May 2, 1995.
23. Cited in Ami Ayalon, "Egypt," in Ami Ayalon, ed., *Middle East Contemporary Survey 1995* (hereafter *MECS 1995*), p. 250; *Civil Society*, January 1997, cited in Meir Hatrina, "Egypt," in Ami Ayalon, ed., *Middle East Contemporary Survey 1997* (hereafter *MECS 1997*), p. 304.
24. MENA, July 27, 1996, in *FBIS*, July 31, 1996; MENA, January 25, 1996, in FBIS, January 26, 1996; MENA, April 27, 1996, in *FBIS*, April 29, 1996.
25. U.S. Department of State, *Patterns of Global Terrorism, 1995*, http://www.state.gov/www/global/terrorism/annual_reports.html.
26. *Radio Cairo*, April 18, 1996, in *FBIS*, April 19, 1996. See also *al-Akhbar* and *al-Ahram*, April 19, 1996; and *Agence France Presse*, April 19, 20, 22, 1996, cited in Ami Ayalon, "Egypt," in Ami Ayalon, ed., *Middle East Contemporary Survey 1996* (hereafter *MECS 1996*), p. 264.
27. *Al-Hayat*, January 11, 1997; *Ha'aretz*, March 4, 1997; *MENA*, December 23, 1997, cited in *MECS 1997*, p. 304.
28. U.S. Department of State, *Patterns of Global Terrorism, 1997*, http://www.state.gov/www/global/terrorism/1997Report/mideast.html.
29. *Al-Hayat*, February 24, 1998; *al-Wasat*, March 9, 1998, cited in Ami Ayalon, "Egypt," in Ami Ayalon, ed., *Middle East Contemporary Survey 1998* (hereafter *MECS 1998*), p. 139.
30. Daniel Brumberg, "Rhetoric and Strategy: Islamic Movements and Democracy in the Middle East," in Martin Kramer, ed., *The Islamism Debate* (Tel Aviv: Moshe Dayan Center, Tel Aviv University, 1997), p. 23.
31. U.S. Department of State, *Patterns of Global Terrorism, 1998*, http://www.state.gov/www/global/terrorism/1998Report/mideast.html#egypt.
32. Ibid.
33. U.S. Department of State, *Patterns of Global Terrorism, 1999*, http://www.state.gov/www/global/terrorism/1999report/mideast.html#Egypt.
34. Ibid.
35. Ibid.
36. Ibid.
37. *Al-Hayat*, February 16 and February 18, 1997, cited *MECS 1997*, p. 305.
38. *Agence France Presse*, March 10, 1990, in *FBIS*, March 11, 1990. See also *al-Jumhuriyya*, March 4, 1990; *al-Akhbar*, March 8, 1990; *Akhir Sa'a*, March 14, 1990; *al-Ahram*, March 15, 1990; and MENA, March 25, 1990, cited in *MECS 1990*, p. 321.
39. MENA, April 15, 1990, in *FBIS*, April 16, 1990; MENA, April 20, 1990, in *FBIS*, April 23, 1990; MENA May 6, 1990, in *FBIS*, May 8, 1990.
40. *Agence France Presse*, February 17, 1993, in *FBIS*, February 21 and April 31, 1993. See also *MENA*, February 29, 1993; *Ha'aretz*, May 3, 1993; and *al-Jumhuriyya*, May 7, 1993, cited in *MECS 1992*, p. 368.
41. *New York Times*, December 17, 1992.
42. Chronology, The International Policy Institute for CounterTerrorism, "Terrorist attacks database," http://www.ict.org.il.

43. *Ha'aretz* quoting *Agence France Presse*, July 29, 1992; *al-Wafd*, August 7, 1992; *Jerusalem Post* quoting *Reuters*, August 10, 1992, cited in *MECS 1992*, p. 370.
44. *Agence France Presse*, November 25, 1992, in *FBIS*, November 27, 1992.
45. *Al-Ahram*, November 8, 1992; *al-Akhbar*, October 14, 1992; *al-Wafd*, November 23, 1992; *Akhir Sa'a*, January 13, 1993, cited in *MECS 1992*, p. 371.
46. *Al-Ahram*, October 30, 1992; MENA, November 16, 1992, in *FBIS* November 16, 1992.
47. MENA, September 27, 1994, in *FBIS* September 28 and September 30, 1994; *Financial Times*, September 29, 1994.
48. The International Policy Institute for CounterTerrorism, "Terrorist attacks database," http://www.ict.org.il.
49. Ibid.
50. Ibid.
51. Ibid.
52. *Le Monde*, November 20, 1997; *al-Hayat*, November 20, 1997; *al-Sharq al-Awsat*, November 22, 1997; *al-Azhar*, December 1997, cited in *MECS 1997*, p. 307.
53. *Middle East International*, November 21, 1998.
54. *Al-Haqiqa*, January 2, 1993, cited in *MECS 1993*, p. 285.
55. Ibid.
56. Al-Wafd, January 11, 1995, cited in *MECS 1995*, p. 254.
57. *Ruz al-Yusuf*, June 29, 1992, cited in *MECS 1992*, p. 372.
58. *Al-Ahram Weekly*, September 17, 1992; *Ruz al-Yusuf*, September 21, 1992; *MEI*, September 25, 1992, pp.11–12, cited in *MECS 1992*, p. 373.
59. Radio Cairo, October 18, 1992, in *FBIS* October 19, 1992; Radio Cairo, October 24, 1992, in *FBIS*, October 27, 1992; *New York Times*, October 21, 1992.
60. *Al-Wafd*, February, 7, 1992; *al-Wasat*, March 23, 1992; *al-Watan al'Arabi*, March 27, 1992; *al-Musawwar*, April 9, 1992, cited in *MECS 1992*, p. 374.
61. MENA, August 26, 1994, in *FBIS*, August 29, 1994.
62. *Al-Jumhuriyya*, June 7, 1992 and MENA, June 7, 1992, in *FBIS*, June 8, 1992.
63. *Ruz al-Yusuf*, October 26, 1992, cited in *MECS 1992*, p. 374.
64. MENA, May 14, May 17, May 18, June 15, and June 28, 1994, in *FBIS*, May 17, May 18, May 19, June 16, and June 29, 1994; *New York Times*, May 17 and May 19, 1994. See also *al-Wasat*, May 12 and May 18,1994; *Agence France Press*, May 15 and June 25, 1994; *al-Ahram*, May 25, 1994; *al-Hayat*, June 16, 1994; and *al-Wafd*, June 19, 1994, cited in *MECS 1994*, p. 266.
65. *Al-Hayat*, May 24 and May 25, 1994; *al-Sha'b*, June 3, 1994, cited in *MECS 1994*, p. 266.
66. *Al-Hayat*, May 17, 1994; *al-Wafd*, May 25, 1994, cited in *MECS 1994*, p. 267.
67. *Al-Sha'b*, May 20, 1994, cited in *MECS 1994*, p. 267.
68. Interview with Radio Tehran, March 22, 1998. Translation in *FBIS*.
69. *Le Monde*, November 17, 1995.
70. MENA, January 23, 1995 and *Agence France Presse*, January 23, 1995, in *FBIS*, January 24, 1995.

71. *Al-Hayat*, November 1, 1995; *CR*, Egypt, No. 4, 1995, p. 12, cited in *MECS 1995*, p. 254.
72. MENA, November 23, 1995, in *FBIS*, November 24, 1995; MENA, November 30, 1995, in *FBIS*, December 1, 1995; *International Herald Tribune*, November 24, 1995.
73. Agence France Presse, November 27, 1995, in *FBIS*, November 28, 1995.
74. *Wall Street Journal*, December 8, 1995.
75. *Filastin al-Muslima*, March 1997; *al-Sha'b*, May 27 and May 30, 1997, cited in *MECS 1997*, pp. 303–311.
76. *Al-Hayat*, January 3 and January 8, 1997, cited in *MECS 1997*, p. 310.
77. *Al-Sharq al-Awsat*, April 13, 1997; *al-Hayat*, November 9, 1997 and May 12, 1998, cited in *MECS 1997*, p. 311.
78. MENA, June 26, 1996, in *FBIS*, June 27, 1996, p.10.
79. *Al-Ahram*, March 10, 1997; *al-Hayat*, March 23, 1997; MENA, August 10, 1997, cited in *MECS 1997*, p. 309.
80. *Ha'aretz*, November 28, 1997.
81. Ibid.
82. *Al-Sha'b*, July 8, 1997; *al-Wasat*, July 14, 1997; *Le Monde*, July 23, 1997, cited in *MECS 1997*, p. 305.
83. *Al-Jumhuriyya*, July 14, 1997; *alHayat* July 27, 1997; *Agence France Press*, August 9, 1997, cited in *MECS 1997*, p. 305.
84. *Al-Ahram*, December 22, 1992, in *FBIS*, December 23, 1992.
85. *New York Times*, January 8, 1995; *Middle East Times*, January 5, 1995. See also *Ha'aretz*, January 10, 1995, cited in *MECS 1995*, p. 117.
86. *New York Times*, August 30, 1995. See also *al-Sharq al-Awsat*, September 7, 1995, cited in *MECS 1995*, p. 117.
87. MENA, August 30, 1997; *al-Sharq al-Awsat*, October 14, 1997, cited in *MECS 1997*, p. 306.
88. *Al-Hayat*, February 11, 1998; Adili's interview in *al-Musawwar*, January 15, 1999, cited in *MECS 1998*, p. 230.
89. *Al-Hayat*, November 2 and November 21, 1998; *al-Sharq al-Awsat*, November 20, 1998, cited in *MECS 1998*, p. 231.
90. "Egypt: Silenced," *The Economist*, Vol. 323, Issue 7763, June 13, 1992.
91. Fauzi Najjar, "Islamic fundamentalism and the intellectuals: The Case of Nasr Hamid Abu Zayd," *British Journal of Middle Eastern Studies*, Vol. 27, Issue 2, November 2000.
92. *Washington Times*, June 28, 1995.
93. *MECS 1997*, p. 311.
94. Ibid.
95. *'Aqidati*, June 3, 1997, cited in *MECS 1997*, p. 311.
96. For a detailed discussion of his family background, see Amir Raafat, "The World's Second Most Wanted Man," *The Star*, November 22, 2001.
97. Ayman al-Zawahiri, *Knights Under the Prophet's Banner*. The text was published in *al-Sharq al-Awsat*, December 2-December 12, 2001. The book was translated by the U.S. Department of Commerce, *FBIS*, December 2-December 12, 2001.
98. Ibid.
99. *Al-Mustaqbal*, March 19, 2002, translated in MEMRI, No. 358, March 22, 2002.

100. *Al-Quds al'Arabi,* July 29, 1996, translated in *FBIS,* July 30, 1996, pp.11–12.
101. *Al-Hayat,* April 25, 2001, translated in *MEMRI* Special Dispatch, No. 211, April 26, 2001 (http://www.memri.org/sd/SP21101.html); *al-hayat,* September 27, 2001, translated in *MEMRI* Special Dispatch, No. 284, October 10, 2001 (http://www.memri.org/ sd/SP28401.html).

Bibliography

ENGLISH-LANGUAGE ARTICLES

The APS Diplomat, "Re-drawing the Islamic Map," 5 (5) (May 25, 1983).
Abdel-Lalifi, Omayma. "Moslem Brotherhood at the crossroads," *The Jerusalem Post,* December 14, 1999, p. 9.
Abdo, Geneive. *No God but God: Egypt and the Triumph of Islam.* New York: Oxford University Press, 2000.
Abed-Kotob, Sana. "The accommodationists speak: Goals and strategies of the Muslim Brotherhood of Egypt," *International Journal of Middle East Studies,* Vol. 27, Issue 3, August 1995.
el Aftendi, Abdelwahab, "The Islamic World in Review," *Arabia* (November 1985) pp. 16–19.
Africa Research Bulletin, 22 (8) (September 15, 1985) pp. 7748–49.
"Al-Alfi Calls Muslim Brotherhood Root Cause of Terrorism," *MENA,* June 15, 1996, translated in FBIS, June 18, 1996, p.17.
Album, Andrew. "Egypt: Egypt faces its moment of economic truth," *Middle East,* July 1995.
Alexander, Yona E. *Middle East Terrorism: Current Threats and Future Prospects.* Aldershot, Dartmouth, 1994.
Alrawi, Karim, "End of an Era," *Inquiry,* 3 (7) (July 1986) pp. 16–17.
Ansari, Hamied, "Sectarian Conflict in Egypt and the Political Expediency of Religion," *Middle East Journal,* 38 (3) (Summer 1984) pp. 397–418.
Arabia, "Democracy Essential for Ikhwan" (February 1982) pp. 9–10.
Arabia, "Egypt's Muslim Brothers" (November 1981) pp. 9–10.
Arabia, "Ikhwan in Parliament: Aiming to Set an Example" (August 1984) pp. 34–35.
Arabia, "Tilimsani on Ikhwan Policy" (November 1981) p. 11.
Baker, Raymaond W. *Sadat and after: Struggles for Egypt's Political Soul.* London, Tauris, 1990.
Barraclough, Steven. "Al-Azhar: Between the Government and the Islamists," *The Middle East Journal,* Vol. 52, No. 2, Spring 1998.
Bazzi, Mohamad. "How radicals hijacked the Muslim Brotherhood," *Los Angeles Times,* October 15, 2001.
Ben-Ner, Yitzhak. "Dr. Farag Foda: the black cloud of Fundamentalism," *New Outlook,* Vol. 35, No. 5 (331–332), September-October 1992, pp.14–17.
Bollag, Burton. "Battling fundamentalism," *The Chronicle of Higher Education,* Vol. 40, Issue 22, February 2, 1994.
Bruce, James. "Arab Veterans of the Afghan War," *Jane's Intelligence Review,* April 1995, pp. 175–79.
Bullough, Vern L. "Some thoughts on Islamic fundamentalism," *Free Inquiry,* Vol. 15, Issue 2, Spring 1995.

Buccianti, Alexandre, "Egypt Faced with Rising Tide of Fundamentalist Violence," *Guardian Weekly*, 134 (21) (May 25, 1986) p. 12.
Campagna, Joel. "From accommodation to confrontation: The Muslim Brotherhood in the Mubarak years," *Journal of International Affairs*, Vol.50, Issue 1, Summer 1996.
Carre, Olivier, "Le Combat—pour—Dieu et L'ttat. Islamique, chez Sayyid Qutb, Pinspirateur du radicalisme islamique actuel," *Revue Franfaise de Science Politique*, 33 (4) (August 1983) pp. 680–703.
Davidson, Lawrence. *Islamic Fundamentalism*. Westport, Conn., Greenwood Press, 1998.
Dickey, Chris, "Islam Fails to Stick," *Guardian Weekly*, 133 (3) (July 21, 1985).
The Economist, "Two legs bad, if they wriggle" (May 21, 1988) p. 46.
"Egypt: Vote or fight," *The Economist*, Vol. 337, Issue 7943, December 2, 1995.
"Egyptian al-Gama'a al-Islamiyya declares cease-fire; Jihad Group vows to Fight On," April 3, 1999. http://www.ict.org.il.
Euben, Roxanne Leslie. *Enemy in the Mirror: Islamic Fundamentalism and the Limits of Modern Rationalism*. Princeton, NJ: Princeton University Press, 1999.
Fahmy, Ninette S. "The Performance of the Muslim Brotherhood in the Egyptian Syndicates: An Alternative Formula for Reform?," *The Middle East Journal*, Vol. 52, No. 4, Autumn 1998.
Friedman, Thomas L. "Birds of darkness," *New York Times*, October 22, 1995.
Wyllie, James. "Egypt: Staying in the Course," *Jane's Intelligence Review*, November 1995, pp. 499–500.
Ganor, Boaz. "The Islamic Jihad: The Imperative of Holy War," January 1, 1993. http://www.ict.org.il.
Gauch, Sarah. "Terror on the Nile," *Africa Report*, May-June 1993, pp. 32–35.
Gerges, Fawaz A. "The end of the Islamist insurgency in Egypt?: Costs and Prospects," *The Middle East Journal*, Vol. 54, No. 4, Autumn 2000.
Ghanem, Fathi, "Profile of a Moslem Militant," *Jerusalem Quarterly*, 34 (August 1985).
Gidron, Avner. "Arresting opponents," *World Press Review*, Vol. 42, Issue 4, April 1995, p.32.
Goodman, Russell W. "The Brotherhood won't go away," *Defense and Diplomacy*, Vol. 9, No. 7–8, July-August 1991, pp.15–17.
Gordon, Joel. "Political opposition in Egypt," *Current History*, Vol. 89, No. 544, February 1990, pp. 65–68, 79–82.
Georgy, Michael. "Egyptian militants vow attacks on Americans," *New York Times*, March 5, 1994.
Grzeskowiak, Martin, "Extremist Islamic Groups in Egypt after 1970, " *Asia, Africa, Latin America*, 10 (1982) pp. 138–56.
el Guindi, Fawda, "The Killing of Sadat and After: A Current Assessment of Egypt's Islamic Movement," *Middle East Insight*, 2 (5) (January 1983).
el Guindi, Fawda, "Veiling Infitah with Muslim Ethic," *Social Problems*, 28 (4) (April 1981) pp. 465–85.
Haim, Sylvia, "Sayyid Qutb," *Asian and African Studies*, 16 (1) (March 1982) pp. 147–56.
Hammond, Andrew. "Egypt: Brotherly love Middle East," *IMDT*, October 1996, pp.14–15.

Hanafi, Hassan, "The Relevance of the Islamic Alternative in Egypt," *Arab Studies Quarterly*, 4 (1) (Spring 1982) pp. 54–74.

Hassan, Sana, "Egypt's Angry Islamic Militants," *NY Times Magazine* (November 20, 1983) pp. 137–38, 140, 142, 144–47.

Hedges, Chris. "A cry of Islamic fury, taped in Brooklyn for Cairo," *New York Times*, January 7, 1993.

Hedges, Chris. "Egypt fears more violent 'Holy War' by militants," *New York Times*, December 19, 1993.

Hedges, Chris. "In Islam's war, students fight on the front line," *New York Times*, October 4, 1994.

Hedges, Chris. "Islamic Group has grown from a splinter to a thorn," *New York Times*, April 1, 1993.

Hedges, Chris. "Mubarak promising democracy, and law and order," *New York Times*, October 12, 1993.

Hedges, Chris. "Muslim militants share Afghan link," *New York Times*, March 28, 1993.

Hedges, Chris. "Unrest Ravaging Tourism in Egypt," *New York Times*, December 17, 1992.

Hottinger, Arnold, "The Problem of the Sharia in Egypt," *Swiss Review of World Affairs*, 35 (4) (July 1985) pp. 30–31.

Ibrahim, Saad Eddin, "An Islamic Alternative—in Egypt: The Muslim Brotherhood and Sadat," *Arab Studies Quarterly*, 4 (1) (Spring 1982) pp. 75–93.

Ibrahim, Saad Eddin, "Arab Social Change: Six Arab Profiles," *The Jerusalem Quarterly* (Summer 1981) pp. 123–40.

Ibrahim, Saad Eddin, "Egypt's Islamic Activism in the 1980's," *Third World Quarterly*, 10 (April 1988) pp. 632–57.

Ibrahim, Saad Eddin, "Egypt's Islamic Militants," *Merip Reports*, 12 (February 1982) pp. 5–14.

Ibrahim, Saad Eddin, "Superpowers in the Arab World," *Washington Quarterly*, 4 (Summer 1981) pp. 81–96.

Ingram, Simon, "Egypt: The Threat Within," *Middle East International*, 247 (April 5, 1985).

Ingram, Simon, "Graduated Crackdown," *Middle East International*, 255 (July 26, 1985) pp. 10–11.

Ingram, Simon, "Sheikh Hafez Challenge," *Middle East International*, 254 (July 12, 1985).

James, Bruce. "Egypt, Country Briefing," *Jane's Defence Weekly*, February 28, 1996.

Jansen, Johannes J. G. *The Dual Nature of Islamic Fundamentalism*. Ithaca, NY: Cornell University Press, 1997.

Jehl, Douglas. "Islamic militants' war on Egypt: Going international," *New York Times*, November 20, 1995.

Karmon, Ely. "The Anthrax Campaign: An Interim Analysis," October 30, 2001. http://www.ict.org.il.

Karmon, Ely. "Who is Behind the Embassy Bombings?," August 7, 1998. http://www.ict.org.il.

Katzman, Kenneth. "Terrorism: Middle Eastern Groups and State Sponsors, 1999," August 9, 1999. http://www.ict.org.il.

Kienle, Eberhard. "More than a Response to Islamism: The Political Deliberalization of Egypt in the 1990s," *The Middle East Journal*, Vol. 52, No. 2, Spring 1998.

McGuinn, Bradford R. "The Islamic challenge in Egypt, has it reached a point of no return?," *Middle East Insight,* Vol. 9, No. 1, November-December 1992, pp. 61–68.
MacFarquhar, Neil. "Egyptian Group Patiently Pursues Dream of Islamic State," *New York Times,* January 20, 2002.
MacFarquhar, Neil. "Islamic Jihad, Forged in Egypt, Is Seen as bin Laden's Backbone," *New York Times,* October 4, 2001.
Mawsilili, Ahmad. *Moderate and Radical Islamic Fundamentalism: the Quest for Modernity, Legitimacy, and the Islamic State.* Gainesville: University Press of Florida, 1999.
Mattoon, Scott. "Egypt: Terror makes its mark," *The Middle East,* Issue 224, June 1993.
Mattoon, Scott. "Islam by profession," *The Middle East,* No. 218, December 1992, pp. 16–18.
al-Menawi, Abdul Latif, "We Must Work Through Legitimate Channels," *Middle East Times,* 3 (28) (July 7, 1985) p. 2.
Middle East Times, "Muslim Brotherhood as Moderate" (July 6, 1985) p. 1.
Mohaddessin, Mohammad. *Islamic Fundamentalism: the New Global Threat.* Washington, DC, Seven Locks Press, c1993.
Moneim, Said and Manfred W. Wenner, "Modem Islamic Reform Movements: The Moslem Brotherhood in Contemporary Egypt," *Middle East Journal,* 36 (3) (Summer 1982) pp. 336–358.
"Muslim Brotherhood Leader Interviewed," *Al-Sharq al-Awsat,* July 16, 1996, p.2, translated in FBIS, July 19, 1996, p.26.
Nash, Jay R. "Day of the Arab: a Murder in Egypt" in *Terrorism in the 20th Century: a Narrative Encyclopedia,* M. Evans, 1998, pp. 219–240.
Nettler, Ron, "Ishim vs. Israel," *Commentary,* 78 (6) (December 1984) pp. 26–30.
Osman, Fathi, "Democracy Essential for Ikhwan," *Arabia,* 6 (February 1982) pp. 8–10.
Paz, Reuven. "Targeting Terrorist Financing in the Middle East," October 23, 2000. http://www.ict.org.il.
Pipes, Daniel. "The Islamic threat, part I: Same difference," *National Review,* Vol. 46, Issue 21, November 7, 1994.
Podeh, Elie. "Egypt's Struggle against the militant Islamic Groups" in *Terrorism and Political Violence,* Frank Cass, Summer 1996, pp. 43–61.
Porteous, Tom, "Religious Activists," *Middle East International,* 290 (December 19, 1986) pp. 11–12.
"President Hosni Mubarak Speech on Prophet's Birthday," *Arab Republic of Egypt Radio,* July 27, 1996, translated in FBIS, July 29, 1996.
Ramati, Yochanan. "Islamic Fundamentalism gaining," *Midstream,* February-March 1993, pp. 2–3.
Reed, Stanley. "The battle for Egypt," *Foreign Affairs,* Vol. 72, Issue 4, September/ October 1993.
Rodan, Steve. "Egypt's terrorist breeding ground," *World Press Review,* Vol. 42, Issue 5, May 1995.
Sackur, Zina. "Islamic Fundamentalist Organisations: The Muslim Brotherhood and the Gama'a al-Islamiya," *ICT,* March 1994.
Sadowski, Yahya, "Egypt's Islamic Movement: A New Political Economic Force," *Middle East Insight,* 5 (November-December 1987) pp. 37–45.

Sagiv, David. "Judge Ashmawi and militant Islam in Egypt," *Middle Eastern Studies*, Vol. 38, No. 3, July 1992, p. 3.
Satloff, Robert B., "Army and Politics in Mubarak's Egypt," The Washington Institute for Near East Policy, *Policy Papers Number 10* (1988).
Schweitzer, Yoram. "Iran-Terror by Proxy," January 5, 2002. http://www.ict.org.il.
Schweitzer, Yoram. "Osama bin Ladin and the Egyptian Terrorist Groups," June 25, 1999. http://www.ict.org.il.
Schweitzer, Yoram. "Suicide Terrorism: Development & Characteristics," April 21, 2000. http://www.ict.org.il.
Shadid, Anthony. "Arrests, deaths undo terror web in Egypt," *Boston Globe*, August 12, 2001, p. A1.
Shahin, Mariam. "Egypt: Egypt cracks down on terrorism," *Middle East Journal*, Issue 256, May 1996, pp.15–18.
"Statement of Interior Minister Hasan al-Alfi on Cooperation Between Egypt and Europe Against terrorism," *MENA*, July 5, 1996 translated in FBIS, July 8, 1996, p. 7.
Shukrallah, Hala. "The impact of the Islamic movement in Egypt," *Feminist Review*, No. 47, Summer 1994, pp.15–31.
Sid-Ahmed, Mohamed, "Egypt: 'Me Islamic Issue," *Foreign Policy* (Winter 1987–1988) pp. 22–35.
Sivan, Emmanuel, "Intellectual Blues," *The Jerusalem Quarterly* (Summer 1981) p. 123.
Sivan, Emmanuel, "Sunni Radicalism in the Middle East and the Iranian Revolution," *International Journal of Middle East Studies*, 21 (February 1989) pp. 1–30.
Sivan, Emmanuel, "The Islamic Republic of Egypt," *Orbis* (Spring 1987) pp. 43–53.
Sivan, Emmanuel, "The Two Faces of Islamic Fundamentalism," *Jerusalem Quarterly*, 27 (Spring 1983) pp. 127–44.
Stahl, Julie. "Islamic Fundamentalists Hold Bush Responsible for Convicted Sheikh's Life," *CNS News*, April 27, 2001 (http://www.memri.org/news/cnsnews1.html).
Taylor, Maxwell and Quayle, Ethel. *Terrorist Lives*. London: Brassey's, 1994.
Third World Quarterly, "Mosque and State in Egypt," 7 (4) (October 1985) pp. xi–xvi.
"Trouble on the Nile," *Time*, Vol. 141, Issue 15, April 12, 1993.
Utvik, Bjorn Olav. "Filling the vacant throne of Nasser: The economic discourse of Egypt's Islamist opposition," *Arab Studies Quarterly*, Vol. 7, Issue 4, Fall 1995.
Waldman, Peter. "Egypt, in shift, to restrain force against suspected Islamic radicals," *Wall Street Journal*, April 28, 1993.
Waldman, Peter. "Unrest on the Nile: As Egypt suppresses Muslim brotherhood, some fear backlash," *Wall Street Journal*, December 8, 1995.
Warburg, Gabriel, "Islam and Politics in Egypt: 1952–1980," *Middle Eastern Studies*, 18 (2) (April 1982) pp. 131–57.
Weymouth, Lally. "'They will never come to power'," *Newsweek*, Vol. 125, Issue 25, June 19, 1995.
Winestock, Geoff. "Seeds of Change: For Egypt's Terrorists, Fertile Ground Lay In Widespread Poverty—Now the State Is Attacking Root Problems to Stem

Resurgence of Extremists—The Many Uses of Sugar Cane," *Wall Street Journal,* January 18, 2002.
Wyllie, James. "Cairo Strives to Keep a Lid on Terrorism," *Jane's Intelligence Review,* July 1996, pp. 309–310.
Yaari, Ehud, "Peace by piece: A Decade of Egyptian Policy Toward Israel," Washington Institute for Near East Policy, Washington (1987).

ARAB ARTICLES

'Abd al-Aziz, 'Isam, "The Jihad Organization Stands before Justice," *Ruz al-Yusuf,* 58 (2844) (December 13, 1982) pp. 12–15.
'Abd al-Basit, Hagan, "al-Jihad and the Brothers: The end of the Honey-moon," *Al-Watan al-Arabi* (May 22,1988).
'Abd al-Fattah, Nabil, "Islam and Religious Minorities in Egypt," *Al-Mustaqbal al-Arabi,* 4 (30) (August 1981) pp. 92–113.
'Abd al-Hadi, Muhammad, "When will the Muslims Reclaim All of Palestine," *al-Nur* (June 12, 1985) p. 3, in Joint Publications Research Service, Near East and South Asia Report (JPRS) (August 8, 1985) pp. 22–25.
'Abd al-Hawi, Muhammad, "After Our Victory We Call on the Government to Recognize Us," *Al-Muftania',* (April 14, 1987) pp. 16–20.
'Abd al-Majid, Wahid, "The 'Brothers' are with the Wafd while the 'Jihad' Awaits Trial and 'Al-Takfir wal-Hijrah' is in Unexpected Danger," *Al-Majallah,* 223 (May 19, 1984) pp. 8–10.
'Abd al-Maqsud, Salah, "Interview with Muhammad Hamid Abu al-Nasir," *atrdsam* (October-November 1986) pp. 16–18.
'Abd al-Qadir, Sayyid, "Inside the Brotherhood," *Ruz al-Yusuf,* 61 (3027) (June 16, 1986) pp. 10–42.
'Abd al-Qadir, Sayyid, "The Islamic Liberation Party," *Akhir Sa'ah* (October 17, 1983) p. 17.
'Abd al-Sami, 'Umar, "I Want a Party: The Br6therhood Did Not Leave the Wafd and Did Not Join the Liberal Party," *Al-Musawwar* (May 2, 1986) pp. 16–19.
'Abu al-Nasr, Hamid, "Open Letter," Al-Sha'b (February 17, 1987) p. 6.
Abduh, Hibah, "Interview with Shaykh al-Ghazali," *Al-Ahram al-Iqtisadi,* 839 (February 11, 1985) pp. 50–53.
Abu Dah, Ibrahim, "How Is the Awqaf Ministry Preparing to Bring 1000 Mosques a Year Under Its Supervision?, *Al-Siyasi* (July 14, 1985) p. 8.
Abu Dawmah, Sayyid, "Muslim Scholars Discuss Islamic Law," *Al-Ahram* (July 5, 12, 19, 26, 1985).
Abu Husayn, Hagan, "Kuwaiti Paper Interviews Islamic Figures," *Al-Anba',* (March 4, 1987) p. 27.
Abu Isma'il, Salah, "An Answer to Al-Mukhtar Al-Islami," *Al-Ahram* (January 12, 1987) p. 6.
Abu-Liwayah, Muhammad, "Kuwaiti Paper Interviews Islamic Leader," *Al-Anba'* (March 4, 1987) p. 27, in JPRS (April 7, 1987) pp. 18–20.
Al-Ahali, "General Guide and a New Guidance Office for Muslim Brotherhood" (May 22, 1985) p. 1.
Al-'Ahd, "Al-iihad in Egypt: What is it? How does it think? What does it want?" (January 17, 1987) p. 8.

Al-Ahram, "Rector of al-Azhar Ask Muslims to Give Help to the Mujahidin of Afghanistan" (December 27, 1986) p. 8.

Al-Ahram, August 14, 2001,translated in MEMRI Special Dispatch 265, August 31, 2001 (http://www.memri.org/sd/SP26501.html).

'Ajjaj, Usamah, "Akhir Sa'ah Reports on Islamic Groups. Where Do Political Parties Stand on Religious Extremism?," *Akhir Sa'ah* (June 11, 1986) pp. 8–10.

Akhir Sa'ah, "Muslim Brotherhood, Jihad Confrontation in Asyut" (April 6, 1988).

'Alam, Hasan, "An Appeal From Shaykh al-Azhar to the Islamic Summit Conference," *Akhir Sa'ah* (January 28, 1987) p. 9.

'Alarn, Hasan, "Interview with the Shaykh of al-Azhar," *Akhir Sa'ah* (April 29, 1987) pp. 12–13.

Al-Akhbar, February 2, 2001, August 23, 2001, August 25, 2001, August 26, 2001, August 28, 2001, August 29, 2001, *Akhbar Al-Youm* and *Aqidati.* Inquiry & Analysis No. 71, September 16, 2001 (http://www.memri.org/ia/IA7101.html).

Al-Arabi, "The Real Situation Between Shaykh al-Azhar and Shaykh Kishk" (February 1982).

Al-Hayat Al-Jadida, November 18, 1999, translated in MEMRI Special Dispatch No. 59, November 19, 1999 (http://www.memri.org/sd/SP5999.html).

Al-Hayat Al-Jadida, October 10, 2000, translated in MEMRI Special Dispatch No. 137, October 14, 2000 (http://www.memri.org/sd/SP13700.html).

Al-Hayat, April 25, 2001, translated in MEMRI Special Dispatch No. 211, April 26, 2001 (http://www.memri.org/sd/SP21101.html).

Al-Hayat, September 27, 2001, translated in MEMRI Special Dispatch 284, October 10, 2001 (http://www.memri.org/sd/SP28401.html).

Al-Jazeera Television (Qatar), September 16, 2001, translated in MEMRI Special Dispatch 277, September 25, 2001 (http://www.memri.org/sd/SP27701.html).

'Asi, Mustafa, "What Does the Meeting of Muslim Ulama in the Soviet Union Mean?," *Al-Ahali* (November 12,1986) p. 8.

'Awad, Mahmud, "Mahmud 'Awad Answers Salah Abu-Isma'il: Do Not Lie, Shaykh," *Uktubar* (January 11, 1987) pp. 15–17.

Baha' al-Din, Ahmad, "The Daily Journal: Sectarian Strife Revisited," *Al-Ahram* (April 12,1987) p. 9.

Bakri, Mustafa, "Interview with the Leader of the Islamic Group in Asyut," *Al-Musawwar,* 3209 (April 11, 1986) p. 17.

Bakri, Mustafa, "Salah Abu Raqiq: We Drove Out Violence for the Third Time," *Al-Musawwar,* 3213 (May 9,1986) pp. 18–20.

Bakri, Mustafa, "The Controversy within the Muslim Brotherhood about the New Guide," *Al-Musawwar,* 3215 (May 23,1986) pp. 10–11.

Bakri, Mustafa, "What Will Happen Following the Escalation of Violence in Egyptian Universities?," *Al-Musawwar,* 3321 (April 25, 1986) pp. 22–24.

Barakat, Muhammad, "To Me a Death Sentence or a Verdict of Innocent Would be One and the Same for the Cause of God," *Al-Yamamah* (October 24, 1984) pp. 38–40.

al-Shinnawi, Muhammad Shams al-Din, "The Real Reasons Behind Liquidating the Muslim Brotherhood," *Al Da'wah* (October 1976).

Al-Dustur, "Religious and Intellectual Figures in Egypt Answer al-Dustur: Why the Factional Strife?" (April 20, 1987) pp. 10–13.

Fawzi, Mahmud, "Now I Write My Articles Accompanied By a Machinegun," *Uktubar* (June 1987) p. 78.

Fikri, Yusuf and Ahman Abu-Kaff, "The Society al-Takfir wal-Hijrah Discloses Its Ideas for the First Time," *Al-Musawwar,* 3010 (June 18, 1982) pp. 66–69.
al-Ghawabi, Shaykh 'Abdallah, "Our Egypt," *Al-Ahram* (March 30, 1987) p. 20.
Al-Gumhuriya, October 7, 2001, translated in MEMRI Special Dispatch 289, October 19, 2001 (http://www.memri.org/sd/SP28901.html).
Hammudah, 'Adil, "Are The Brothers Abandoning Violence?," *Ruz alYusuf,* 3032 (July 21, 1986) pp. 30–34.
Hammudah, 'Adil, "Exit From the Cave: Violence Climbs to the Top," *Ruz al-Yusuf,* 3039 (September 8, 1986) pp. 30–33.
Hammudah, 'Adil, "Islamic Groups," *Ruz al-Yusuf,* 57 (2781) (September 28, 1981) pp. 22–25.
Hammudah, 'Adil, "Sayyid Qutb," *Ruz al-Yusuf,* 3030 (July 7, 1986) pp. 30–34.
Hammudah, 'Adil, "The Brothers and Sadat Face to Face," *Ruz al-Yusuf,* 3033 (July 28, 1986) pp. 28–32.
Hammudah, 'Adil, "J'he Leader of the Hippies of Asyut," *Ruz al-Yusuf,* 3035 (August 11, 1986) pp. 28–32.
Hammudah, 'Adil, "The Story of Religious Extremism from al-Banna to al-Islambuli," *Ruz al-Yusuf,* 3037 (August 25, 1986) pp. 26–29.
Hammudah, 'Adil, "The Trial," *Ruz al-Yusuf* 3036 (August 18, 1986) pp. 26–30.
Hamrush, Ahmad, "Issue Is not Shari'ah but Government," *Ruz al-Yusuf* (August 12, 1985) pp. 16–17.
Harhish, Ilyas, "Islamic Groups in Egypt," *Al-Majallah,* 88 (October 17, 1981) pp. 41–42.
Al-Hawadith, "Independent Party for Muslim Brotherhood" (February 14, 1986) p. 9.
Al-Hawadith, "We Do Not Believe in Sectarianism" (April 10, 1987) p. 30.
Al-Hawadith, "Will Secret Contacts Between the Nasirists and Islamists Bring Two Opposites Together?" (January 9, 1987) pp. 22–23.
al-Hayawan, Muhammad, "Word of Love," *Al-Jumhuriyyah* (August 17, 1987) p. 5.
Huwaydi, Fahmi, "What is the Real Situation Between Shaykh al-Azhar and Shaykh Kishk," *Al-'Arabi,* 279 (February 1982) pp. 41–44.
'Immarah, Muhammad, "Pioneers of Muslim Rejection," *Al-'Arabi,* 297 (August 1983) pp. 23–29.
Irshadi, Samir, "Islam in Egypt is Shaking the Dust Off Itself and Moving Forward Unrelentlessly," *Kayhan al-'Arabi* (February 21, 1987) p. 6, in JPRS (April 10, 1987) pp. 4–8.
"Islamic Jihad Vows to Send U.S. Soldiers Home 'in Coffins'," *Al-Quds al-'Arabi,* July 29, 1996, translated in FBIS, July 30, 1996, pp.11–12.
Ismail, Jamal, "Shari'ah Laws for Those Who Hurry and for Those Who Procrastinate," *Al-Dustur,* 15 (376) (May 20, 1985) pp. 13–14.
Ismail, Jamal, "Will 'The Society' Become a Political Party?," *Al-Dustur,* 16 (434) (June 23, 1986) pp. 18–20.
Jabr, Karim, "The Next Step of the Islamic Groups," *Ruz al-Yusuf* 61 (3021) (May 5, 1986) pp. 12–15.
Jabr, Karim, "The Split between the Wafd and the Muslim Brotherhood," *Ruz al-Yusuf* 2924 (June 25, 1984) pp. 10–12.
Jabr, Karim, "The University of Asyut under the Protection of the Islamic Groups," *Ruz al-Yusuf* 61 (3020) (April 28, 1986) pp. 16–20.
al-Jamal, 'Isam, "I Predict an Improvement in Arab-Egyptian Relations," *Al-Watan al-Arabi* (February 4, 1987) p. 12.

al-Jiyar, Sawsan, "The Weapons of Those Who Claim to be Prophets," *Ruz al-Yusuf* 61 (3019) (April 21, 1986) pp. 39–42.

Al-Khalij, "Muslim Brotherhood Leader Discusses Relations with Wafq" (July 23, 1986).

Al-Liwa' al-Islami, "Islamic Society: Why is It Being Subjected to Sedition and Conspiracies?" (March 13, 1986) p. 3.

Mahmud, Mustafa, "Against Whom Are the Powers of Islamic Law Being Invoked?," *al-Ahram* (July 9, 1985) p. 7.

Al-Majallah, "Interview with Tilimsani," (January 16, 1982) pp. 1–5.

Al-Majallah, "The Islamic Societies in Egypt: The Most Prominent Obstacle Facing the New Government" (October 17, 1981).

Al-Majallah, "The Private World of Khalid Islambuli," (January 2, 1982) pp. 1–6.

Mamduh, Mihrad, "Important Confessions from the Leader of the al-Takfir Organization in Egypt," *Al-Musawwar*, 3108 (May 4, 1984) pp. 20–25.

Ma'tuq, Muhammad, "Egypt's Mufti Replies to the Booklet, 'The Invisible Religious Duty,'" *Al-Majallah*, 2 (97) (December 19, 1981) p. 14.

al-Minawi, 'Abd al-Latif, "After the Death of 'Umar al-Tilimsani, the Muslim Brotherhood: Middle Solution or Extremism?," *Al-Majallah* (May 28-June 3, 1986) pp. 16–17.

Muhammad, Muhsin, "From the Heart," *Al-Jumhuriyyah* (August 17, 1987) p. 5.

Mu'awwad, Mahmud, "Broad Debate at People's Assembly on Islamic Call and the Shari'ah," *Al-Ahram* (May 5, 1985) p. 6.

Al-Muftama', "Belief, Before Book, Binds Me to My Father" (May 5, 1987) pp. 20–23.

Al-Mujtama', "Design to Exclude al-Azhar Ulamas from Political Action" (March 18, 1986) pp. 30–32.

Al-Muftama', "Egyptian Student Movement Rejects All Forms of Custodianship and Containment" (May 7, 1985) pp. 45–47.

Al-Muftama', "Muslim Brotherhood Leader Interviewed on Palestinian Problem" (August 12, 1986) pp. 16–17.

Al-Muftama', "Mustafa Mashur Says 'I Expect Us to Gain 40 Seats,'" (April 7, 1987) pp. 18–21.

Al-Muftama', "Shaykh Salah Abu Isma'il Relates His Experience with the New Wafd Party to a]-Mujtama'" (December 10, 1985) pp. 22–24.

Al-Muitama', "When Will the Egyptian al-Da'wah Magazine Be Published?" (July 2, 1985) pp. 28–29.

Mukarram, Muhammad, "The Full Secrets of the Most Dangerous Terrorist Organization," *Al-Musawwar*, 3024 (September 24, 1982) pp. 4–9.

Muntasir, Salah, "The Strength of the Muslim Brotherhood," *Al-Ahram* (April 12, 1987) p. 9.

Al-Musawwar, "Inside the Prison with the Islamic Societies," 2990 (January 29, 1982) p. 18–24.

Mustafah, 'Abduh, "Phenomenon of Veiling Researched," *Al-Wafd* (May 23, 1985) p. 9.

Al-Nur, "Muslim Fundamentalists Express Hope in Joining Existing Parties" (May 8, 1986).

Nafi', Ibrahim, "The Personal Theories of a Moslem," *Al-Ahram* (July 5, July 12, 1985).

Nuwayshi, Mursi, "Religious Leaders Discuss Application of Islamic Law," *Al-Watan al-'Arabi* (July 19–25, 1985).

al-Qadi, Mustafa, "Islamic Leader on Islamic Groups, Camp David," *Al-Anba'* (February 23, 1987) p. 23.
al-Oassas, Nada, "We Approve the Establishment of a Communist Party and One for the Copts," *Al-Dustur* (May 4, 1987) pp. 20–2, in JPRS (June 30, 1987) pp. 50–56.
Sald, Ulfat et al., "The Terrorists Deviate from Religion," *Ruz al-Yusuf,* 58 (2785) (October 26, 1981) pp. 14–15, 55.
Sa'd, Muhammad, "The Truth about the al-Jama'at al-Islamiya," *Al-Siyasi,* 6 (305) (September 6, 1981) p. 6.
Sadiq, Mahmud, "Muslim Brotherhood Outlines Aims, Methods," *Al-Sharq al-Aswat* (January 11, 1988) p. 10.
Al-Safir, December 7, 2001, translated in MEMRI Special Dispatch 311, December 11, 2001 (http://www.memri.org/sd/SP31101.html).
al-Sa'id, Sana', "Interview of the Week: Islam as a Philosophy Emphasizes Democracy of Dialogue, Opinion and the other Opinion," *Mayu* (June 10, 1985) p. 160.
Salim, Jamal, "Why Does the Brotherhood Put Its Hand in Wafq's Hand?," *Ruz al- Yusuf* (August 12, 1985) pp. 14–15.
Al-Sha'b, "Solution of Economic Problems Begins with Faith, Ethics, and Virtues" (March 31, 1987) p. 3.
Shadi, Salah, "'Umar al-Tilimsani Interview," *Al-Watan al-Arabi* (July 26-August 1, 1985).
al-Shabashiri, Muhammad, "Television Cried Out From Within," *Al-Nur* (June 12, 1985) p. 3.
al-Sharayan, Da'ud, "Jalal Kishk: The Islamic Movement has Gone Beyond Tilimsani," *At-Yainamah,* 33 (829) (November 21, 1984) pp. 42–46.
al-Siba'i, lqbal, "There is No Such Thing as Religious Extremism," *Ruz al- Yusuf,* 59 (2904) (February 6, 1984) pp. 40–41.
Sirhan, Majdi, "Muhammad Muhawid, and Mahmud Ghallab, The Evil Persons Manipulating Egypt's Security in the Shadows," *Al-Wafd* (March, 5, 1987) pp. 3–8.
Sulayman, Hamid, "The al-Shaykh Abu Isma'il Phenomenon: Uncovered," *Akhir Sa'ah* (January 21, 1987) p. 14.
'al-Suyufi, Ahmad, "'Umar al-Tilimsani in Confrontation with the Religious Government," *Al-Sha'b* (June 11, 1985) p. 9.
Al- Tadamun, "Grand Imam of al-Azhar Interviewed" (July 8, 1986).
Tahiri, Amir, "Secret Plans of the Islamic Groups to Overthrow the Regime in Egypt,"
Al-Majallah, 2 (92) (November 14, 1981) pp. 18–20.
al-Tawilah, 'Abd-al-Sattar, "Terrorism Against the People," *Al-Siyasi* (June 7, 1987) p. 7.
al-Tawilah, 'Abd-al-Sattar, "Who Pushed the Extremist Religious Movements?," *Ruz al-Yusuf* 3037 (August 25, 1986) pp. 14–15.
al-Tilimsani, 'Umar, "The Gradual Application of Islamic Law," *At-Sha'b* (July 16, 1985) p. 6.
al-Tilimsani, 'Umar, "The Muslim Brotherhood is Preparing to Announce its Party," *Al-Sharq al-Awsat* (February 18, 1985) p. 8.
al-Tilimsani, 'Umar, "Wafd and the Brotherhood, Once Again," *Al-Wafd* (October 11, 1984) p. 7.
Uktubar, "How Can We Extinguish the Fires Burning Throughout the Islamic World?" (January 18, 1987) pp. 54–55.

Al-Watan al-Arabi, "Cairo: Strange Encounters with Radical Thought," (September 3, 1982) pp. .30–32.
Al-Watan al-Arabi, "Interview with 'Umar al-Tilimsani" (September 25, 1981) pp. 35–37.
Al-Watan al-Arabi, "'Umar al-Tilimsani Remembers" (July 20, 1984) pp. 22–25.
Al-Yamamah,_ "Shaykh Salah Calls for 'Return to Islam'" (July 23, 1986) pp. 34–35.
Al-Yamamah, "We Are Not a Party and We do not aspire to Power" (January 26, 1983) pp. 32–34.
Al-Yamamah, "Will the Muslim Brotherhood Seize Power?" (July 10, 1985) pp. 32–34.
www.lailatalqadr.com, October 4, 2001, translated in MEMRI Special Dispatch 288, October 17, 2001 (http://www.memri.org/sd/SP28801.html).
www.lailatalqadr.com, October 11, 2001 translated in MEMRI Special Dispatch 296, November 2, 2001 (http://www.memri.org/sd/SP29601.html).
Zaydan, Hamid, "Hiwar al-Sha'b ma' al-Shabab al-Muslim," *Al-Sha'b* (March 22, 1984).
Zaytun, Salih, "Application of Islamic Shari'ah in Egypt Inevitable," *Al-'Ahd* (June 4, 1985) pp. 23–26.

ARTICLES—FRENCH

Burgat, Francois. "Cacher le politique: les representations de la violence en Egypte," *Maghreb Machrek,* No. 142, October-December 1993, pp. 32–60.

BOOKS—HEBREW

Ayalon, Ami, *Mishiar ve-Opozitzya be-Mitzrayim* (Tel Aviv, 1983).

BOOKS—ARABIC

Faraj, Muhammad 'Abd al-Salam, *Al-Faridah al-Gha'ibah* (The Missing Obligation).
Mujahid, 'Abd al-Haqq, *Al-Tayyar al-Islamifi Misr* (Islamic Trend in Egypt) (Cairo: Ittihaday A-Talabah wal-Ummal al-Muslimin fi Urubah, 1982).
'Immarah, Muhammad, *al Faridah al-Gha'ibah: Ard wa-hiwar wa Taqyin;* (Beirut: Dar al-wahdah lil-Nashr, 1983).
Ibrahim, Saad Eddin, *Misr Turaji'u Nafsaha* (Cairo, 1983).
Mardini, Zuhayr, *al-Ludaden: Al Wafd wa-al-Ikhwan* (Beirut: Dar Iqra', 1984).

BOOKS—ENGLISH

Ajami, Fouad, *The Arab Predicament* (Cambridge: Cambridge University Press, 1981).
Esposito, John, *Islam and Politics* (Syracuse: Syracuse University Press, 1984).

Hinnebusch, Raymond, *Egyptian Politics Under Sadat* (Cambridge: Cambridge University Press, 1985).
Ibrahim, Saad Eddin, *Egypt: Internal Challenges and Regional Stability* (London: Routledge & Kegan Paul, 1987).
Jansen, Johannes, *The Neglected Duty* (New York: Macmillan, 1986).
Kepel, Giles, *Muslim Extremism in Egypt: The Prophet and the Pharaoh* (Berkeley: University of California Press, 1986).
Kramer, Martin, *Political Islam* (Beverly Hills: Sage, 1980).
Legum, Colin, Haim Shaked, and Daniel Dishon (eds.), *Middle East Contemporary Survey,* vols. 2–8 (New York: Hilmer & Meier, vols. 2–7; Westview, vol. 8, 1978–1985).
Mitchell, Richard, *The Society of Muslim Brothers* (London: Oxford University Press, 1968).
Rubin, Barry, *The Arab States and the Palestine Conflict* (Syracuse: Syracuse University Press, 1982).
Sadat, Anwar, *In Search of Identity* (New York: Macmillan, 1978).
Sivan, Emmanuel, *Interpretation of Islam* (Princeton: Princeton University Press, 1985).
Sivan, Emmanuel, *Radical Islam* (New Haven: Yale University Press, 1985).
Waterbury, John, *Egypt: Burdens of the Past, Options for the Future* (Bloomington: Indiana University Press, 1978).
Yadlin, Rivka, *Anti-Zionism as anti-Judaism in Egypt* (Jerusalem: Zalman Shaza Center, 1988).

Index

'Abd al-Azziz Hijazi 82
'Abd al-Azziz, Muhammad Kamal 36
'Abd al-Fattah, Isma'il 15
'Abd al-Ghaffar, Muhammad 'Aziz 131, 132
'Abd al-Halim, Mahmud 18, 82
'Abd al-Halim, Musa 164
'Abd al-Harith al-Madani 164
'Abd al-Jawwad Yasin 121
'Abd al-Latif Hamzah 82
'Abd al-Nasir, Gamal 11–17, 94, 95, 96, 122, 144, 171
'Abd al-Qudus, Muhammad 21
'Abd al-Rahman, Ali 73
'Abd al-Rahman, 'Umar 23, 46–8, 57, 77, 111, 114–5, 141, 146, 166–7
'Abd al-Sabur Shahin 168–9
'Abd al-Salam, Arif 50
'Abd al-Salam Faraj, Mohammed 58, 114, 141
    assassination of Sadat, involvement in, 23, 41, 148
    on *jihad* 44–5, 48, 139, 169
Abu Basha, Hassan 42
Abu Isma'il, Salah 7, 21, 33, 75, 77, 128, 129, 131, 133
Abu al-Nasr, Muhammad Hamid 25, 34, 36, 38–9, 53, 135, 138, 145, 165
    Iran, position toward, 119
    Israel, position toward, 107–8, 112
    United States, position toward, 105

Abu Zayid, Nasir Hamid 168–9
Ahmad, Makram Muhammad 23, 42
Ahmad, Yusu Mahmud 25
Ajami, Fouad 6
Ala, Ahmad 168
al-Alfi, Hasan 159
Ansari, Hamied 54
Arab Socialist Union 17
al-Ashmawi, Muhammad Sa'id 164
Ashmawi, Salih 21
Ataturk, Kemal 122
Awqaf and al-Azhar Affairs, Ministry of, 9, 18, 20, 25, 77, 80, 90, 151, 155
Ayatollah Ruhollah Khumayni 19, 50, 75, 95, 102, 116, 118, 135, 144
al-Azhar, Islamic university of, 8, 9, 14, 18, 20, 25, 80–1, 86, 91, 156, 159

al-Badri, Yusuf 33, 121
Baha al-Oin, Husayn 166
al-Banna, Hasan 10–11, 30, 146
Bar Association 164, 166
Battle of the Hajj 120
Begin, Menahem 111

Camp David agreements 19, 20, 97, 108, 110
Central Security Unit riots 39

al-Dhahabi, Husayn 18
al-Din al-Aryan, 'Isam 35, 66
al-Din Ghazi, Badr 140

Index

Egypt 5, 6, 13, 94, 96–7
   and Israel 6, 15, 19, 94, 97, 171
     see also Camp David agreements
   and Islam 4, 5, 13, 20, 90
     see also Suez Canal area

Fahim, 'Asim 103, 147
al-Fakhrani, Mahmud 158
Farouk 11
Free Officers group 11
Fuda, Faraj 163, 168

General Union of Egyptian Students 64
al-Ghazali, Muhammad 121, 149, 161, 165
Global Front for Fighting the Jews and the Crusaders, statement of, 170

Hamas 171
Hanafi, Hasan 168
al-Haqq, Ziya 136
Hizballah 171
al-Hudaybi, Hasan 12, 51

Ibbrahim, Saad Eddin 4, 29, 42, 54, 79, 83
Ibn Taymiyah 50
Iran 7, 79, 95, 115, 117–18, 146
   Iranian Revolution 19, 75, 116, 171
   subversion of 120–1
     see also Battle of the Hajj
   and the USSR 116
Iran-Iraq war 118–19
Islam 4, 6, 8
Islamic Fundamentalism 1, 3–5, 8, 10, 60–1, 143, 152, 157
   and Arab Nationalism 121–4
   conflict with the government 19, 94–5, 97
     see also "Law of Shame"
   and Iran 7, 115–18
   and Israel 107–9, 113–15, 172
   and *jahiliyyah* 1, 50–2, 139
   and Marxism 14, 16, 146–7
   and minorities 6, 21, 68, 70, 144–6, 151, 160
   repression of, 157–60, 166
   and the United States 2, 3, 6, 98–100, 102–5, 170–3
   and the USSR 106–7
   and violence 7, 18, 35, 74, 139–42, 157, 167
     see also Muslim Brotherhood, al-Jihad, Jama'at, Jam'iyat
al-Islambuli, Khalid 44, 49, 64, 142
Islamic Conference 14
Islamic Dawn Association (Jam'iyat Fajr al-Islam) 73
Islamic Group 37, 67, 156, 159, 166, 167
   violence, use of, 161–2
Islamic Liberation Organization 17, 41–3, 56–7, 61, 142
Islamic Research Council 14
Islamic Society 58
Isma'il, Nabawi 23, 42
Jadd al-Haqq, 'Ali 88, 100, 110, 112, 119, 123, 169
Jalal, Su'ad 83
Jama'at 1, 43, 47, 53–5, 151, 153–4
   and violence 41, 42, 48
al-Jamal, Hasan 21, 126
Jam'iyat 1, 22, 41, 63–4, 69, 75, 151, 153–4
   political activity 65–7, 70–1
   and use of violence 72, 157
al-Jazzar, Hilmi 22,
al-Jihad 35, 37–8, 42–3, 45, 56–8, 60, 103, 137, 156
   and violence 22–3, 41, 46, 59, 104, 142, 157–8

Kazim 'Abd al-Qawi, Muhammad 59
Kepel, Gilles 57, 71, 73, 76, 142
Kishk 8, 21, 75–6, 83, 96, 111–12, 122, 138, 144
Knights Under the Prophet's Banner 169, 174–185
   see also Ayman al-Zawahiri

bin Ladin, Usama 157, 160, 171
  see also al-Qa'ida
"Law of Shame" 19
Liberal Party 33, 129, 130
Libya 24
Luxor attacks 161–62, 167
  see also Islamic Group

Mabruk, Ahmad Salamah 170
Madkur, Rajab 55
Mahfuz, Najjib 168
Mahgub, Rifa't 158
al-Mahjub, Muhammad 'Ali 117
al-Mahjub, Rif'at 133
Mahmud, Mustafa 84
Mahmud, Zaki Najib 20
al-Ma'mun al-Hudaybi, Muhammad 26, 28–9, 128, 149, 162–3, 165
al-Maraghi, Muhammad 73, 138
Mashhur, Mustafa 30, 38, 165
Matrawi, Muhammad 36
Mubarak, Husni 22, 23, 26, 97, 156, 159, 165
  assassination attempt of, 158
Muhammad Khalid, Khalid 136
Muhyi al-Din, 'Ala 140
Muhyi al-Din, Khalid 23
Mujahaddin-i-Khalq 107
Murad, Mustafa Kamil 5, 23
Muslim Brotherhood 10–11, 13, 18, 147
  critics of, 130–1
  ideology 28–30, 125, 131, 143
  and Iran 95, 116
  and Israel 93, 95, 107–9, 110–13
  political activities 14, 23, 30, 33–4, 133, 163–4
    see also Wafd party, Liberal party
  relationship with government 17, 32, 134
  repression against 12–13, 15, 20–2, 95, 156, 158
  and Shari'ah, 131–4
  strategy 126–30
  and the United States 93, 103, 105
  and violence 7, 113, 138, 150, 162–3
    see also Islamic Fundamentalism
Mustafa, Shukri 18, 41, 49, 56, 83, 115
Mutawalli al-Sha'rawi, Muhammad 83, 89, 149

Nassar, Mumtaz 23
Navon, Yitzhak 110
The Neglected Duty (al-Faridah al-Gha'ibah) 44
  see also Mohammed 'Abd al-Salam Faraj
Nuqrashi, Mahmoud Fahmi 11, 35, 95

People's Assembly 133–4, 140
Personal Status Law 81

al-Qadhafi, Mu'ammar 123, 136, 146
al-Qa'ida 169, 170, 171, 173
  see also Usama bin Ladin
Qutb, Sayyid 6,12, 14, 15, 36, 49, 51, 64, 98, 100–1, 106, 109, 146
  and *jahiliyyah* 50–2, 149
  on *jihad* 140–1
    see also *Signposts Along the Way* (Ma'alim fi al-tariq)

Rahal, Muahammad Salim 142
Ramadan, Sa'id 15
Rushdi, 'Usama 71–2

al-Sadat, Anwar 14, 19, 97
  assassination of, 3, 22, 46, 150, 166
al-Safti, Majd 59
Salamah, Hafiz 8, 75, 76–7, 91, 133–4, 136
Sariyah, Salah 41, 49, 56
Sayf al-Islam Hasan al-Banna, Ahmad 127, 165

al-Sayyid Habib, Muhammad 37, 68, 128
Secret Organization 11, 28, 38
September 11, 2001 attacks 173
Signposts Along the Way (Ma'alim fi al-tariq) 49
  see also Sayyid Qutb
Shadi, Salah 32, 38, 101, 127
Shahin, Yusuf 168
Shaltut, Mahmud 83
Shari'ah (holy law) 4, 17, 24, 26, 34
Shukri, Ibrahim 23, 81, 103
Siraj-al-Din, Fu'ad 21
Sivan, Emanuel 20
Special Organization 38, 39
Suez Canal area 11, 12, 96
Sultan, Fu'ad 161
Survivors from [Hell] Fire 23–4, 42, 59

al-Tahrir al-Islami 42
al-Takfir wal-Hijrah 18, 35, 42, 43, 56–7, 61, 115, 142
Tantawi, Muhammad Sayyid 136, 169
al-Tayyib al-Najjar, Muhammad 82, 149
Technical Military Academy, attack of 17, 41, 43, 57

Technical Military Organization
  see Islamic Liberation Organization
Terrorism 159–62, 166–7
al-Tilimsani, 'Umar 19, 21, 28–31, 35, 54, 74, 105, 116, 122, 145, 148
  Israel, position toward, 108, 110, 111, 112–13
  on politics 129, 133, 136, 138

Ulama 79–80
United States 7, 94, 145
  embassies, bombings of, 170
USSR 94–5, 106–7, 145

Wafd party 21, 25, 30, 33, 78, 129
Wasat party 166
al-Wasil, Nasir Farid 169

al-Zawahiri, Ayman 169, 170, 173
  on Arab-Israeli conflict 94, 171–2
  see also *Knights Under the Prophet's Banner*
al-Zawahiri, Muhammad 170
al-Zummur, Abbud 166

GPSR Compliance

The European Union's (EU) General Product Safety Regulation (GPSR) is a set of rules that requires consumer products to be safe and our obligations to ensure this.

If you have any concerns about our products, you can contact us on

ProductSafety@springernature.com

In case Publisher is established outside the EU, the EU authorized representative is:

Springer Nature Customer Service Center GmbH
Europaplatz 3
69115 Heidelberg, Germany